T0312059

.

Exploring General Equilibrium

Exploring General Equilibrium

Fischer Black

The MIT Press
Cambridge, Massachusetts
London, England

First MIT Press paperback edition, 2010

© 2010 Massachusetts Institute of Technology

This book was set in Times New Roman by the MIT Press.

Library of Congress Cataloging-in-Publication Data

Black, Fischer, 1938–
Exploring general equilibrium / Fischer Black. — New ed.
    p.   cm.
Includes bibliographical references and index.
ISBN 978-0-262-51409-5 (pbk. : alk. paper) 1. Equilibrium (Economics) 2. Business cycles. I. Title.
HB145.B54 2010
339.5—dc22

2010008318

To Cathy,
Althea, Melissa, Ashley, Paige,
and Terry

Contents

It is sometimes claimed in economic literature that discussions of the notions of utility and preference are altogether unnecessary, since these are purely verbal definitions with no empirically observable consequences, i.e., entirely tautological. It does not seem to us that these notions are quantitatively inferior to certain well established and indispensable notions in physics, like force, mass, charge, etc. That is, while they are in their immediate form merely definitions, they become subject to empirical control through the theories which are built on them—and in no other way. Thus the notion of utility is raised above the status of tautology by such economic theories as make use of it and the results of which can be compared with experience or at least with common sense.

—John von Neumann and Oskar Morgenstern

Foreword

Edward Glaeser

Fischer Black's *Exploring General Equilibrium* remains an interesting and unusual book, fifteen years after it was first published. In his quite positive review of the volume in the *Journal of Economic Literature*, Laurence Kotlikoff wrote that "the book could well have been titled 'Black's Notes,'" and he was right. The volume represents an explosion of opinions and insights about contemporary macroeconomics by a great financial economist. Black's thoughts weren't fettered by the norms of circumspect, academic discourse. Nor did he feel compelled to back up each of his claims with the weight of statistics or formal models. This book is Fischer Black unbound, and Fischer Black is always worth reading.

Black's career is now the stuff of legend. He received his Ph.D. in applied mathematics from Harvard in 1964. His drift into finance occurred when he went to work for Arthur D. Little and came into contact with Jack Treynor, who was beginning his work on the equilibrium approach to asset pricing. The key implication of that approach, which was also being developed on the West Coast by Harry Markowitz and William Sharpe, is that there should be few opportunities for risk-adjusted excess returns in well-functioning markets. There is an absence of arbitrage and higher observed returns are compensation for more systematic risk.

The no-arbitrage equilibrium would be the guiding principle for Black's work in both finance and macroeconomics. In 1971, Black moved to the University of Chicago, and two years later, together with Myron Scholes, Black published his most famous paper, "The Pricing of Options and Corporate Liabilities," in the *Journal of Political Economy*. The paper derived "a theoretical pricing formula for options," using the principle that "it should not be possible to make sure profits by creating portfolios of long and short positions in options and their underlying stocks." This is the no-arbitrage equilibrium in practice, and the resulting Black-Scholes formula became one of the most widely used results in economic history. Myron

Scholes received a Nobel Prize for this work in 1997, which Fischer Black surely would have shared if he had not died in 1995, the year *Exploring General Equilibrium* was first published.

This book is also an application of Black's belief in the power of equilibrium theory, although it is here applied to macroeconomics rather than asset pricing. Several of Black's earliest papers, such as his first published paper, "Banking and Interest Rates in a World Without Money" (in the *Journal of Bank Finance* in 1970), "Active and Passive Monetary Policy in a Neoclassical World" (published in the *Journal of* Finance in 1972), and "Uniqueness of the Price Level in Monetary Growth Models with Rational Expectations" (published in the *Journal of Economic Theory* in 1974), were forays into the great debates of macroeconomics. Black's application of his equilibrium approach to monetary policy led him to conclude that price levels were generally indeterminate and that "monetary policy can affect neither the real sector nor the price level" (Black 1972), which put him at odds with both Keynesians, who thought that monetary policy could impact the real economy, and monetarists who argued that "inflation is always and everywhere a monetary phenomenon" (Friedman and Schwartz 1963).

For many reasons, including Black's disagreement with both major schools of macroeconomic thought in the early 1970s, this macroeconomic work has received relatively little attention. It did, however, lead him to views about the business cycle similar to those that became increasingly popular in the 1980s. Black believed that since "monetary policy does not influence the economy," "business cycles are a natural result of uncertainty in a general equilibrium model." Researchers on "real business cycles" (RBCs) held similar views, although Black takes great pains in this volume to distinguish his views from that school of thought. Despite those differences, Black joins RBC theorists in emphasizing that business cycles come from real economic shocks to tastes and technology rather than from monetary interventions. He would also have surely agreed with the many economists in this school who opposed the anti-recessionary tactics of the Obama administration because, after all, Black thought that "there is very little the government should do to influence the economy."[1]

While Black never had the influence in macroeconomics that he had in finance, he certainly thought deeply about macroeconomic issues and this book provides a compendium of his conclusions. Black clearly believed that many macroeconomists, and microeconomists too, were using mistaken models and faulty methods, and he wanted his viewpoint heard. While economic models have changed since the early 1990s, many of the debates remain hotter than ever, and Black's provocative perspective and healthy skepticism remain valuable.

At its core, the book argues that a simple general equilibrium model can explain much of the movement in the aggregate economy. Black argues that fixed factors of production are irrelevant, and that the world is characterized by constant-returns-to-scale production, at least over sufficiently long time periods. He argues that physical and human capital are poorly measured things, and that in reality, these stocks of capital include essentially everything that makes the world productive, including the current state of technology. Any mismatch between theory and data can be explained by either a faulty theory or bad data. Black argues that the seeming failures of a general equilibrium model tell us more about the difficulties and problems of measuring inputs and outputs than about the general applicability of the model.

The general equilibrium model with constant returns to scale and no limits on accumulation of human and physical capital is certainly compatible with the long-run economic growth that the world has experienced. Black attributes the measured differences in growth rates across countries to differences in savings rates, political stability, and "just luck" (92). For example, he argues that Japanese growth in the 1980s reflected the fortuitous combination of Japan's decision to invest heavily "in the capacity to produce high-quality cars and consumer electronic products," combined with the fact that "demand for such products soared during the 1980s" (92). The prescient implication was that Japanese growth was unlikely to continue at such heady rates.

Macroeconomics in the 1980s was, to a certain extent, divided between the pragmatic, often Keynesian, "saltwater" economists who resided in Cambridge, Massachusetts, and Berkeley and the more theoretically disciplined "freshwater" economists of Minneapolis, Chicago, and Carnegie-Mellon, who generally saw fewer benefits from countercyclical public activity. Black does not reside in either camp, but he certainly has more sympathy toward the freshwater school. He shows little belief in the existence of market failures or externalities, and, even if they do exist, he is skeptical of the ability of government intervention to make things better.

The book's enduring value comes from the fact that these issues are still unresolved. The recession that started in 2007 has only made macroeconomic debates more relevant. Three academic macroeconomists, Benjamin Bernanke, Christina Romer, and Lawrence Summers, sit at the center of economic policy making today. Black has interesting thoughts on the work of all three, and his comments still sparkle with insight.

Neutral Technical Change

The major difference between the original *Exploring General Equilibrium* and this new edition is the inclusion of Fischer Black's last paper, titled "Neutral Technical Change," at the end of the volume. In what appears to have been one of Black's last acts, he mailed me a copy of the paper in the hope that I would be able to find it a publisher. It was never quite clear why Black picked me, except for the fact that I had given him fairly copious notes on an early draft of this volume.

Like this book, "Neutral Technical Change" is not written like any standard economics paper and it is not finance. Instead, it is a discussion of whether the events of the 1980s should be understood as skill-biased technical change. My imagination failed me, and I was unable to figure out where to publish the piece. It set on my shelf for fourteen years, and I felt quite guilty about my inability to satisfy Black's last request.

I was, therefore, thrilled when the MIT Press contacted me about publishing a new version of *Exploring General Equilibrium*. While "Neutral Technical Change" is not stylistically suitable for most standard economic journals, it fits perfectly with the style of this volume. Like the rest of this book, it applies Black's general equilibrium model to important economywide events, it hints at a model rather than rigorously defining one, and it contains a flurry of interesting insights about important papers. Luckily for my conscience, the MIT Press was happy to include this paper in this new edition, provided that I edit the paper.

I altered the paper in two major ways. First, I shortened it considerably in keeping with the wishes of the MIT Press. Second, I restructured the paper slightly to make its progression somewhat more linear. I made almost no word changes. The importance of this document is that it provides a view into the mind of Fischer Black. Replacing his words with my own would only reduce their value.

The 1980s were marked by a remarkable increase in income inequality, which is often referred to as the rise in returns to skill. While that increase abated somewhat during the 1990s, it has continued since then. A vast literature has tried to both measure and understand the increasing dispersion of wages both in the United States and throughout the world. "Neutral Technical Change" is Fischer Black's contribution to that literature.

Much of the debate over the rise in returns to skill focused on the relative importance of increasing trade, skill-biased technical change, and institutional factors, such as the decline of unionization. Black argues that the increasing compensation of more skilled workers is best seen as purely neutral technical change. He suggests that the 1980s experienced an increase in physical capital, and "if human capital measures 'skill,' we will see the original increase in physical capital create an increase in the returns to skill and the accumulation of human capital" (266). What others call the rise in returns to skill, Black sees as an increase in the amount of skill, measured appropriately in efficiency units.

Readers will have to come to their own conclusions about whether Black's interpretation of rising inequality is correct. But I am convinced that even those who are skeptical of Black's primary thesis will get something out of this essay. It is a novel, interesting take on one of the most important labor market phenomena of the past fifty years. Like so much that Fischer Black did, it is fascinating and utterly unique. It is a great loss for the world that Fischer Black died at such a young age, but at least we have his words that continue to enlighten our minds and warm our hearts.

Note

1. Quotations in this paragraph are from Fischer Black, *Business Cycles and Equilibrium*, updated edition with a new foreword by Perry Mehrling (New York: Wiley, 2009), xxii, xxvi.

Preface

I began this research about twenty-five years ago, when Jack Treynor introduced me to equilibrium models of economic and financial markets. I was fascinated. In finance, I set out to build an equilibrium model of warrant and option pricing. In economics, I started trying to model bond pricing, which led me to monetary theory, business cycles, labor markets, and growth.

Sometimes individual securities, or even broad classes of securities, seem mispriced. Sometimes economic happenings seem to call for more than an equilibrium model can provide, but these instances are infrequent and relatively insignificant. I see the world through equilibrium glasses; I don't think they fail me very often.

I have had no formal training in economics or finance. I do not fully understand some of the tools and concepts used by those who have had that training. Sometimes I think I'm close, but then they slip away. I question many conventions in economic research; but in some cases, it's just that I don't fully understand them.

I can't help trying to look at the big picture. The world is becoming more specialized, as my own theories suggest. I too try to specialize, but my mind keeps wandering. As a result, I make errors, both small and large. I don't like errors, and I'd appreciate help in finding them.

I try hard to say things clearly. This means confronting the work of others directly, rather than citing it and moving on. It means a nonacademic writing style. It sometimes means stating as fact things that are clearly opinion. No doubt the reader's glasses differ from mine. But we are all looking at the same world, and the technology for making glasses is constantly improving. Someday it will all be clear.

The people who helped me are too numerous to list. Special thanks, though, to Edward Glaeser and Boyan Jovanovic, who gave me extensive comments on the entire manuscript, and for production help to Beverly Bell and Kathryn Randall.

The literature most closely related to my work includes Aghion and Howitt (1992), Alchian (1959), Arrow (1953), Barro (1990b), Boeri (1994), Caballero, Engel, and Haltiwanger (1994), Davis (1987a), Davis and Haltiwanger (1990, 1992), Debreu (1959), Fischer and Merton (1984), Greenig (1986), Hall (1988a), Hamilton (1988), King, Plosser, and Rebelo (1988a, 1988b), King and Rebelo (1988), Kydland and Prescott (1982), Long and Plosser (1983), Loungani, Rush, and Tave (1991), Mayshar and Solon (1993), McCloskey (1985, 1990), McLaughlin (1991), Merton (1973), Neumann and Topel (1991), Rebelo (1991), Rogerson (1987, 1990), Sargent (1980), Schultz (1961), Shapiro (1993), Summers (1991), Uzawa (1965), von Neumann (1945), Yang and Ng (1993), and, of course, Walras (1874).

Fischer Black
E-mail: black_f@gs.com

Part I

Introduction

The general equilibrium model, as developed by Walras (1874), von Neumann (1945), Arrow (1953, 1964), and Debreu (1959), is remarkable. When we allow the most general utility functions, as suggested by von Neumann and Morgenstern (1946), the model makes few assumptions, yet allows strong normative conclusions. In its unrestricted form, it is simple and elegant.

In the general equilibrium model, people trade claims on output to maximize expected utility, with utility functions limited by a few axioms. At the start, they trade claims to future payoffs, with or without the intermediation of firms. They do not ask for opportunities to trade later on. As time unfolds and uncertainty is resolved, they may be disappointed in what they receive; but at the start, there is no way to rearrange the claims that improves expected utility for everyone.

This model has no role for government. It suggests nothing about how to organize or manage firms, and it has no real trading in securities after the initial burst of trading. Yet under the model's assumptions, we can't make some people better off without making others worse off.

When we want a single unified theory of almost everything, I like the general equilibrium model. I feel it is consistent with most of what we see in the world: both labor markets and the markets for goods and services; both general and specific aspects of the economy; and both short-run variability and long-run growth. Many people seem to feel, however, that the model is not general enough to explain what they see in the world. They create lots of models inconsistent with general equilibrium.

Those who do use models consistent with general equilibrium add assumptions that make their models much more specific. They may still aim for models general enough to explain many things, but they speak of "identifying restrictions," or restrictions that make it possible to "reject" the models by looking at conventional economic data. I like creating more specific models, too, but only when I have strong economic reasons for the restrictions I add. I think about adding investment, costs of operating markets, private information, and continued trading as time unfolds.

For example, I have created a version of the model including money, banks, central banks, and open market operations (Black (1987)). I argue that this model can explain observed business cycles, even though monetary policy must be largely passive. I am unable to find a version of the model that allows a significant role for effective monetary policy. More generally, I like creating many "examples," which are very simple versions of the general equilibrium model, each designed to explain a single stylized fact. I would not dream of "testing" an example on a broad sample of data, since I know in advance that we can reject it if we look hard enough.

Many of the models in the literature are not general equilibrium models in my sense. Of those that are, most are intermediate in scope: broader than examples, but much narrower than the full general equilibrium model. They are narrower, not for carefully-spelled-out economic reasons, but for reasons of convenience. I don't know what to do with models like that, especially when the designer says he imposed restrictions to simplify the model or to make it more likely that conventional data will lead us to reject it. The full general equilibrium model is about as simple as a model can be: we need only a few equations to describe it, and each is easy to understand. The restrictions usually strike me as extreme. When we reject a restricted version of the general equilibrium model, we are not rejecting the general equilibrium model itself. So why bother "testing" the restricted version? If we reject it, we will just create another version.

I think it's better to "estimate" a model than to test it. I take "calibration" to be a form of estimation, so I'm sympathetic with it, so long as we don't take seriously the structure of a model we calibrate. Best of all, though, is to "explore" a model. This means creating many specific examples of a general model, where each one explains a single stylized fact or perhaps a few features of the world. It means using some of these examples to elucidate microeconomic evidence. I don't think we are ready to create a model with intermediate scope that explains in numerical detail many different kinds of evidence at once.

Some people claim that the general equilibrium model is untestable; that it can't be rejected and is therefore "vacuous." At one time, the same claim was made about utility theory, as described by von Neumann and Morgenstern (1946). Yet that theory is now widely used with little comment. Some people even claim to reject it, at least in some respects. In my view, the main purpose of a general theory like theirs is to spawn examples to illustrate specific points. Few use von Neumann–Morgenstern utility in its most general form; but many use examples of utility that satisfy its axioms.

In principle, we can estimate and even test the general equilibrium model. We can analyze large quantities of marketing and engineering data along with more conventional data on wages, hours, production, and the like. We can use data on individual skills, preferences, and personalities along many dimensions. We can experiment with the economy by trying out different kinds of monetary and fiscal policy. Hall (1988c), among many others, even claims to reject the competitive general equilibrium model using aggregate data from the national income and product accounts.

In practice, we probably won't try to estimate or test the most general version of the model. The costs of gathering detailed data on tastes and technology, and of experimenting with the economy, are too high. If we decide not to test the general equilibrium model, I think we should keep it around to help organize our thinking about stylized facts and other data. Whenever we use a theory inconsistent with general equilibrium, we should also try out versions of the general equilibrium model. If we can create versions of both theories that fit the data, then we should probably keep our minds open about which theory is best. In fact, since general equilibrium theories usually imply fewer profit opportunities than other theories, I think we should give them the edge.

"Exploring general equilibrium," then, means generating examples and specific versions of the full general equilibrium model, to explain stylized facts and other data. It means changing examples quickly when they don't fit the facts. It means avoiding formal testing, or even estimation, of heavily restricted models. When a general equilibrium model and another kind of model both fit the facts, it means favoring the general equilibrium model.

Classical Theories

In some ways, the general equilibrium approach is a traditional "classical" approach to macroeconomics. Walras and other economists in the nineteenth century often imagined a world where markets clear and prices are flexible. They thought about equilibria with many commodities. They even debated the "real bills" doctrine, which is closely related to my notion of passive monetary policy.

But we now have concepts that classical economists didn't have— concepts that help us understand how general equilibrium works. We understand general equilibrium itself better, because of the work of Arrow, Debreu, and many others. In particular, we have added *time* to the description of goods and services. We understand expected utility better, because of the work of von Neumann, Morgenstern, and many others. We think about unemployment and career paths. We know better what it means to run a monetary system on credit rather than hard currency. We can now think about the match between wants and resources in a world with uncertainty about investment payoffs along many dimensions.

We even have data that classical economists didn't have. We know that inventories play a major role in cycles, and that consumption is smoother than output. Perhaps most important, we now have data on output, sales, and prices for a huge array of individual goods and services, and on compensation and hours worked for lots of individuals and groups. We even have data on stock and bond prices for many countries, going back centuries in a few cases. Finally, we have mathematical tools that classical economists didn't have. I think much of today's research is *too* mathematical, but sometimes a mathematical model captures in a few equations what would otherwise take thousands of words to explain. In these ways, the general equilibrium approach goes beyond classical macroeconomics.

Puzzles

When people claim to find "puzzles" in the data, they usually mean that the data seem to conflict with their models. Here are some of the puzzles people have cited:

1. Why does consumption seem smoother than income?

2. Why does income seem smoother than investment?

3. Why do wages seem so acyclical?

4. Why does the equity premium seem so high?

5. Why does the real interest rate seem so low?

6. Why does part-time work pay less (per hour) than full-time work?

7. Why does production vary more than sales?

8. Why do most broadly defined sectors move together?

9. Why are output changes correlated across countries?

10. Why are consumption changes less correlated across countries than output changes?

11. Why does the number of help-wanted ads increase in good times?

12. Why does labor turnover go up in good times?

13. Why doesn't growth ever seem to slow down?

14. Why do some countries grow faster than others?

15. Why don't capital-output ratios vary much?

16. Why do capital prices vary more than measured replacement cost?

17. Why are some people unemployed?

18. Why does unemployment fluctuate?

19. Why does labor migrate toward capital?

20. Why aren't returns to capital high where capital-labor ratios are low?

I think we can explain all of these puzzles using sample models derived from the full general equilibrium model with general von Neumann–Morgenstern utility. In most cases, these puzzles dissolve when we relax artificial restrictions that people have placed on models that are otherwise consistent with general equilibrium.

Stylized Facts

I feel that I understand all these puzzles, so I don't think about them much. I think more about a group of stylized facts that summarize the world as I see it. These are my observations, derived from everyday experience, from reading newspapers and magazines, and from studying technical publications. Some of these stylized facts are the same as those others have listed; some are different; and some actually conflict with what others see.

I think the full general equilibrium model is consistent with all of these facts, but knowing that doesn't help us much. What's important, I think, is to *explain* the stylized facts in a deeper sense. We want to understand the underlying economics. We may even want a separate model for each stylized fact—a model that shows most clearly what that fact means.

Unlimited growth

For hundreds of years, output, income, wealth, and consumption have grown all over the world, without any apparent limits. Neither land nor energy nor population nor pollution has prevented this growth.

Persistent inequality

Within a country, individuals vary enormously in wealth and income. Countries and regions vary enormously too. Neither revolution nor redistributive taxation nor state ownership of capital has succeeded in eliminating inequality.

Growing specialization

Every year, workers, firms, products, and services become more specialized. I can see no limits to the increasing specialization of both tastes and technology.

Continual innovation

Partly because of the increase in specialization, growth often takes the form of innovation. We don't just produce more of the same goods at lower cost; we produce new goods and services using new kinds of capital in new ways.

Stable consumption rates

Consumption rates vary among people, and on average across regions and through time, but overall consumption as a fraction of wealth or income has no obvious trend. This is one reason we see continued growth.

Stable risk and expected return

Changing risk tolerance or changing investment opportunities could give us drift in overall variability and expected income as a fraction of wealth, but no such drift is apparent. While risk and expected return fluctuate, I see no long term trend.

Unobservable cost of capital

The estimate error for the expected return on aggregate capital is high. It is so high that we usually can't tell whether the cost of capital is higher or lower than average in any given country. Also, we can't tell how it varies over time, or what it's related to.

Units and unit value
Whenever assets trade, we can see sharp changes in their values. However we decide to count the number of units of capital in the economy, unit value changes more than the number of units, at least in the short run. These unit value changes are mostly permanent.

Temporary and permanent changes
Changes in output are erratic. Permanent changes are part of growth, and temporary changes we call "business cycles." But the unanticipated permanent changes and the unanticipated temporary changes are highly correlated.

Common movements
Both permanent and temporary changes in output have a substantial component that is common to different regions, sectors, and even countries. Virtually all the cross correlations are positive with broadly defined sectors, though in specific instances one sector can do well while another is doing badly.

Smoothed consumption and wages
Measured consumption and wages both vary less than income and wealth from quarter to quarter or year to year. Over days or hours, though, both can be highly variable, and both show greater annual variability over five- or ten-year intervals.

Volatile investment
Investment and saving (which differ in an open economy) are more volatile than output and income (which also differ). Similarly, output of durables is more volatile than output of other goods and services.

Volatile production
Production is more volatile than sales. Thus inventories are used more to avoid stockouts in sales situations than to smooth production. Firms vary production to maintain inventories more than they vary inventories to maintain production.

Stable output shares
The shares of output going to capital and labor (or rather to physical and human capital) are fairly stable. We see no apparent trends in these ratios, especially since World War II.

Correlated human and physical capital

Partly because output shares are stable, I think market values for human and physical capital are highly correlated in the aggregate. While some events help workers and hurt the owners of physical capital (or the reverse), most events affect them both in the same direction. Properly measured returns to human capital are low when returns to physical capital are low, and low returns anticipate increases in unemployment.

Correlated hours and earnings

Similarly, total labor compensation and hours are highly correlated. Wages and hours seem uncorrelated because we use average rather than marginal wages; because we ignore varying unemployment and overtime; and because we don't measure added human capital through on-the-job learning.

Full-time work

Most people work full time, though some have multiple jobs. They don't want part-time work. The hourly pay for part-time work is below that for full-time work. People who are not working full time generally work at finding a new full-time job.

Career advancement

People who keep the same job don't usually get big raises. Raises come with job changes, either within the same firm or across firms. Job changes of this kind are more common than terminations, and occur at a greater rate when times are good. Thus labor mobility, in the broadest sense, is procyclical.

Unemployment and leisure

Unemployment may be voluntary, in the sense that people may choose a career knowing that periods of unemployment are likely, but most people are still unhappy when it comes. It does not give them pleasure in the same way that leisure gives them pleasure.

Procyclical vacancies

Some vacancies represent openings for temporary jobs, while some represent offers to join a permanent team. Vacancies of both kinds go up when times are good.

Countercyclical dispersion
The dispersion of employment growth rates across plants, or across broadly defined sectors, is countercyclical. This means that "job destruction" is more volatile than "job creation" over the cycle. In a recession, the number of workers who lose their jobs increases a lot, while the number of workers who gain jobs doesn't change much.

Average hours and employment
For an individual plant, average hours per worker and employment are negatively correlated. For example, adding an extra shift increases employment and reduces average hours per worker. For the economy as a whole, though, average hours per worker and employment are positively correlated.

Uncorrelated volatility and growth
When we look across countries, we find that the less stable countries are about as likely to show high income or growth as the more stable ones. Similarly, changes in volatility over time are not obviously correlated with growth.

What Matters

I claim that we can use the general equilibrium approach to explain all of these stylized facts. In fact, we can use very simple models that incorporate only the most basic economic processes. Here are some of the key features I put into many of the specific models I use in understanding the stylized facts.

Human capital
The primary labor input to production is neither hours nor weighted hours. It is human capital, measured at estimated market value, possibly decomposed into units and unit value. It has mostly permanent rather than temporary shocks.

Physical capital
The primary capital input to production cannot be measured using the perpetual inventory method. It is physical capital, measured in "efficiency units" at estimated market value. We use the market value changes we see to estimate those we don't see.

Utilization

Utilization of human and physical capital is procyclical. More utilization of human capital can mean more hours per worker, more effort per hour, or greater employment. Utilization of human capital and utilization of physical capital are highly correlated.

Team production

When we produce something, we combine inputs, such as human and physical capital, experienced and inexperienced workers, domestic and foreign capital, or capital from different sectors. Because they are used together in production, the rents and values of these different forms of capital are related: when one does well, the others on the same team usually do well too.

Units and unit value

We can decompose the market value of composite capital into units and unit value, where most of the variation is in unit value. Variation in unit value represents variation in the "relevance" of composite capital.

Roundabout production

Many investments in both tangible and intangible assets have significant returns for years and years. Thus people must estimate conditions in the world for many years in the future when making their investments. These estimates can be very wrong.

Slow response

Shocks to tastes and technology affect the economy for many years. The reallocation implied by a shock costs less when done slowly. We normally implement both public and private innovations by investing in new human and physical capital, which also takes time.

Durable goods

Output of durable goods is highly cyclical relative to output of the services of durables. Utilization of human and physical capital tends to be low when durables output is temporarily low.

Career growth

Some forms of human capital are very durable. Production of this kind of human capital is very roundabout. It occurs through a lifelong process of career growth. In good times, people add human capital rapidly by working and gaining experience. In bad times, they lose it through obsolescence.

Numerous sectors

To understand growth and cycles, we must think of the world as divided into billions of sectors along many dimensions. Specialization in production and consumption makes the distinctions among these sectors more and more important. Variation in the match between wants and resources along all these dimensions drives variation in growth rates, business cycles, and asset price volatility. Common assumptions when making investments create comovement among sectors, especially when we aggregate to just a few sectors.

Complex utility

For many purposes, we must define tastes in great detail across many sectors; and we must write utility as time-nonseparable and state-dependent. Despite this complexity, though, we can stay within the simple world of von Neumann–Morgenstern utility.

Political stability

While they do not fall within the normal scope of the general equilibrium model, governments and social conventions often affect growth and business cycles. Violence, sharp changes in government policy, poorly defined property rights, and use of governments to promote rent seeking can lead to high volatility and low growth. High levels of government activity and large transfers to government officials or others can lead to low volatility and low growth.

What Doesn't Matter

I list here some factors that are inconsistent with general equilibrium, and some that are consistent with it but add unnecessary complexity. My general equilibrium approach is defined as much by what doesn't matter as by what does.

Fixed factors

While we can point to certain fixed factors that might someday constrain growth, we can see little evidence that any of these have been binding in recent centuries. For most purposes, we can ignore them.

Special sectors
Sectors that produce durables or that have especially roundabout production processes play an important role in business cycles. For brief periods, particular factors or resources can be crucial. But sectors like "oil" or "real estate" or "equipment" or "banking" or "research and development" or "education" do not have a consistently special role.

Economies of scale
Economies of scale are important at the plant level, and possibly at the firm level up to a certain size, but I doubt that they matter much for any of the developed countries.

Externalities
Knowledge has positive externalities as a nonrival input to production and consumption, and negative externalities, since new knowledge steals markets from old knowledge. I don't know whether the positive or negative ones dominate, so I ignore both and treat knowledge as a form of capital. Cities have both positive and negative externalities, but neither seems important at the level of a whole economy.

Nonconvexities
Thus we can treat production as convex. We can ignore, as a first approximation and probably also as a second approximation, any nonconvexities in production.

Public technology
The arrival of public technology that we embody in new investments acts just like the creation of technology through private research and development. We can have continuing growth in output through accumulation of capital, including technical capital, even in a world without growth in public technology.

Adjustment costs
I don't see any special role for adjustment costs in the installation of new capital (though I do see a role for costs in shifting capital between sectors or subsectors). I assume that market value and replacement cost are always equal, so I include all "internal" adjustment costs in replacement cost.

Leisure
In general, part-time work doesn't pay. I assume people are always either working or waiting for recall or looking for a new job. Neither waiting for recall nor job hunting is leisure. While it sometimes matters that people enter and leave the work force, we can explain business cycles without thinking about leisure at all.

Real interest rate
The real interest rate is one component of the cost of capital. (The price of risk is the other.) While the real interest rate does seem to change over time, those changes do not have any special significance for business cycles.

Cost of capital
The cost of capital has two components: the real interest rate and the price of risk. The price of risk probably fluctuates more than the real interest rate, but we can't see it clearly. We might as well assume that both components are constant.

Aggregate demand
I don't know how to define "aggregate demand," so I don't know how to measure it or use it in a theory of business cycles. Thus I ignore it.

Money
I think monetary policy must be largely passive in an economy with fully developed financial markets. It can't influence either inflation or the real economy. Money doesn't matter.

Inflation
So long as inflation is high enough to keep the nominal interest rate positive, I don't think it affects the real economy much. I take hyperinflation as a symptom of a country's inability to collect enough taxes to pay its bills: this political or fiscal instability has real effects, but the hyperinflation is just a symptom. In countries without hyperinflation, we might as well assume that inflation is constant.

Part II

Aspects of General Equilibrium

We often think of the general equilibrium model as one where commodities appear from time to time in amounts that depend on the state of the world at that time. We may even take the commodities to be perishable consumption goods, as in Lucas (1978).

But we can equally well use a model, as in Merton (1973), where real production processes allow us to transform goods at one time into goods at another time. We can even assume that the production processes are so rigid that they fix the relative prices of all pairs of goods. Relative prices vary over time and with the state of the world, but they do not depend on tastes.

In the first kind of model, quantities are fixed and prices are floating. In the second kind, prices are fixed and quantities are floating. Yet the two approaches are equivalent. For each model of one kind, there is an observationally identical model of the other kind. All state-contingent prices and quantities are identical at all times across the two models.

For a simple illustration of this, imagine two worlds with identical people. Each world has two goods, and each person has symmetric preferences. Everyone is indifferent between (a) x units of good 1 plus y units of good 2; and (b) y units of good 1 plus x units of good 2. For example, the utility function might be:

$$u(x, y) = \log x + \log y. \tag{1.1}$$

World L is a Lucas world. Each person has an endowment of goods, where the aggregate amounts of the two goods are equal. People trade to maximize utility. In equilibrium the two goods trade for the same price. Everyone ends up with equal amounts of the two goods. Individual i has wealth w_i, measured in units of the first good.

Now we construct world M, which is the corresponding Merton world. In this world, each person starts out with w_i units of good 1 only. There is a freely available technology for converting good 1 into good 2 on a one-for-one basis. Everyone again ends up with equal amounts of the two goods.

The two equilibria are identical, in that the equilibrium allocations and prices are the same in world M as in world L. But in world L, aggregate quantities are fixed and the relative price is free to move; while in world M, the relative price is fixed and quantities are free to move. This means the absence of production in the Walras–Arrow–Debreu model is not a defect. The model cannot explain any new facts if we put production in. The advantage of a model with production is purely conceptual: it helps us think about certain aspects of the world. This also means that we should not characterize a general equilibrium model as one where quantities are fixed while prices are free to move. If we picture deviations from equilibrium as taking the form of "sticky prices," then we should also put up the picture showing deviations from equilibrium as "sticky quantities." Indeed, sticky quantities sound more plausible than sticky prices.

This symmetry means that in a certain deep sense, "adjustment costs" cannot be important. The first kind of model allows no adjustment at all, while the second has no adjustment costs and allows free adjustment at given state-dependent prices. Similarly, "irreversible investments" cannot really make a difference to the kinds of equilibrium we can generate. In the Merton sort of model, investments are reversible; in the Lucas model, they are not. Yet the two models generate identical equilibria.

In the discussion below I use an example where production has "fixed proportions." Assuming that the fixed proportions can change over time, this is really just a stylistic device. In a sense, it has no economic content, since I can describe the same equilibrium assuming "fixed relative prices" instead of fixed proportions, where the fixed relative prices also change over time.

General Utility

Most of the time we write utility as time-separable and state-independent. It is the discounted sum of local utilities from future periods, so neither past consumption nor the state of the world affects utility of consumption in any period.

With this kind of utility, risk tolerance (willingness to accept gambles that may change wealth) and intertemporal elasticity of consumption (willingness to shift consumption between the present and the future) are inextricably linked. We can't vary one without varying the other; yet conceptually they are totally different features of our preferences. This linking causes endless mischief in both theory and empirical work. That alone is reason to move to more general utility.

For some applications we may want to use state-dependent utility. If we plan to look at data, we can choose observable state variables—the kinds that marketers use in tracking demand for their products and services. Tastes change, and they sometimes change unpredictably, but taste changes are usually observable. When tastes change, buying patterns change. Firms even do experiments—test marketing and consumer panels—to find out their customers' tastes.

For other applications, as when we want to construct extreme examples of utility, we can use a "fixed proportions" utility function, where people derive utility only from a fixed combination of goods and services, both past and future. Given available supplies of things, just one is likely to be in short supply and to be crucial to utility. Today's crucial item probably won't be tomorrow's, though: our tastes may change, and we will struggle to produce more of today's crucial item so it won't be so crucial tomorrow.

In fact, this kind of utility may not be as extreme as it looks at first. I think unwillingness to shift, either across time or across different goods and services, explains more than willingness to shift. Rather than assuming that people are willing to substitute one thing for another freely, I think we will come closer if we assume they are not willing to substitute at all. For example, when researchers like Kydland and Prescott (1993) see that hours worked tend to be strongly procyclical, they think that shows that people are very willing to shift leisure between present and future. I interpret it differently. I think people are shifting leisure very little; rather, they are shifting between working and waiting for recall, or between working and looking for a new job.

Consumption Smoothing

For still other applications, we can simply make the utility of current consumption depend on past consumption. For example, suppose we want to explain consumption smoothing. In the United States, quarterly and annual fractional consumption changes are not independent. As we increase the differencing interval, volatility rises faster than it would if successive changes were independent. One reason for this, I believe, is that people have an aversion to changes in consumption. This goes beyond risk aversion, since it shows up even when all changes in consumption are known. Given two consumption paths with equal present values, people prefer the one with smoother consumption.

Ryder and Heal (1973), Sundaresan (1989), and Constantinides (1990) discuss utility functions that show "habit formation," in the sense that past consumption creates a "floor" for current consumption. This may make sense for drug addiction, but I doubt that it applies to consumption generally. It has the unfortunate feature that an increase in current consumption, holding fixed past and future consumption, can reduce utility.

Greenig (1986) has a utility function that I find more appealing. (His utility function is a special case of Uzawa's (1968); and Abel (1990) discusses a special case of Greenig's.) With Greenig's approach, we can replace each period's consumption in the conventional separable utility function with a product of powers of that and prior consumptions.

Write c_t for consumption, β for the discount factor, and F for a weighted geometric average of current and past levels of c_t. In general, F can depend on many past levels of c_t. Local utility U is a conventional power function. Then we can write Greenig's general utility function as:

$$u = \sum_t \beta^t U[F(c_t, c_{t-1}, \ldots)]. \tag{2.1}$$

An individual maximizes the expected value of this utility subject to the usual constraints. To begin, we also need imaginary past consumption levels for the function F.

This is not the most general utility function, but it is general enough, I think, to eliminate the "equity premium puzzle" as described by Mehra and Prescott (1985) and the "real interest rate puzzle" as described by Weil (1989). In other words, it is general enough to explain why the consumption series is smoother than the wealth series at market value.

I can see no economic reason for assuming that utility of consumption is time-separable. Rather than saying that the utility function in equation (2.1) "explains" these puzzles, I prefer to say that the puzzles arise only when we impose inappropriate and unmotivated restrictions on the utility function. Sometimes time separability doesn't matter, and we can assume it for convenience; where it does matter, I think we should quickly abandon it.

Local Substitution

At intervals of a quarter or longer, aggregate consumption shows evidence of a preference for smoothing. At much shorter intervals, though, people seem very willing to shift consumption through time.

They exhibit "local substitution." Indeed, at very short intervals, individuals may even show satiation, which is almost the opposite of consumption smoothing.

Hindy, Huang, and Kreps (1992) and Hindy and Huang (1992, 1993) have proposed utility functions that show local substitution. Their idea is simply to replace current consumption in the utility function with an exponentially weighted average of current and past consumption. This allows them to write a plausible utility function over a continuous stream of consumption. We can combine their idea with Greenig's to create a utility function that shows willingness to substitute in the short run but smoothing in the medium to long run. We simply substitute a weighted arithmetic average of current and past consumption for current consumption in the weighted geometric average that defines a preference for smoothing.

As before, write c_t for consumption, β for the discount factor, and U for a conventional local power utility function. Write G_t for a weighted arithmetic average of consumption at time t and prior times, and F for a weighted geometric average of current and past levels of G. Now our utility function is:

$$u = \sum_t \beta^t U[F[G_t(c_t, c_{t-1}, \ldots), G_{t-1}(c_{t-1}, c_{t-2}, \ldots), \ldots]]. \tag{3.1}$$

The function G puts more weight on the recent past, while the function F puts more weight on the distant past. This allows us to combine local substitution and smoothing. Heaton (1993) uses a similar technique to combine local substitution with habit formation.

Production

We use human and physical capital, with effort, to produce output. Human capital includes skills, abstract knowledge, and the ability to learn more. Physical capital includes tangibles like land, equipment, and inventories, and intangibles like reputation, blueprints, and the experience a firm's employees have in working with one another.

We often focus on the last stages of production, when soft drinks are rolling off the assembly line, or movie images are dancing on the screen. When we take a broader view, we can see people formulating soft drinks and ordering ingredients, or learning the movie business from the ground up.

Production takes time—lots of time. In agriculture, for example, it takes research that makes tractor engines more efficient;

development of tires that will last through many growing seasons; construction of a factory to make tractors; teaching farmers to read and understand maintenance manuals; plowing; planting; and waiting for the crop to grow. What people learn and build this year will affect output for decades into the future.

Final output is what we care about, but before we get there, we plan and scheme and try things out; we adjust production methods and redesign products; we buy the raw materials to make the components that go into the finished goods we send to the retail stores. Only a little of what we do each year is to produce final goods and services. Most of what we do is to turn this year's capital into next year's capital.

Our technology is such that if we don't consume anything, we expect to have more capital next year than we had this year, no matter how we measure it. In fact, the rate at which we expect composite capital to grow (when we don't use it up) seems to stay about the same decade after decade or even century after century.

At the highest level, we can model this process as if capital grows on its own at an uncertain rate, while people convert bits of capital to consumption along the way. Write r_t for one plus the return on composite capital K_t, and c_t for consumption. Everything is per person.

$$K_{t+1} = r_t K_t - c_t. \tag{4.1}$$

Think of r_t as chosen independently in each period from a distribution with mean μ and standard deviation σ in log space.

With this way of writing production, K_t is "effective" capital and incorporates the cumulative benefit of any quality improvements in human or physical capital over the years. Any temporary shocks to tastes or technology, plus this year's permanent shock to technology, show up in r_t. Thus we do not need to put a separate technology factor, or technology "shock," in front of $r_t K_t$.

Also, r_t combines output and depreciation from all sources. Writing y_t for output and d_t for fractional depreciation (including obsolescence), we have:

$$r_t = 1 + y_t/K_t - d_t. \tag{4.2}$$

Output and depreciation have temporary components that partly offset one another. When output is high, expected depreciation is high too. Thus, as a first approximation, we can assume that r_t is drawn independently in each period from an unchanging distribution.

Again as a first approximation, we can take consumption to be a constant fraction γ of effective capital.

$$c_t = \gamma K_t. \tag{4.3}$$

When consumption satisfies (4.3), effective capital follows a geometric random walk over time. Its expected growth rate is $\mu - \gamma$ in log space. There are no fixed factors in this production process, so expected growth can continue at a constant rate indefinitely, if γ is low relative to μ. Actual growth depends on both γ and the realizations r_t.

Because people can choose among different production methods (and different forms of political and economic structure) with various levels of risk and expected return, μ and σ depend on both tastes and technology. Because people take μ and σ into account when choosing consumption, γ also depends on both tastes and technology. To separate the influences of tastes and technology, we need far more detail in the model.

Output

I like thinking of production as taking us from this year's composite capital (both human and physical) to consumption plus next year's composite capital. With a little more detail, we can go from this year's inputs to "output" plus what's left of this year's composite capital. We divide output into consumption and investment, and add investment to this year's composite capital.

Output is like the "maturation" of production processes that may have been going on for many years. When parents start teaching their children or when firms start developing their brand names, they base their decisions on their views of what the world will be like in the future. The investments they make will have little value without supplementary investments along the way, but the payoffs from successful investments can also continue for many years.

When a successful investment matures, it usually does so with a final burst of effort. Employment jumps up, hours are high, and machines are used intensively. Out comes a specific product or service. A less successful investment matures with more of a whimper, or doesn't mature at all. Its owner may try to defer its maturation until later, when conditions for it may be better. An initial or intermediate investment is successful if the investor's guesses turn out to be more right than wrong—if tastes and technology develop the way he expected them to. The details matter: it does no good to be right about computers if you make big ones with tape drives when people want small ones with removable disk drives.

Some investment decisions have short horizons, but many have long horizons. Those with long horizons are especially risky, because investors must see far into the future to know how to place their bets. If they make mistakes this year, they are apt to make the same mistakes next year, because they won't know much more about the distant future next year than they know this year. Investors make long-horizon bets, though, because when they do succeed they sometimes succeed spectacularly.

Output and the utilization of both human and physical capital jump up when successful investments mature, and are apt to stay high for a while as subsequent investments mature. Some of the increase in output is permanent. The temporary part stays high for a while because expectations about the distant future change incrementally. If we were making good estimates about this year five years ago, we were probably making good estimates about next year four years ago. Similarly, when early investments turn out to have been misdirected, output jumps down permanently, and both output and utilization can be temporarily low for an extended period.

Changes in utilization and the associated changes in output we call "business cycles." Changes in what output would be at normal levels of utilization we call "growth." This normalized output follows a process that looks like a smoothed geometric random walk—in fact, a process that looks like smoothed values of composite capital at market value.

Changes in utilization are temporary, while the smoothed changes in normalized output are permanent, in the sense that shocks to the underlying geometric random walk are permanent. The random walk is smoothed because adjustments to shifts in tastes and technology are slow and costly. Even a major new invention takes time to affect output, because it has an impact only after we incorporate it in newly created human and physical capital.

Business cycle shocks and growth shocks and shocks to effective composite capital measured at market value are all correlated. Thus shocks to utilization and shocks to normalized output are correlated. Perhaps the best way to identify business cycles is to use a measure of utilization like weighted hours worked per person; and perhaps the best way to identify growth is to use a measure of capital in efficiency units, like the market value of an economy's securities.

When we decompose output into cyclical and "trend" components, we can use these measures of business cycles and growth as guides. The cyclical component will be stationary, and the trend component will look like a smoothed geometric random walk. Hodrick and Prescott's (1981) way of decomposing output fails to bring out these statistical features of output or the underlying economic ties between business cycles and growth.

In good times, we see permanent growth in effective capital, smoothed permanent growth in output, temporary jumps in utilization, and temporary jumps in output. In bad times, we see the reverse. Looking across broadly defined sectors, permanent shocks everywhere are correlated; temporary shocks everywhere are correlated; and the permanent and temporary shocks are correlated with one another.

What is it about the evolution of tastes and technology that makes some investments successful? High payoffs are good, but only if they are in forms that people want to consume now or want to apply to ongoing production processes. Investments fail when the payoffs differ in detail from what we expected, or when what people want turns out to differ in detail from what we expected them to want.

In general, then, we can define "good times" as when we see a good "match" between wants and resources, and "bad times" as when we see a poor match. The match stays good in a boom or stays bad in a bust because shifts in tastes and technology are partly permanent. If we were right about this year, we're likely to be right about next year.

Since output depends on the details of investments made in the near and distant past, and on the evolution of tastes and technology since the investments were made, I am reluctant to summarize it as depending on today's composite capital, or on today's components of capital. I'm reluctant to include measures of utilization like hours worked, because high utilization causes high output only in the most immediate sense. In a deeper sense, both high output and high utilization are caused by successful investments.

If I do write output as depending on a "capital input" and a "labor input," I at least want to make it *symmetric*. If the capital input is physical capital, then the labor input should be human capital. If we include a measure of effort like hours worked, we should also

include a measure of utilization of physical capital. I can't see any
sense in using physical capital as the capital input, and hours or
weighted hours or workers as the labor input.

The simplest approach we can take is to write output y_t as
depending on human capital h_t and physical capital k_t. Assuming
Cobb–Douglas production, we have:

$$y_t = a_t h_t^\alpha k_t^{1-\alpha}. \tag{5.1}$$

Sometimes we use examples where the factor a_t is constant. When it
varies, though, it is not just a "technology factor." It is affected by
both tastes and technology in complex ways. Shocks to tastes and
technology affect a_t, h_t, and k_t simultaneously, but the changes in a_t
are temporary. To add more detail, we can write a_t as depending on
a coefficient A_t and on effort e_t and utilization f_t of physical capital:

$$a_t = A_t e_t^\alpha f_t^{1-\alpha}. \tag{5.2}$$

"Effort" here means both hours per worker (or potential worker)
and effort per hour. Thus we can also write output as:

$$y_t = A_t (e_t h_t)^\alpha (f_t k_t)^{1-\alpha}. \tag{5.3}$$

With this way of writing output, we emphasize the absence of any
fixed factors limiting growth. As human and physical capital
accumulate, output grows. The marginal products of human capital,
physical capital, effort, and utilization can all vary, but none of
them must decline steadily as capital and output grow.

Effort is utilization of human capital. A person who is unemployed
or out of the labor force has human capital, though he is not using it
as part of the formal economy. Thus variation in effort includes
moves between unemployment and employment, and moves into or
out of the labor force.

Writing output as (5.1) or (5.3) has a striking implication, which I
will use repeatedly in different contexts. A change in one of the
inputs causes a change in the marginal products of all of the inputs.
More human capital or more effort means a higher rental rate on
physical capital. More physical capital or more intense use of
physical capital means a higher wage.

As we add more detail and use separate descriptions of output in
different sectors, this implication spreads. A good event in one
sector that causes effective capital to increase in that sector is also
good for all the other sectors that join with it in production. When

production involves inputs from different countries, this can mean that growth spreads from one country to another. The idea that an input's marginal product depends on the amounts of other inputs that combine with it in producing something can help explain common movements across different sectors, convergence among countries that interact a lot, and even migration from poor countries to rich ones.

Finally, let's summarize. We combine human and physical capital into composite capital K_t, and we combine effort and utilization of physical capital into utilization E_t of composite capital.

$$E_t = e_t^\alpha f_t^{1-\alpha}, \tag{5.4}$$

$$K_t = h_t^\alpha k_t^{1-\alpha}, \tag{5.5}$$

and

$$y_t = A_t E_t K_t. \tag{5.6}$$

This "production function" shows constant returns to scale in the sense that multiplying K_t by a constant multiplies y_t by the same constant. I think of K_t as the market value of composite capital, but I do not think of this function as separating the effects of tastes and technology, or the effects of freely available and privately owned technology, or the effects of government and private actions. It is a "reduced form."

Thus we can create a version of (5.6) where we take A_t as constant. Changes in K_t are permanent and capture growth, while changes in E_t are temporary and capture business cycles. Changes in K_t and changes in E_t are correlated.

Writing Y_t for output in this simple model, we have:

$$Y_t = A E_t K_t. \tag{5.7}$$

This model captures business cycles and growth in broad statistical outline. Before we take it seriously, though, we should smooth out the relation between output and permanent shocks to composite capital.

Firms

To understand production fully, we need to go to the level of the individual unit: the plant or assembly team; the office or department. Production in process moves through these units, which add a little here, and take out a little for final goods and services there. The possible inputs and outputs for each unit are very specific, and each has an array of possible processing methods. Understanding technology means understanding all of these possibilities, not just the ones actually used during a particular period.

In principle we can do that. We can look at a firm's engineering data, including the specifications and maintenance history of all of its plant and equipment. We can look at the background and skills of its employees and its ties with suppliers and customers. We can look at studies of different ways of staffing and organizing production. We can look at its plans for dealing with emergencies like strikes and power outages.

In practice this is almost impossible. Even if we succeed in summarizing the firm's production process, how are we to combine these processes for all the firms in the economy? If growth and business cycles depend on the varying match between wants and resources, too much aggregation will destroy the detail we need to follow the match. We'll certainly lose it if we aggregate physical capital at book value, or if we estimate the labor input by summing worker-hours, weighted or unweighted.

In principle, we can keep all the detail and build up a true picture of the economy's technology. In practice, the cost of doing so would be staggering. Measuring production possibilities in detail would be so costly that it would take much of total output just to estimate how we create the remaining portion of output. The production process must remain something of a mystery. Thus the production side of the economy is parallel to the preference side. In principle, we can observe both tastes and technology, actual and potential, in full detail. In practice, the cost of doing so would be prohibitive.

The aggregation problem is similar for tastes and technology. Even if we could map out individual utility functions in all their sectoral detail, how could we combine them into a representative utility function defined on composite consumption? Even if we could map out each firm's technology, how could we combine these maps into an overall technology for the economy?

In practice, we can't know or aggregate tastes or technology accurately enough to distinguish general equilibrium from its alternatives. If we can't aggregate tastes or technology, then we can't define or measure "marginal cost," for an individual product or for a firm's entire output. I especially don't know how to define marginal cost when production processes are long and variable, so that many of the inputs contributing to today's outputs occurred in the more or less distant past. So we can't really ask, as Hall (1988c) wants to do, if price exceeds marginal cost for the typical firm.

A manager spends much of his time looking for cases where the firm pays a worker more than his marginal product, or a machine more than its contribution to output. An economist doesn't have much chance of outguessing the manager. Competitors do a good job of bidding away underpaid workers, so normally an economist can only assume that each factor is paid its marginal product in a generalized sense.

The facts that cause firms to do most production also make it hard to answer questions about marginal cost and price. If all inputs were traded freely at observable prices in competitive markets, we would not need firms. Firms exist because a contractual arrangement among workers and managers and owners of other inputs allows more efficient production than handling all transactions in spot markets.

These contractual arrangements are more efficient partly because the people in the firm come to know one another and learn how best to work together. They are efficient because the managers work out ways to induce the workers to act more in the firm's interest than in their own. Some of these ways require continued use of the same workers for many months or years.

In other words, the very notion of a firm implies the kind of long-maturity investment that I consider crucial to growth and business cycles. It also makes implausible any aggregate production function that presumes to express technology as distinct from tastes.

Inputs

To repeat, production takes too many years and too many distinct inputs to be summarized by an aggregate function that depends only on the current values of a few inputs. If we ignore these problems and write down an aggregate production function anyway, what shall we use for the inputs?

As noted above, we certainly don't want asymmetric inputs, like tangible physical capital for the capital input, and hours for the labor input. We want symmetric inputs, like human and physical capital, or foreign and domestic capital, or effort and utilization of physical capital.

Many of the examples I use make sense in a world of certainty, but to understand business cycles and varying growth across countries and time, we need models with uncertainty. In particular, we need to deal with varying values of the capital inputs to production.

Variation in value, as a first approximation, reflects variation in the "effectiveness" of capital. When the match between wants and resources improves, where "resources" means capital as allocated to numerous sectors, the value of the capital stock rises; and when the match worsens, the value falls. Variation in patience or in risk tolerance can sometimes affect value, but we can understand the economy's behavior without those effects.

More effective capital is just as good as more capital: in fact, I suggest that we define the capital inputs to production so that more effective capital *is* more capital. To do this, we can define capital at estimated total market value. This is like measuring capital in efficiency units.

I can't think of any consistent way to aggregate capital except at market value. When we want to know how much physical capital a firm is using, we generally add the market values of its securities, as estimated from market prices. The book value of the firm's securities, taken from its financial statements, is a very noisy estimate of market value; one reason is that book value omits entirely the values of many of the firm's intangible assets.

The Bureau of Economic Analysis estimates aggregate physical capital using the "perpetual inventory method." The BEA takes investment in each of various asset classes, applies a customized but unvarying depreciation rate to each class, and adds the results across investment years and asset classes. The BEA ignores intangible assets completely and treats cost data inconsistently. We enter an asset at market value, since cost is initial market value, but we don't value it at market after that. This problem is especially severe for intangible assets, which vary more in value than tangible assets. As a result, the BEA's estimate of capital hardly varies at all, except that it grows at a steady pace. An estimate like this can't help us much in understanding the variation we see in output.

We know we can't aggregate physical capital by counting machines, or by combining the "capacity" of different machines, when they produce such a variety of outputs. The BEA sensibly tries to assign a dollar value to each part of physical capital.

Apparently, the BEA thinks of the value it assigns to a machine as the "replacement cost" for that machine. I think the only sensible definition of "replacement cost" or "reproduction cost" for physical capital is market value. To replace an item, we simply buy it in the market. Building a similar item from scratch is not replacing it, since a newly built item differs from an existing one, and since building takes time.

Some people like to think of replacement cost as excluding "adjustment costs" like the cost of shutting down an assembly line to install a new machine. I prefer to think of replacement cost as inclusive of all adjustment costs, since I can't figure any clear way, even in principle, to separate adjustment costs and other costs. In a sense, all costs are adjustment costs.

We can't easily estimate the market value of a machine or an idea that a firm uses as part of its production process. We can, however, estimate the market value of the firm's entire stock of physical capital whenever the firm's securities trade in the markets. We just add up the market prices of the securities.

I assume that market price is the best estimate of value for this purpose. I trust the judgment of the market, where people have real money at stake, more than the results of an arbitrary valuation method devised by economists. I do not see much merit in the tests that seem to detect "excess volatility" in the markets.

If we take firms' market values seriously, as estimated from market prices for selected firms, we will probably conclude that market values for firms that don't have traded securities fluctuate in much the same way as market prices for firms that do. This is especially true of an index of market prices.

If market value or replacement cost for all physical capital fluctuates like market price for firms that have traded securities, the BEA estimates are far too stable. If we measure the physical capital input to production my way, using market prices whenever they exist as guides, we will find that the physical capital input varies enormously. Measured this way, shocks to the physical capital input are largely permanent, and changes in the physical capital input come more from revaluation than from new investment or expected depreciation.

We can also think of capital at market value as the present value of all its future rents. This makes the use of capital at market value seem circular: rents are like outputs, yet the present value of rents is an input. The problem here is that everything we measure is endogenous, including current and expected future rents. Thus capital is as much an output as an input.

How are we to estimate the market value of human capital? Since claims on human capital almost never trade in the market, we must reason by analogy with physical capital. We make our human and physical capital investments using the same assumptions about the future, so when we are right about physical capital, we are probably right about human capital too. Human capital, like physical capital, lasts a long time, but both can become obsolete with alarming suddenness. Human and physical capital take relatively stable shares of output.

For all these reasons, I think human and physical capital vary in value in much the same way. In fact, I think the returns on human and physical capital are highly correlated. We always seem to have more human capital than physical capital, but the fractional changes are similar. Thus we can use the market prices for firms that have traded securities to suggest market values for human capital. We assume that the return on total human capital is equal to the return on total physical capital. We do the same for the physical capital of firms that have no traded securities.

What does it mean to talk about the market value of human capital? In theory, the market value of a person's human capital is the present value of his future wages, less the present value of any direct investments in human capital. (Investments that we make by taking lower wages on the job are already accounted for.)

Effort and utilization of physical capital clearly vary with the business cycle: in general, utilization is high when successful investments mature and low at other times. We may want to add hours across people to figure a rough measure of effort; or we may want to use weighted hours, as Hansen (1993) and Kydland and Prescott (1993) do, increasing the weights for people with greater skill or compensation. Similarly, we may want to figure a weighted average of capacity utilization for machines and other physical capital, using survey results to estimate utilization.

Many aspects of effort, though, are hard to observe. People stay on the job and work at a slower pace when business is down but they expect it to pick up soon, partly to maintain their skills. Capacity utilization for physical capital is almost undefinable, since I don't know how to define "full capacity" for an asset or a firm. What is capacity utilization for a personal computer that sits idle, as planned, 99% of the time?

Since it's so hard to measure utilization of either human or physical capital directly, I suggest that we do it indirectly, as part of a statistical decomposition of output that combines temporary shocks and smoothed permanent shocks. Does this decomposition mean the decline in labor income during a recession is caused by an attack of laziness? Not at all. For the most part, variation in effort is a symptom rather than a cause of business cycles.

This indirect method of measuring utilization gives us a single number, rather than separate estimates for human and physical capital. In effect, we are assuming that effort is the same as utilization of physical capital. Similarly, when we use market value variation from securities to estimate changes in the values of both human and physical capital, we are assuming that these two inputs remain in a constant ratio.

For many purposes, then, we can simplify equation (5.3). Write α for human capital's share of output, k_t for physical capital at estimated market value, and K_t for composite capital at market value.

$$K_t = k_t/(1 - \alpha). \tag{6.1}$$

Now write y_t for output and E_t for composite utilization. As in (5.6), we have:

$$y_t = A_t E_t K_t. \tag{6.2}$$

We can also combine (4.2) and (6.2) to relate utilization, return, and depreciation:

$$r_t = 1 + A_t E_t - d_t. \tag{6.3}$$

In the case where return is drawn from the same distribution each period, and where A_t is relatively stable, a cyclically high level of utilization means a correspondingly high expected depreciation rate for composite capital.

How can we tell when a shock to output is temporary? An increase in capital at market value can mean higher rent now or higher rent later. It can mean higher rent now followed by further increases in rent, or a big increase now followed by reversion to a mean.

We want to define utilization so that its shocks are temporary. I suggest that we define A_t as a multiple of a weighted geometric average F of current and past levels of the market value of capital, all divided by the current level. This weighted average roughly captures what output would be at normal levels of utilization.

$$A_t = B F(K_t, K_{t-1}, \ldots)/K_t. \tag{6.4}$$

Then (6.2) becomes:

$$y_t = B E_t F(K_t, K_{t-1}, \ldots). \tag{6.5}$$

I believe we can always choose the weights so that E_t, as defined by (6.5), usually increases when we have a positive shock to capital at market value, and then gradually declines again. In other words, we choose the weights so that shocks to utilization are both temporary and positively correlated with shocks to capital at market value.

By analogy, if we want a separate measure of effort (utilization of human capital), we can imagine dividing total wages by a multiple of a weighted geometric average of current and past levels of human capital at estimated market value. The weights may differ from those in F. Again, we choose the weights so that shocks to effort are both temporary and positively correlated with shocks to human capital. We can do this in a model more easily than we can do it in practice, because we can't easily estimate the value of human capital.

Smoothed Output

What would output look like if utilization never changed? Would it be proportional to capital at market value?

Not necessarily. The market value of capital is the present value of its rents, which means it is a kind of weighted average of current and state-dependent future output. Even without changes in utilization, we can have anticipated and possibly state-dependent changes in the ratio of output to capital at market value.

In fact, we can use the weighted average F that appears in (6.4) and (6.5) to define a smoothed output series. In addition to choosing the weights so that shocks to utilization are both temporary and positively correlated with shocks to composite capital, we can choose them so that smoothed output shows only positive autocorrelation in its changes.

A shock to utilization is reversed in subsequent periods, while a shock to smoothed output is extended in subsequent periods.

We define smoothed output z_t so that

$$z_t = B F(K_t, K_{t-1}, \ldots), \tag{7.1}$$

where B and F are defined as in (6.4). From (6.5), we have:

$$y_t = E_t z_t. \tag{7.2}$$

We normalize E_t so that it averages about one. Then it seems reasonable to call z_t "smoothed output." Since z_t is a multiple of an average of current and past capital stocks, it naturally tends to have percentage changes that show positive serial correlation. We can also think of (7.2) as giving a decomposition of output into "cycle" and "trend." Unlike Beveridge and Nelson's (1981) decomposition, innovations to the cycle and trend components of output in (7.2) show a positive correlation.

Units and Unit Value

Some people like the BEA's physical capital estimates because they feel that the physical capital input to production doesn't really vary much. They distinguish between physical capital and its value. They don't think value is very important; for example, they say a shortage of a particular kind of physical capital may increase its value without increasing its effectiveness in production.

I believe this view confuses engineering effectiveness and economic effectiveness. A shortage doesn't affect the production possibilities for a piece of capital in the engineering sense, but it means that the rental rate on that kind of capital goes up along with its value. Its economic effectiveness increases.

I think market value measures economic effectiveness quite precisely. Market value is the present value of the net rents we expect from a piece of capital, so it summarizes the economic contribution we expect that capital to make throughout its lifetime. If we want to estimate the instantaneous effectiveness of a piece of capital, we can use its rental rate.

Similarly, some people think human capital doesn't vary much. They may use average years of schooling or job experience to measure it. Since these measures don't take account of changing tastes and technology, which affect the relevance of schooling and job experience, I don't think they have much economic meaning.

At least in principle, though, I think we can decompose the total market value of physical capital into a units series and a unit value series that have some economic meaning. The units series varies slowly, like the BEA estimates, while the unit value series varies like an index of security prices. For some purposes, we may want to use these two components of capital separately, though I still believe the best measure of aggregate physical capital is its total market value.

Assume that we use (6.1) to estimate composite capital K_t at market value. Write y_t for output, c_t for consumption, q_t for units of capital, and p_t for unit value. Choose the initial value for p_t arbitrarily. At the start of each period, total capital is units times unit value:

$$p_t q_t = K_t. \tag{8.1}$$

Each period, we invest the difference between output and consumption in new units at the next period's unit value:

$$q_{t+1} - q_1 = (y_t - c_t)/p_{t+1}. \tag{8.2}$$

In effect, we are assuming that depreciation takes the form of changes in unit value rather than loss of units. Combining (8.1) and (8.2) in the usual way, we have:

$$p_{t+1}/p_t = (K_{t+1} - y_t + c_t)/K_t \tag{8.3}$$

and

$$q_{t+1}/q_t = (K_{t+1}/K_t)/(p_{t+1}/p_t). \tag{8.4}$$

With these definitions, the units series will be quite stable. Some may view it as measuring the "amount" of capital, but then the unit value series measures the "effectiveness" of each unit, so total market value measures capital in "efficiency units."

In a sense, the BEA estimates of physical capital together with estimates of Tobin's q give us another way of dividing capital at market value between units and unit values. But the BEA is only trying to measure tangible physical capital, while I'm thinking about total capital, including human capital. Tobin's q never strays too far from one, while this unit value series is nonstationary and follows something like a geometric random walk.

When we look at composite capital in separate sectors of the economy, we can continue to use a single unit value series derived for the whole economy, and estimate a separate units series for each sector. Then the units in different sectors will be comparable, since they will all have the same value. We'll be able to add units of capital across sectors.

Rather than decomposing output into a multiple of smoothed composite capital and utilization, we might look at the statistical relation between output and the components of capital. For example, we might regress the fractional change in output on current and lagged fractional changes in units and unit value of capital.

I suspect we'll find that both units and unit value help explain output in this sense. We may find that an unusually large increase in units leads more quickly than an increase in unit value does to an increase in output. Unit value may predict output only with long and variable lags. Indeed, Fischer and Merton's (1984) and Barro's (1990b) results suggest exactly that.

Consumption

Consumption, for individuals and in total, depends on both tastes and technology. High expected returns on investments increase the amount we *can* consume; impatience and other elements of utility increase the amount we *want to* consume.

In the long run, consumption seems to grow at the same rate as wealth, income, and other measures of available resources. Consumption is roughly proportional to wealth, measured at market value, and people consume less than the expected return on composite capital, so we expect continuing growth.

I find this continued growth surprising, since we might naturally assume that people consume all of the expected return on composite wealth and all of the gains from the spread of freely available technology. Growth can continue only when people are sufficiently patient and their investments are sufficiently productive. Apparently both conditions have been satisfied all around the world in recent centuries.

In the medium term, consumption is remarkably stable. I think this is partly because of "consumption smoothing," as expressed through the kinds of utility discussed above, and partly because consumption is geared to take-home pay, which is itself quite stable. Actually, consumption seems more stable than it is, because we assume a mechanical depreciation process for consumer durables. Thus estimated consumption from consumer durables is smoother than it would be if we had accurate implied rental rates for them. Rental rates on spot markets often change sharply.

For a simple aggregate model of consumption that illustrates some of these features, write c_t for consumption, W_t for composite wealth at market value, and F for a weighted geometric average of current and past levels of wealth. For a constant b, we can write:

$$c_t = bF(W_t, W_{t-1}, \ldots). \tag{9.1}$$

This will give a consumption series that is smoother than wealth when changes in wealth are mostly permanent. It is, of course, only an approximation. When b is less than the expected return that people face on wealth, it will give continuing growth.

Income follows wealth more closely than consumption does. If we ignore the difference between income and output, and between saving and investment, we can define "investment" as income less consumption. Investment defined this way will automatically be more volatile (in the medium term) than consumption. Consumption smoothing alone makes measured investment more volatile than output and consumption.

Temporary changes in output and income magnify these effects. People look past these temporary changes in figuring consumption. Even if consumption were strictly proportional to wealth, temporary changes in output would make investment more volatile than consumption. In the short term, consumption often changes very sharply. People are flexible (and erratic) about exactly when they consume many things. We can capture some of this variability with utility that shows "local substitution," as discussed above.

Innovation

Much of the growth that we see in the world comes jointly with innovation. Does this mean that growth is driven primarily by the spread of a freely available technology created largely by scientists unmotivated by profit? Does it mean that investing in human or physical capital has external benefits? Does it mean that firms and individuals who invest in knowledge gain nonrival inputs to consumption and production whose benefits can be widely shared at low cost?

I think we can understand innovation largely within the general equilibrium framework. All the positive externalities mentioned above exist, but they are largely offset, or more than offset, by negative externalities. We might as well assume that the positive and negative externalities cancel each other, and model the world as having no externalities.

For example, take freely available technology. It sounds nice for the "haves" of the world to simply transfer the technology they have painfully acquired to the "have nots." What does it cost them?

For one thing, the transfer itself costs money. Education can be as painful as research and development. Moreover, this free transfer reduces the incentives that firms and individuals have for creating new technology. If an inventor can charge people for the use of technology based on its value to them, he will usually charge the "haves" more than the "have nots," and he will create more technology. The resulting equilibrium can be close to efficient, and it even has some attractive distributional features. On balance, I suspect that world welfare is maximized, using any of several utility functions, when we enforce property rights in knowledge and ideas, at least up to a certain point, and when we allow price discrimination in the sense that heavy users pay more than light users.

Creating new knowledge has a negative externality in the impact that new ideas have on the values of old ideas. A new idea can make an old idea obsolete overnight, and can thus "steal" the old idea's market. When ideas are costly and property rights are enforced, this can mean the amount spent on creating the old idea was largely wasted. It helped neither its creator nor society. Aghion and Howitt (1992) show that when the negative externalities in market stealing offset the positive externalities in ideas, the resulting equilibrium can be efficient.

Knowledge, after it is created, earns rents, but rents need not imply an inefficient equilibrium. Imagine that many people each create a small amount of a specialized input to production. When that input is a limiting resource, it earns rents for its owners, yet it may always earn competitive rental rates, and its owners may face normal expected returns when they make their investments.

Knowledge is different because current knowledge tends to be owned by just a few people at a time. To model that feature, imagine that people compete to create valuable knowledge. A person who succeeds collects rents from users, until his knowledge is made obsolete by the next discovery. Under certain assumptions, the total rents he collects equal (in present value) the amounts everyone spent on the competition. We can even have a kind of constant-returns technology, where doubling the amount you spend to create knowledge doubles the present value of your anticipated rents. This makes investment in knowledge very much like investment in any other kind of capital.

Do I gain when you become educated? If we work together to produce something, my wage will be higher if you are educated than if you are not, but this is not an external benefit. The external benefit comes when you give me valuable ideas without expecting valuable ideas in return, or perhaps when I simply take pleasure in knowing that you are educated. I find it hard to believe that these external benefits are significant.

Some sectors of the economy seem to show a continuing rapid pace of innovation. For example, we see more rapid innovation in "equipment" than in other sectors. Certainly electronic equipment has had more rapid innovation than most sectors. Does that mean we should treat equipment as a special kind of capital?

Not really. Rapid innovation in computers means a rapid decline in the price of a unit of computing or data storage capacity. This implies that today's computers depreciate rapidly as new generations are introduced. The rental rate on a rapidly depreciating asset must be high relative to its value, but the expected return on the asset can be normal.

Also, the production process in this kind of business is especially long-lived. Firms and individuals gain experience with one generation of equipment that they use in producing the next generation. Jumping into the middle of this sequence can be hard. But many sectors have long-lived production processes; another example is the development of a brand name in packaged consumer goods.

To model a sector like this, write p_t for the computer price, d for its fractional depreciation rate per period, y_t for the computer rental rate, and r for the interest rate. In a world of certainty with no taxes, we have:

$$p_{t+1} = (1 - d)p_t \qquad\qquad (10.1)$$

and

$$y_t = (r + d)p_t. \qquad\qquad (10.2)$$

Now suppose that a computer maker has experience capital worth k_t which allows him to produce current generation machines at cost

c_t. If he produces n_t of the current machines, which implies a market share proportional to his share of industry capital, he ends up with experience capital k_{t+1} equal in value to his experience capital today. Firms with higher market share have more capital, but they all produce at the same cost. The number of machines he sells next period increases to exactly offset the reduction in his gross profit per machine, so his total gross profit remains the same.

$$n_{t+1} = n_t/(1-d), \tag{10.3}$$

$$c_{t+1} = (1-d)c_t, \tag{10.4}$$

$$n_t(p_t - c_t) = rk_t, \tag{10.5}$$

and

$$k_{t+1} = k_t. \tag{10.6}$$

So long as he keeps on innovating, the computer maker earns a competitive return on his initial capital investment. No one can enter the business, except by splitting off from an existing firm, because next period's capital depends on this period's capital plus current production.

Note that (10.6) says that the values of next period's capital and this period's capital are the same; but they take different forms. Next period's capital is as much an output of the production process as this period's machines.

This sector is special only because innovation is rapid, the product depreciation rate is high, the rental–purchase price ratio is high, and an outsider must buy existing industry capital to enter the business. None of these factors implies any externalities or lack of competition.

In sum, innovation does not seem to force us outside the general equilibrium approach. It does not even imply that we need a changing technology factor in front of our production function. We can treat the accumulation of technology as just the growth of a form of capital, and we can capture this growth in the inputs to production.

Actually, we can interpret this model in many ways. We can imagine that the technology needed to produce each generation of computers arrives just in time, but that a manufacturer can benefit from the technology only by using it in new plant and equipment or in new skills; or we can imagine that each manufacturer creates the ability to produce each new generation through private research and development. In this model, public and private technical advances are indistinguishable.

Return

Return, as defined by equation (4.2), is the ratio of output to composite capital at market value, less depreciation (or plus appreciation) on start-of-period capital. For many purposes, we can assume that expected return is constant, since variation in the output–capital ratio is offset by variation in expected depreciation.

Even though expected return may vary, actual return varies far more than expected return. Variation in actual return, which is mostly luck, swamps variation in expected return. That's one reason we can't tell whether expected return varies, as Merton (1980) points out.

Variation in the return on capital is the single biggest reason for variation in growth across countries or across time. In other words, the most important reason for variation in growth is *luck*.

Return is mostly unanticipated. This does not mean, though, that we find no correlation across countries between return and initial conditions in those countries. Returns across countries are correlated in various ways: in a given period, some kinds of countries do well, while others do badly. After the fact, we may be able to use initial conditions to explain those differences almost fully. That does not mean owners of capital know in advance what their returns will be.

What counts is whether we made the right investments months or years ago as the production process unfolded. If recent developments put a rosier hue on those investments, return and growth are high. If recent developments put a bluer hue on them, return and growth are low.

As always, the details matter. What we hope is that we succeeded in investing in areas, defined across many dimensions, that gave large returns of goods and services that people turned out to value highly. Throughout the production process, the *match* between wants and resources along all these dimensions plays a crucial role in the return to capital. When the match is poor, we have to regroup by reallocating capital across sectors. Regrouping is costly, because capital is specialized in many ways. The loss in capital we incur by regrouping is permanent.

While variation in realized return matters more, variation in expected return plays some role in economic growth, both across countries and across time, especially over very long periods. Up to a certain point, a more stable political system means lower risk and higher expected return. Better defined property rights, for a given level of specialization, can have the same effects. When stability comes at the cost of high taxes and a large government sector, though, it may reduce expected return. Very specialized investments, sometimes combined with free trade and investment, can increase both risk and expected return.

Often, though, factors that affect a country's welfare do so via the value and composition of its capital stock, rather than its risk or expected return. I count a country as poor when it has relatively little human and physical capital, though it may have become poor in part because the expected return on its composite capital was low.

Risk

Risk is uncertainty in the return on composite capital at market value. It is uncertainty about the payoffs from our investments, where some payoffs will occur far in the future. It is uncertainty about whether we will have what we want in the future, and about whether we will want what we have.

High risk means lots of reallocation when things turn out badly. It means high adjustment costs as we shift resources to more promising areas. It means high average unemployment as people switch to better careers. It usually means great inequality across individuals and countries. In the end, risk means uncertainty about the composition and level of future consumption.

To some degree, risk comes from nature, and we can't avoid it. It comes from the uncertain outcome of contests among firms or political leaders. But to some degree, we choose the risks we face. We choose extensive specialization in our production methods, and in the inputs to and outputs of production. We choose roundabout production methods where the payoffs from our investments are delayed so long that we don't know whether we'll want them when they arrive. We even choose political systems with lots of violence or frequent revolution or erratic redistributions of wealth because they seem "fairer," or because we don't understand how they'll work, or because a ruthless minority is doing the choosing.

Risk and expected return are related. The risks we bear unwillingly seem associated with low expected return; while the ones we choose are most often associated with high expected return. That's why we choose them. We choose to specialize in production and consumption because specialized production is more efficient, and because specialized consumption is more satisfying. We choose roundabout production methods because investments at each stage increase the expected payoffs from investments at later stages. (See Black (1972).)

Because risk and expected return are related in so many different ways, we need not see a positive correlation between risk and expected return across countries or over time. Because actual return differs greatly from expected return, we especially need not see a significant correlation between actual return and risk.

To the extent that people choose risk, though, they usually choose it to increase expected return. People push toward higher expected return until the pain of the added risk just offsets their extra expected return. Along this margin, risk and expected return must be equally important.

To model this, assume that each country faces two sorts of risk: an "environmental" risk, σ_0, associated with its political and physical environment; and an "added" risk, σ_1, associated with the extent to which it uses roundabout production and the degree of specialization in its production processes and its consumption. We treat the environmental risk as given, though in fact it can vary, as when a country strengthens its property rights by writing a new constitution. Investors who are more tolerant of risk choose more added risk.

Write σ for total risk and assume that environmental risk and added risk are independent. Then we have:

$$\sigma^2 = \sigma_0^2 + \sigma_1^2. \tag{11.1}$$

Assume that expected return μ consists of a given portion μ_0 plus an added portion μ_1 associated with added risk.

$$\mu = \mu_0 + \mu_1. \tag{11.2}$$

Investors increase σ_1 to increase μ_1 and thus μ. At the margin, the resulting extra risk hurts utility as much as the extra expected return helps it.

If we could estimate μ reliably for different countries, though, we might not see a positive relation between risk and expected return. The negative relation between σ_0 and μ_0 may dominate the positive relation between σ_1 and μ_1. Kormendi and Meguire (1985) try to separate the two effects and claim to find a positive relation between risk and expected return (as reflected in growth) at the margin, but their results may be heavily influenced by the difference between actual return and expected return.

Thus the general equilibrium approach doesn't restrict the sign of the correlation between risk and expected return, across countries or through time; and it especially doesn't restrict the sign of the correlation between risk and actual return.

Shocks

We can see the risk in the economy as a series of shocks, representing the resolution of uncertainty. Any revision in our expectations about the future gives us a shock. Finding out where our expectations were right and where they were wrong gives us a final shock.

Shocks come in permanent and temporary flavors. Any series that looks something like a geometric random walk (with drift) has permanent shocks. As a first approximation, we can see a geometric random walk in such measures of economic activity as wealth, output, and consumption. We can see a geometric random walk more clearly in composite capital measured at market value, and we can see it in the value of a unit of capital, when we decompose total capital into units and unit value.

Temporary shocks come in periodic and mean-reverting subflavors. After a periodic shock, we see cyclical variation like the echoes of replacement activity following a spike in output of durables. Mean-reverting shocks look like random noise followed by gradual reversion toward a mean, but with no tendency to overshoot the mean. Taste shocks that show up as fads or fashions often have this form.

Because it is bounded, the unemployment rate has only temporary shocks. Though I question its usual interpretation, Tobin's q, as conventionally computed, has only temporary shocks. Output has both permanent and temporary shocks. Investment has bigger temporary shocks than output.

Both temporary and permanent shocks reflect revised expectations about tastes and technology at various future times, across a huge range of sectors along many dimensions. Thus they are correlated; but they are not perfectly correlated, because the revisions can affect economic variables in a variety of ways.

As Clark (1987), Stock and Watson (1988), and Quah (1992) note, we cannot uniquely decompose the shocks to a single series like output into temporary and permanent components. We must add conditioning variables, like measures of utilization and the market value of capital, to create a plausible decomposition. Moreover, I think we should allow for smoothing of the permanent shocks.

The Match

Both temporary and permanent shocks to many economic variables reflect revisions in expectations about future tastes and technology. I think we can summarize many of these revisions as variations in the expected "match" between wants and resources, where we specify both wants and resources in great detail along many dimensions.

We make investments in human and physical capital in the light of our best estimates of future tastes and technology. When these estimates turn out to be more right than wrong, we have a good match between wants and resources, and times are good. When we are wrong, we have a bad match and times are bad. The more specialized the economy, the more detail we need in order to understand the match.

To a considerable extent, we *choose* the relative sensitivity of the economy to taste shocks and to technology shocks. When we demand and supply highly differentiated goods and services, we increase our exposure to taste shocks. When we demand and supply highly specialized skills and production processes, we increase our exposure to technology shocks. We increase sensitivity to each until we stop increasing expected utility. Along these margins, then, taste and technology shocks should be equally important.

We can look at the match at many levels: at the level of consumer goods and services, at the level of inventories and work in process, or at the level of labor inputs to production. Since we invest at all levels using common assumptions, the match is often good or bad at all levels at once, but it can be good at one level and bad at another. For example, a better way to grow soybeans may improve the match at the commodity level by increasing output of beans. It may degrade the match at the labor input level, though, by reducing demand for available farming skills.

The match has a temporary component, because we tend to shift resources away from areas of plenty, and toward areas of shortage.

It has a permanent component, too. Continuing drift in a huge array of variables naturally causes it to become worse and worse, to the extent that we don't shift resources around. Also, a bad match means we must bear adjustment costs in shifting resources, which reduces our capital.

I think the permanent component of the match explains much of the variation in actual return or growth across countries and across time. The temporary component explains the cycles we see in such quantities as output, unemployment, effort, equipment utilization, and help-wanted ads.

Let's illustrate with a simple model that has fixed proportions in tastes and a simple technology. This is only an example—I do not mean to imply that real world tastes or technology are like this.

Write k_t for total capital. We can divide it arbitrarily among n sectors, where a unit of total capital becomes a unit of sectoral capital k_{it}.

$$k_t = \sum_i k_{it}. \tag{12.1}$$

One unit of sectoral capital produces sectoral services at the rate b_{it}, which is a random variable chosen from a lognormal distribution that is common to all sectors and all times. The technology variables b_{it} and b_{jt} for different sectors may be correlated, but they are all serially independent. Writing y_{it} for sectoral services, we have:

$$y_{it} = b_{it} k_{it}. \tag{12.2}$$

We use a factor a_{it} to measure tastes for sectoral services. Like b_{it}, it is a random variable chosen from a log-normal distribution that is common to all sectors and all times. Taste variables may be correlated across sectors, and may be correlated with technology variables across sectors, but they are all serially independent. Everyone has the same tastes and resources. Local utility is simply the minimum of the products of taste factors and outputs of sectoral services.

$$u = \min[a_{1t} y_{1t}, \ldots, a_{nt} y_{nt}]. \tag{12.3}$$

From (12.2) and (12.3), we see that utility depends only on the products of the taste and technology factors. If they come from identical distributions, we can say that uncertainty in tastes and uncertainty in technology are equally important. We assume that the realized values of all taste and technology factors are observable, so we don't have to worry about decomposing the products.

$$u = \min[a_{1t} b_{1t} k_{1t}, \ldots, a_{nt} b_{nt} k_{nt}]. \tag{12.4}$$

Because the example is completely symmetric, maximizing expected utility means allocating capital equally across the sectors. Since everyone is identical, we have a competitive equilibrium, even though investments in at least one sector will have large payoffs that we can describe as "rents." In other sectors, we will have unemployed resources and zero rents.

In this model, we can refer to the inverses of the products $a_{it} b_{it}$ as "wants," and the allocations k_{it} as "resources." Wants and resources depend on both tastes and technology. A good match between wants and resources means an allocation where capital in each sector is proportional to the inverse of the product $a_{it} b_{it}$ for that sector, or as close to proportional as possible.

At a different level, we can refer to the inverses of the taste factors a_{it} as "wants," and the outputs y_{it} as "resources." The quality of the match may differ between the two levels.

To model a match with permanent shifts, suppose further that capital for the next period is equal to this period's utility times the number of sectors. In other words, the capital allocated to a sector in excess of the minimal useful amount is wasted for future periods as well. No matter how we discount future local utility, this makes global expected utility proportional to capital.

$$k_{t+1} = n(\min[a_{1t} b_{1t} k_{1t}, \ldots, a_{nt} b_{nt} k_{nt}]). \tag{12.5}$$

This is a crude way to model adjustment costs. The farther a sector is from being a limiting sector, the more costly its capital reallocation is.

To model a match with temporary shifts, assume that initial capital in each period is the same.

$$k_{t+1} = k_t. \tag{12.5'}$$

This makes next period's expected utility the only source of variation in global expected utility, as we vary the allocation of today's capital to sectors. In either version of the model, there is a limiting sector in each period, but the limiting sector can change from period to period.

This happens in the world, too. In the 1970s and 1980s, the oil sector limited many of the world's economies. Changes in the availability and price of oil had major effects on employment and output in many sectors. At other times other sectors have been crucial. During famines or population spurts, food has even been a limiting sector in some regions. In fact, Fogel (1994) claims that food was a consistent limiting sector until very recently.

Limiting sectors change because conditions change, because we expand capacity in those sectors, and because we change production methods so that we make less use of the outputs of those sectors. Eventually, we face different limiting sectors. Thus limiting sectors are only temporary. They do not restrict the long-run growth of the economy.

Sectors

In the real world, the match between wants and resources is defined over a vast number of sectors along many dimensions. To make our investments in human and physical capital, we must form expectations about tastes and technology in each of those sectors for an array of future times.

Will we have war or peace? Will we live in cities or suburbs or small towns? Will the life expectancy in the twenty-first century be closer to 80 or to 90? Will medical progress mostly take the form of new drugs, fancy diagnostics, or elegant surgical procedures? Will we experience a major earthquake or volcanic eruption or meteor impact? Will rugby become as popular in the United States as it is in England? Will parents abandon day care because they decide to take time off to watch (and help) their children grow up? What games will people play at home next year? At what rate will we cut back our agricultural subsidies? Will unisex clothing sweep the world?

People making career decisions, or starting new businesses, or investing in plant and equipment, or finding new locations for stores must answer such questions repeatedly. If their answers turn out to be right (and if they have the right talents), their careers and businesses will thrive.

I think of the world as having *billions* of relevant sectors. Davis and Haltiwanger (1990, 1992) come close to this view when they look at job gains and losses in specific plants. They find large numbers of job gains and job losses in all phases of the business cycle. New plants are created and closed all the time.

When we define a sector as a plant, or as a single job within a plant, or as an individual product or service, some sectors are expanding and some are contracting all the time. The net number of expanding sectors is smaller in recessions than in booms, but some are always expanding, as capital moves into more promising areas. The dispersion of performance across sectors is greater in bad times than in good times.

When we define sectors broadly, though, we see that they generally expand and contract together. In a boom, almost all expand; in a recession, almost all contract. This is a natural result of looking at the world in cruder terms. We use the same assumptions when investing in different sectors. When our assumptions turn out to be generally right, most broadly defined sectors do well; and when they turn out to be generally wrong, most broadly defined sectors do badly.

A general equilibrium version of Hall's (1991) "temporal agglomeration" can also play a role in explaining comovement among sectors. It's the team nature of production. My marginal product is higher when you're working than when you're not. Yours is higher when I'm working. Thus we tend to work at the same times; in daylight, on weekdays, during our busy season, and in booms. The same applies to my firm and its suppliers and customers. By following the network of suppliers and customers, we can go from one firm to almost any other firm, so team production is another reason for broad comovement among firms.

To model this, write y for output of a production process that uses capital inputs h and k from two different sectors. For constants a and α, assume that:

$$y = a h^\alpha k^{1-\alpha}. \tag{13.1}$$

Assume that all of the capital in each sector is used in this process. The rental rates r_h and r_k satisfy:

$$r_h = \alpha y / h \tag{13.2}$$

and

$$r_k = (1 - \alpha) y / k. \tag{13.3}$$

Total outputs y_h and y_k in the two sectors are:

$$y_h = \alpha y \tag{13.4}$$

and

$$y_k = (1 - \alpha)y. \tag{13.5}$$

Thus a shock that increases the effective amount of capital in either sector will increase output in both sectors, in proportion to their respective shares.

In the more realistic case where capital in each sector participates in multiple production processes, this effect is not so strong. Still, this is one reason for the comovement of broadly defined sectors.

Sometimes, as in the simple model of the match given in the last section, we have a limiting sector that is crucial to a country's output and employment across many broad sectors for a period of time. Variation in the availability and price of that sector's output contributes to comovement, even among broadly defined sectors.

In other words, the patterns of sectoral comovement we see are perfectly consistent with general equilibrium. We need not attribute any of this comovement to variation in "aggregate demand," whatever that might be.

Growth

How can we use these elements to explain the persistence and variability of growth?

As a first approximation, we can ignore fixed factors in production and the exact nature and timing of investments. We can treat growth as the accumulation of composite capital, plus possibly a change in freely available technology that affects both old and new capital. Capital's market value grows as people add new units of capital, or as existing units grow in value as they become more effective. Thus market value provides the best estimate of the capital input to production in efficiency units.

Actual growth can differ greatly from expected growth, since actual return on capital can differ greatly from expected return. Actual return varies across countries and through time largely because of variation in the match between wants and resources. When we make investments, some of which will pay off only in the distant future, we estimate what the world will be like at all times along the way. The more right those estimates are, the higher the return is.

Because we make similar investments in similar countries, returns in different countries are positively correlated, and the correlations are more positive for more similar countries. Certain kinds of countries do well in each period, but the relation between return and country type (as measured by "initial conditions") tells us little about the relation between expected return and country type.

Growth might have external benefits from increasing market size or the gains to one person from added human capital in another, or external costs from pollution or the obsolescence in old ideas caused by creation of new ideas. I see no way to tell whether net external benefits are positive or negative, so I suggest that we stick to the general equilibrium approach by assuming they are zero.

Innovation can be just one form of investment: we can treat research and development as the creation of a particular form of capital. Sectors with consistently rapid innovation have higher rental-to-value ratios and a higher obsolescence rate than other sectors. Because such sectors exist, the expected return on composite capital is consistently positive.

Risk and expected return can be related negatively, as when political stability and government expropriation are the crucial factors; or positively, as when risk tolerance and the price of risk are the crucial factors. Thus risk may not help much in estimating expected return. Along one margin, though, people take more risk to increase expected return. They choose the aggressiveness of their investments to maximize expected utility.

Growth is return on composite capital less consumption of capital, as in equation (4.1). Expected growth is expected return less consumption. We can have persistent growth only if people consume less than the expected return on their capital—if they are sufficiently patient.

As I see it, then, persistent growth depends on the factors affecting expected return (including talent, culture, risk tolerance, political stability, size of government, and openness to trade and investment) plus patience. Actual growth depends on expected growth plus luck. To illustrate, let's write down a model where growth depends on risk tolerance, patience, and luck.

Write β for the discount factor that measures patience, U for local utility, c_t for consumption, and F for a weighted geometric average of current and past levels of c_t. Writing utility this way lets us separate risk tolerance and willingness to shift consumption through time. Assume everyone is identical.

Write k_t for composite capital at market value and γs_t for one plus total return, where γ measures the aggressiveness of an individual's investment strategy. The distribution for s_t is log-normal with a mean greater than 1.0. Each person solves:

$$\max_{\gamma, c_t} E[\textstyle\sum_t \beta^t U[F(c_t, c_{t-1}, \ldots)]], \tag{14.1}$$

subject to:

$$k_{t+1} = \gamma s_t k_t - c_t. \tag{14.2}$$

Future levels of c_t will depend on all of the then prior values of s_t.

Higher levels of β mean faster expected growth, as people reduce current consumption to increase expected future consumption. Greater risk tolerance means faster expected growth, as people increase γ to invest more aggressively. The biggest factor in growth, though, is luck, which shows up in the realized values of s_t. It's the difference between actual growth and expected growth.

Because the individual is maximizing over γ, expected growth and consumption volatility must be equally important along this margin. The benefits of higher expected growth must equal the costs of higher consumption volatility. Thus the claim by Lucas (1987) that policies to increase growth are more important than policies to reduce volatility does not hold in this model.

If we are moving along another margin, though, we may not even face a trade-off between volatility and growth. For example, adding political stability, strengthening property rights, and reducing the size of government may simultaneously reduce volatility and increase expected growth for a country that starts with little political stability.

Convergence

What does my simple growth model imply about convergence of output or growth rates across countries?

Since I have no fixed factors, and since the key reason for variation in growth is the difference between realized and expected return, my model implies divergence among isolated economies. This fits the facts. Throughout history, isolated economies have diverged enormously. At one extreme we have countries like the United States and Japan, while at the other we have the indigenous populations of the Americas, Africa, Australia, and New Zealand.

Most modern economies, though, are not isolated. They trade with one another, invest in one another, and sometimes take technology without paying for it. Conventional growth models emphasize the free transfer of technology, while I consider that inessential and probably undesirable. Interaction through trade and investment is sufficient to explain why many countries don't diverge; and indeed, why the OECD countries may be converging.

Among many of the developed and developing countries, this interaction is intense. We see cross-industry trade and intra-industry trade. With intra-industry trade, different countries often handle different stages of production. Cross-border direct investment is part of this, since the country controlling production often invests in the countries playing smaller roles. All this implies that different countries are combining their efforts in producing various goods and services.

Whenever economies are connected by production involving inputs from different countries, divergence is limited. For example, adding domestic human capital adds to the marginal product and value of all foreign human capital that joins with it in various production processes. Thus we expect to see completely isolated economies diverge, while interacting economies diverge less or converge, depending on how strongly they interact. This is consistent with what Parente and Prescott (1993) find: the distribution of countries between rich and poor seems to remain about the same, which means those at the extremes tend to move toward the middle.

To model this, take an extreme case where a large country with human capital h interacts with a small country with human capital k. They are the only two countries in a world of certainty, and they jointly produce a single good that everyone consumes. People are immobile, and all quantities are per person.

Write y for total output. For constants a and α, assume that output is:

$$y = a h^\alpha k^{1-\alpha}. \tag{15.1}$$

This means that the returns r_h and r_k to added investments at home and abroad are:

$$r_h = \alpha y / h \tag{15.2}$$

and

$$r_k = (1 - \alpha) y / k. \tag{15.3}$$

Dividing, we have:

$r_h/r_k = \alpha k/(1 - \alpha)h.$ (15.4)

In equilibrium, the returns r_h and r_k are equal, and the levels of human capital satisfy:

$h/k = \alpha/(1 - \alpha).$ (15.5)

If human capital in the small country is below this equilibrium ratio compared to human capital in the large country, the return to investment in human capital is higher in the small country. Human capital investment is then higher than normal in the small country and lower than normal in the large country.

This means we see convergence in capital and output across those two countries. The convergence takes time, even when physical capital seems to be fully mobile, because we can't shift human capital instantly from one country to another. We subtract human capital mostly through obsolescence, and add it mostly through job experience and education: all these things take time.

Note that this puts a very different slant on Lucas' (1990) observation that capital per head in India is only a tiny fraction of U.S. capital per head. In his competitive model, this implies an enormous and unrealistic difference in interest rates between the two countries. In mine, it implies that we use production methods where Indian human capital is only a minor input.

To add more realism, we can assume that we choose among many ways of organizing production, using different combinations of inputs from different countries. Some methods take all their inputs from the same country. We choose the method that gives the lowest cost.

Migration

Why do people from poor countries try to migrate to rich ones? Is it, as in Lucas (1988), because of externalities in human capital, so that doubling all capital more than doubles output? Is it, as in Rebelo (1991), because countries that are poor because of higher taxes on physical capital have lower physical capital and thus lower wages? Is it because rich countries have extensive transfer programs that give poor migrants net benefits in health care, schooling, or welfare?

Externalities, taxes, and transfers all play a role, but we don't need any of them to explain migration. We can explain it using the idea that people work in teams that mix workers at different skill levels. A low-skill worker earns a higher return on his human capital than a high-skill worker, but because he has a lot less human capital, his total labor compensation is low.

Low-skill workers lack schooling or experience or both. They can be young people or migrants. Thus a worker normally earns a high return on human capital early in his career and a low return later on when he has more human capital. When we think about a typical worker, we can use a blended amount of human capital and a blended return on human capital, where we combine amounts and returns for different kinds of workers.

Using "rich" and "poor" to refer to relative human capital levels, we can say that a person migrating from a poor country to a rich one may be rich in his own country but poor in his adopted country. Thus he may increase the return on his human capital by migrating. His gains from migrating are similar to those of a person who switches career paths in a recession.

Let's illustrate with a model just like our convergence model. Imagine that production in every country uses teams of two people, where one has several times the other's human capital. Assume a world of certainty. Write y for output, h for the poor person's human capital, and k for the rich person's human capital, and assume that production looks like this for a constant a:

$$y = ah^{\alpha}k^{1-\alpha}. \tag{16.1}$$

Write r_h for the return on the poor person's human capital and r_k for the rich person's return. We have:

$$r_h = \alpha y/h \tag{16.2}$$

and

$$r_k = (1 - \alpha)y/k. \tag{16.3}$$

Dividing, we have:

$$r_h/r_k = \alpha k/(1 - \alpha)h. \tag{16.4}$$

Total labor income is the return on a person's human capital times the amount of his human capital. Thus the labor-income ratio is:

$$r_h h/r_k k = \alpha/(1 - \alpha). \tag{16.5}$$

Assume that production has the feature that α is less than $1 - \alpha$, so the poor person plays a minor role; but the rich person is very rich, so r_h is much larger than r_k. If the ratios in (16.4) and (16.5) apply in his home country, but the migrant is rich there, he adds to the return on his human capital by migrating.

More generally, we can assume that we choose among many production methods that have the same form as (16.1), but differ in detail. The qualitative results remain the same.

Migration is not a mystery. People who migrate from poor countries to rich countries clearly earn more, even without differences in externalities, taxes, or transfers. They earn more because they are worth more. A model that doesn't capture this is simply an incomplete or overrestricted model.

Indeed, we can use this same model to explain how a person can increase his compensation as he advances along his career path. Each time he is promoted, he moves from a job where he is relatively senior to one where he is relatively junior. Even though his relative contribution goes down, his marginal product goes up.

Volatility

Why are asset prices so volatile? Or, if we decompose capital at market value into units and unit value, why is unit value so volatile?

I have never found this question as interesting as Shiller (1989) has. He looks at current news and finds that prices seem to change even when there's no news. I think about expectations, which are constantly changing as people process old news. He looks at the smooth path of dividends and finds that prices seem to change more than the present value of dividends. I think of dividends as depending on current and past prices, rather than of prices as depending on expected future dividends, so smooth dividends seem natural to me.

Given the volatility of expectations, I'm surprised that asset prices aren't *more* volatile than they are. We see asset volatility for the same reasons that we see variation in growth rates across countries and through time, and for the same reasons that we see business cycles. The questions are different, but the answer is the same. Asset prices vary because we make highly specific investments while looking far into the future; as time goes by, we change our beliefs about the future along many dimensions, which makes our investments seem more relevant — or less relevant — and thus changes the values of claims on those investments. Sometimes asset prices change because we become more patient — or less patient — and sometimes they change because we become more tolerant of risk — or less tolerant of risk — but we don't need those sources of volatility to understand why prices often change for no apparent reason.

The details matter. We can't understand the powerful role of varying expectations without looking at outputs that range from peanuts to spaceships, and at inputs that range from truck driving skills to experience in doing coronary bypass operations. We just can't understand volatility using a model that has two inputs and one output, or even one that has 200 inputs and outputs.

Prices will continue to change in response to forces that we can't easily measure, and people will continue to claim that markets have "excess volatility." To me, the volatility in market prices seems normal and consistent with the volatility in national growth rates and in cyclical measures of business activity.

Business Cycles

As we have seen, the things that cause growth rates to vary across countries and through time also cause business cycles. Most fundamentally, we make investment decisions that are enormously specific, yet that rely on forecasts of tastes and technology into the distant future. As time unfolds, we revise our expectations and adjust our investments. When our forecasts turn out to have been right, we have a good match between wants and resources; otherwise, a poor match.

The match, in the sense of an allocation of available resources, is a stationary, cyclical variable. It can be cyclical in the periodic sense, but more often it is cyclical in the mean-reverting sense. Defining the match at different stages of production gives different cycles: they are all correlated, but imperfectly.

Business cycles and growth fluctuations are related most fundamentally because they have the same causes. They are related because more aggressive investments — which are more specialized and more forward-looking — cause bigger fluctuations in growth and bigger business cycles. They are related statistically in that temporary and smoothed permanent shocks to output and especially to investment are correlated.

At the finest level of detail, resolution of uncertainty about tastes and technology causes many sectors to expand and many to contract. In a boom they mostly expand, and in a bust they mostly contract. When we define sectors very broadly, though, they generally expand and contract together. At times, a single sector becomes critical and most other sectors march to the tune it plays.

We don't need Keynesian concepts like "aggregate demand" and "sticky prices" to understand business cycles. We don't need "bubbles" or "excess volatility": the natural volatility from making big bets on the future is sufficient. We don't need "overlapping generations" or "imperfect markets"; they don't hurt, but they don't help us understand business cycles either. We don't need "imperfect competition," "economies of scale," or "strategic complementarities." All we need is a standard general equilibrium model.

There is now a large literature on "real business cycle" (RBC) theories. That name makes them sound like general equilibrium theories, but they are severely restricted in ways that general equilibrium theories are not. To further define the general equilibrium approach, let's list the features of RBC theories that seem arbitrary and unmotivated.

Exogenous shocks
RBC models treat the driving force behind business cycles and growth as a "shock" that is simply a multiplicative factor on the production function. They call it a "technology shock," but do not explain how technology is involved. I don't believe we can define or measure an aggregate technology shock.

Temporary shocks
The factor in front of production function usually has temporary rather than permanent shocks. That seems strange for a technology factor, and it doesn't fit the fact that the major economic series like output and consumption have larger permanent shocks than temporary ones.

Future shocks
In an RBC model, a change in expected future technology, holding current technology fixed, has peculiar effects. An expected

improvement in future technology *reduces* current consumption by changing the interest rate.

Fixed factors
RBC models usually use a nonreproducible factor of production, so the exponent on reproducible capital in the production function is a lot less than one. This means the expected return on capital tends to decline as the economy grows. Since we have no evidence of such a decline in recorded history, these models add a particular kind of nonstochastic exogenous growth to the factor out front, so the model will look more reasonable.

Local certainty
Capital follows a locally smooth path rather than a path with Brownian motion in RBC models. These models have a real interest rate but no price of risk, so they have only part of the cost of capital. They can't show the trade-off between risk and expected return or expected growth.

Asymmetric inputs
RBC models usually use capital and hours (or "efficiency units of labor") as the inputs to production. These inputs are not symmetric. Human and physical capital are symmetric; so are human capital modified by effort and physical capital modified by utilization.

Current inputs
Recent RBC models use only current inputs of capital and labor. They do not recognize the importance of specific investments in particular kinds of human and physical capital in the near and distant past.

Steady-state path
The typical RBC model has a nonstochastic steady-state path for output. Actual output fluctuates around that path, which lets people "linearize" their models and treat deviations from the steady-state path as business cycles. A model with smoothed permanent shocks and no fixed factors has no steady-state path in this sense.

Capital at book value
When they estimate the stock of physical capital for their production functions, RBC researchers typically use the perpetual inventory

method with fixed depreciation applied to investments at cost. This gives a very smooth series with no apparent economic meaning. When they estimate human capital, they often just add years of schooling or work experience and ignore variation in the cost or relevance of acquired skills.

Noncyclical depreciation
Since RBC models use fixed depreciation, variation in the rental rate on capital looks like variation in its expected return. In a more realistic model, expected return is fixed, so cyclical rental rates imply offsetting cyclical depreciation rates.

Uniformity
Most RBC models have a single capital good, a single representative consumer, and a single kind of worker who has no human capital. They can't look at detailed differences between expectations and realizations, or at the effects of specialization and long-term planning on expected growth and risk.

Separable utility
RBC models usually use time-separable, state-independent utility. This encourages people to write down simple Euler equations that are unmotivated and very restrictive. It makes consumption smoothing, and sometimes the equity premium and the real interest rate, seem puzzling.

Leisure
RBC models identify unemployment with leisure, which just doesn't sound right to me. We like leisure, but we don't like unemployment. Since they don't have sectors, they identify the business cycle with shifts of leisure through time. That doesn't sound right either.

Calibration
Despite all these serious problems, people try to use RBC models to match certain stylized facts numerically. They have some success at this, but I don't see what we learn from it. We can easily use other versions of the general equilibrium model to match the same facts. Successful calibration does not imply that a model has correct structure any more than correlation implies causation.

Durables

All of capital is durable. Capital includes human capital, intangible physical capital, consumer durables, and even inventories of things that are perishable in use.

A durable good provides services throughout its life. Higher demand for the services of a durable means higher demand for the stock of durables. Output of the durable goes up temporarily to build up the stock. Since we count output of durables as investment, this is a big reason why investment is more volatile than output or consumption. Output of durables is highly cyclical.

In sectors producing very durable goods, we see lots of temporary layoffs when times are bad. Both firms and workers expect employment to pick up after the economy works off its "excess" stocks of durables. Similarly, we see lots of vacancies and temporary hires when times are good. Both firms and workers expect employment to drop after the economy builds up its stocks of durables.

To illustrate, write x_t for the services of durables and k_t for the stock of durables. Assume that x_t is proportional to k_t.

$$k_t = bx_t. \tag{17.1}$$

Each period, we produce new durables to cover depreciation in existing durables, plus an amount to cover the change in the stock of durables due to a change in demand for their services. Writing y_t for output of durables and d for the depreciation rate, we have:

$$y_t = dk_t + b(x_t - x_{t-1}) = bdx_t + b(x_t - x_{t-1}). \tag{17.2}$$

Take demand for the services of durables as given, and assume all of its changes are permanent. Then x_t follows something like a random walk. Changes in x_t are far more volatile than x_t itself. Thus y_t is more volatile than x_t. Investment is more volatile than output, from this point of view, simply because capital is durable.

Inventories

Inventories are durable, so they share the traits of all durables. Even inventories of things that are perishable in use are durable.

Inventories provide two very different services: they allow us to produce things in a time pattern that gives low cost, and they make it convenient for buyers who want to pick things up on short notice. Low production cost need not mean production smoothing; it may mean producing one item very intensely and then refitting the production line to handle the next item. In general, inventories help us balance production cost and stockout cost, as in Kahn (1992).

For specific goods in specific locations, sales rates can vary sharply. When we group goods by category and location, sales rates smooth out. For many categories, sales rate changes are largely permanent.

Let's illustrate with a model like the general durables model above. Write x_t for the current sales rate and k_t for inventories. Assume that sellers keep their inventory-to-sales ratios constant. In other words, ignore the production cost side of the problem.

$$k_t = bx_t \tag{18.1}$$

Each period, we produce new goods for inventory to cover the amount sold that period, plus an amount to cover depreciation in inventory, plus an amount to cover the change in inventories due to the change in sales rates. Writing y_t for production and d for the inventory depreciation rate, we have:

$$y_t = x_t + dk_t + b(x_t' - x_{t-1}). \tag{18.2}$$

From (18.1) and (18.2), we have:

$$y_t = (1 + bd)x_t + b(x_t - x_{t-1}). \tag{18.3}$$

Since sales rate changes are mostly permanent, the difference term on the right-hand side of (18.3) is far more volatile than the level term.

When we bring in production costs, we may find that sellers allow their inventory-to-sales ratios to vary so they can reduce production costs. But I see no reason to assume that production ends up smoother than sales; more likely, stockout costs dominate production costs, and production is more volatile than sales.

Careers

A career is a sequence of jobs, each providing skills and experience needed for the next. In effect, an employer uses part of the extra revenue a worker generates to train him and pays him the rest in wages. As the worker accumulates human capital, his pay rises.

A person pursuing a career usually has a sharply rising wage profile in his early years. In the early years, his human capital is low, and he is taking part of his total pay in added human capital, so his measured wage is especially low. Later he has more human capital, and adds it more slowly, so his measured wage is high. In effect, the worker invests in his own human capital by taking a job more as a stepping stone to better jobs than for its current pay and working conditions. As always, these investments are very specific. A career can turn out well or badly along many dimensions.

A worker invests in his career in the light of conditions he expects in the future. He tries to gain valuable skills and knowledge at each stage of his career, but things are bound to turn out better than he expects in some ways and worse in others. Overall, if it turns out that he made good choices, he advances quickly; otherwise, he advances slowly or loses his job.

Outcomes are not independent. Since people have similar beliefs, they often make similar decisions about human capital investments. They may use the best information available when making their investments, but if that information turns out to be wrong, lots of people will find themselves on poor career paths. In other words, this is the same process that causes variation in country growth rates, volatility in asset prices, and business cycles. When investment decisions turn out well, in detail along many dimensions, we see strong growth, a cyclical boom, high asset returns, and rapid career advancement.

Most job changes are promotions, and occur within a single firm. Even those that involve moving to a new employer usually represent progress along a career path, without intervening unemployment. When we count promotions within a single firm as job changes, labor mobility is strongly procyclical. In good times promotion probabilities go up; in bad times most people just stick with the jobs they have.

Let's illustrate some of these points with a simple career path model. Assume that a worker's total pay is a fraction r_t of his human capital k_t at age t. He faces a probability p_t of promotion; if he is not promoted, he simply keeps his current job. The event that leads to his promotion also causes his effective human capital to rise by 20%. The worker's measured wage w_t is his total pay less his expected gain in human capital.

$$w_t = (r_t - .2p_t)k_t. \tag{19.1}$$

His human capital grows by:

$$k_{t+1} = 1.2k_t \text{ with probability } p_t, \tag{19.2}$$
$$= k_t \text{ with probability } 1 - p_t.$$

If r_t remains constant and p_t falls with age, his measured wage rises rapidly. It rises with his human capital; and ironically, it rises further as his chance for promotion falls. He is receiving less of his total pay in added human capital, so he receives more in his measured wage.

Obsolescence

Capital, if not replenished, loses its value through age-related deterioration, through use, and through obsolescence. Wear and tear tend to be pretty steady, but obsolescence is highly erratic. It can often be negative, as when an antique car or piece of furniture acquires value.

Obsolescence is the dark side of innovation. When we create new ideas, we reduce the values of old ideas. Existing knowledge becomes less relevant. We can't have "technical regress" in the scientific sense, since we keep building on what we already know, but we can have it in the economic sense. In effect, new knowledge destroys old knowledge.

Obsolescence affects human capital as much as physical capital. What we learn through experience, we lose through obsolescence. Some human capital is long-lasting, but some depreciates very quickly.

This explains why full-time workers earn more per hour than part-time workers, and why people who work very long hours earn still more per hour. If we learn from each hour of work, but obsolescence comes only through time, hard workers will have higher levels of human capital. They earn more per hour *and* they work more hours, so full-time workers will earn much more per year than part-time workers, and people who put in lots of overtime will earn much more per year than those who don't.

At first glance, higher pay per hour for people who work more hours seems to violate the principle that the marginal product of labor declines as we use more labor. Once we bring in the dynamics of the stock of human capital, though, the puzzle vanishes.

To model this, write k for human capital and h for hours worked per day. Human capital depreciates at a constant rate d, and the worker adds human capital at a rate equal to a constant g times hours h times human capital k. Writing $\dot{k}$ for the growth rate of k, we have:

$$\dot{k}/k = gh - d. \tag{20.1}$$

If d and g are really constant, this makes human capital unstable. For high enough hours, human capital can grow indefinitely, while for low hours per day, it shrinks indefinitely.

Now let the hourly wage be a constant c times human capital, and write w for the daily wage. We have:

$$w = ckh. \tag{20.2}$$

This means that working long hours can have a huge effect on the daily wage, especially when sustained for many years. It has a direct effect because the worker is paid for more hours, but its indirect effect through the dynamics of the stock of human capital can be even bigger. People have a strong incentive to work longer hours.

Total compensation rises sharply with work intensity, which helps explain why so few people work only part time, and why overtime shift differentials are large. For many purposes, we can assume that while people are working, they work full time.

Finally, this helps explain why unemployment takes the form of layoffs and job hunting rather than widespread part-time work. Fifty people working full time can produce more than a hundred people working half time.

Human Capital

What are the differences between human and physical capital?

One difference is that the market for human capital is quite limited. Selling part of your human capital has overtones of "slavery," so we have not developed the legal structure that would make it efficient. Perhaps alimony agreements embody the closest thing to transactions in human capital: some of them provide for one spouse to receive a percentage of the other spouse's earnings.

The "adverse selection" in a human capital transaction might be large. A person who wants to sell might have lower true earnings potential than an apparently similar person who wants to buy shares in his human capital. In effect, even a developed market would be thin, and people wouldn't buy or sell very much of it.

"Moral hazard" might be significant too. After a person sells some of his human capital, he faces a higher "tax" on his future earnings. This will cause him to work fewer hours. To some degree, moral hazard reduces the amount of human capital people would want to sell in a more developed market.

Some people say that production of human capital is more "labor-intensive" than production of physical capital. In my models, that would mean that we use more human capital than usual relative to physical capital when producing new human capital. It may be true that production of human capital makes use of a larger than usual proportion of human capital, but I don't see what that implies. Many sectors use inputs in unusual proportions. For example, it may also be true that production of physical capital makes use of a larger than usual proportion of physical capital.

What *is* special about human capital is that people mostly own their own human capital, with all of its specific risks. They could diversify or hedge out some of these risks by trading in shares of physical capital, but as Baxter and Jermann (1993) note, they generally don't.

Also, adding or subtracting human capital through investment or disinvestment takes time. People don't just borrow to go out and buy more human capital. They accumulate it gradually through years spent in school and on the job. They expect to lose it through obsolescence.

Finally, human capital moves between countries almost entirely through migration. When migration is small, as it is for most countries most of the time, we can view human capital as immobile.

Output and Effort

Now let's look at the relation between output and effort as business conditions change. Let's measure effort by hours worked, assuming that effort per hour does not vary. Write A for a constant, e for effort, h for human capital, f for utilization of physical capital, and k for physical capital. Assume that we capture variation in effective capital by measuring human and physical capital at market value. Write output y as:

$$y = A(eh)^{\alpha}(fk)^{1-\alpha}. \tag{21.1}$$

To find the wage w, which includes both measured and unmeasured components, we take the derivative of y with respect to e.

$$w = \alpha Ah(fk/eh)^{1-\alpha}. \tag{21.2}$$

We capture permanent shocks to output in k and h, and temporary shocks in f and e. (In a more detailed model, we would smooth the human and physical capital inputs to production.) Permanent and temporary shocks are correlated because they have common causes.

Imagine that in equilibrium, changes in h and k are proportional, and changes in e and f are proportional. That means the wage has only permanent variation as h varies.

For a worker deciding how much to work, we have a different calculation. He sees utilization of physical capital (and perhaps effort of other workers) change. If he doesn't increase his effort with everyone else, his wage w_0 is:

$$w_0 = \alpha Ah(fk/e_0h)^{1-\alpha}. \tag{21.3}$$

Thus he sees a higher wage from higher human capital (which is permanent) and from higher utilization of physical capital (which is temporary). He responds to the temporary increase in his wage by increasing his effort.

From (21.1) we see that output rises for two reasons. It has a permanent increase from h and k, and a temporary increase from e and f. If output reflected only the temporary shifts in e and f, it would rise by the same percentage as effort. Because the permanent shifts in h and k are correlated with the temporary shifts in e and f, output rises more than effort. This is one reason we see an increase in conventional measures of "labor productivity" in booms.

Unmeasured Activity

On-the-job learning creates human capital. The worker owns most of this capital, even though he loses some of it if he leaves the firm. Some is associated with the entire team working together in the firm, and is more like intangible physical capital. The firm owns most of this capital.

The human capital created on the job is part of output, investment, and wages, though it is not measured in the national income and product accounts. All of this activity is unmeasured, and it is large. Since labor's share of output is more than capital's, I imagine that human capital exceeds physical capital. If human and physical capital grow together, average net investment in human capital must exceed average net investment in physical capital, too.

In other words, the numbers are huge. They are comparable to the unmeasured activity in the "underground economy." Measured investment is less than half of total investment, because it includes only investment in physical capital. Measured saving is less than half of total saving. Measured output and wages are substantially less than total output and wages. Labor's share of output is even bigger than we thought.

This unmeasured activity is strongly procyclical. In good times, every hour you work adds a lot to your human capital; but in bad times, the skills you add are less valuable because they are less relevant. They lose even more value if you are laid off or decide to change careers. People work more hours in good times, and they learn more for every hour they work, so on-the-job learning is doubly procyclical.

This means that total output is more procyclical than measured output, and that total investment and saving and wages are more procyclical than measured investment and saving and wages. Moreover, the total real wage is more procyclical than the measured real wage, even if we don't count shifts into and out of the labor force and shifts into and out of overtime work.

Unmeasured activity can help explain the differences between workers with more and less experience. When a worker enters the labor force, a big part of his total wage is unmeasured. Later on, he continues to learn, but added human capital forms a smaller and smaller part of his total compensation. The total wage rises less steeply with experience, on average, than the measured wage.

Since young workers have a lot of unmeasured pay, and since unmeasured pay is strongly procyclical, it's easy to understand why they change jobs and become unemployed and reemployed and move into and out of the labor force at such a high rate. This is not the only reason, but it's a big one.

In effect, the firm provides training for its employees along with its other products and services. The employees take this training as part of their compensation. This training or learning by doing is an unmeasured part of output, labor compensation, and investment.

When Arrow (1962) talks about "learning by doing," he really means "learning by investing in physical capital." It makes more sense, though, to talk about "learning by investing in human capital." Then learning by doing and learning by investing are aspects of the same thing.

To model this, write y for income or output, and divide it into income from human and physical capital:

$$y = y_h + y_k. \tag{22.1}$$

Divide income from human capital into measured and unmeasured parts:

$$y_h = y_m + y_u. \tag{22.2}$$

The unmeasured part of income represents training or on-the-job learning, which shows up as investment in human capital. Write x for investment and divide it into human and physical capital components:

$$x = x_h + x_k. \tag{22.3}$$

Investment in human capital takes the form of schooling and learning by doing:

$$x_h = x_s + x_d. \tag{22.4}$$

The unmeasured part of labor income is then equal to investment in human capital through learning by doing.

$$y_u = x_d. \tag{22.5}$$

Write labor income as depending on the total hourly wage w and hours or effort e.

$$y_h = we. \tag{22.6}$$

Divide the total hourly wage into measured and unmeasured components.

$$w = w_m + w_u. \tag{22.7}$$

Thus the measured part of labor income is the measured wage times hours.

$$y_m = w_m e. \tag{22.8}$$

The unmeasured part of labor income is then:

$$y_u = w_u e. \tag{22.9}$$

I claim that the unmeasured part of hourly pay is much more volatile than the measured part. When times are good, on-the-job learning is rapid (per hour on the job). High total hourly pay induces high effort, which means doubly high total labor compensation.

This is why measured wages seem so sluggish, and it's one reason why the measured real wage doesn't seem to vary much over the cycle. (Also, we figure an average wage rather than a marginal wage, and we exclude people who are not working.) When we include unmeasured pay and average the marginal wage over everyone, the real wage becomes highly procyclical.

As equation (22.5) says, this unmeasured compensation is part of investment in human capital. It is highly volatile, since both hourly pay in this form and hours are procyclical. Since it is a form of investment in a durable good, this volatility is natural. Investment in human capital through working may be even more volatile than investment in physical capital.

World Human Capital and Effort

Sometimes people like to think of production as depending on domestic human and physical capital plus a measure of world human capital. This is one way to model freely available technology or the external benefits of an educated population. It's an example of a "strategic complementarity."

If world human capital matters, I like to use a similar model that stays within the general equilibrium approach. We can use world human capital without assuming freely available technology or external benefits from education or research.

Once we say that world human capital matters, we are saying that output depends on human capital inputs from different locations. We can model that with a simple Cobb–Douglas production function that takes human capital from different places as inputs. To create the simplest example, let's ignore physical capital.

We can also include utilization of human capital, or "effort," to model the apparent strategic complementarity in team production. For an extreme example, let's include each individual separately. Write h_i for his human capital, e_i for his effort, and α_i for his contribution to output. Writing y for output, we have:

$$y = A\Pi_i(e_i h i)^{\alpha_i}. \tag{23.1}$$

Write h for world human capital and e for world effort.

$$e = \Pi_i e_i^{\alpha_i}. \tag{23.2}$$

and

$$h = \Pi_i h_i^{\alpha_i}. \tag{23.3}$$

World effort and human capital are simply weighted geometric averages of individual effort and human capital. Combining, we have:

$$y = Aeh. \tag{23.4}$$

Output depends only on world human capital and effort. Separating out one individual, output depends on his human capital and effort combined with a weighted geometric average of human capital and effort from everyone else in the world. Those averages are very close to world human capital and effort.

This production function is extreme: looking at (23.1), we see that output is zero if any individual fails to pitch in. Thus it captures all we can ask for in the way of strategic complementarities: the contribution of my effort to world output depends on everyone else's effort. Still, because it's Cobb–Douglas, my compensation is just my share of world output.

$$e_i \frac{\partial y}{\partial e_i} = \alpha_i y. \tag{23.5}$$

Saving and Investment

Immobile human capital can help explain why saving and investment are highly correlated.

The "home bias" in physical capital investments is sufficient by itself to explain the high correlation between saving and investment. Everyone invests mostly at home, even when free to invest anywhere, so saving and investment move together no matter what causes them to change.

Human capital can explain the high correlation, though, even when all investors hold fully diversified portfolios of physical capital around the world. When times are good at home, investments in both human and physical capital are attractive. As successful investments mature, they take heavy inputs of intermediate goods, effort, and utilization of physical capital. When people hold most of their physical capital abroad, most local investments in physical capital must come from abroad.

Meanwhile, local labor income is temporarily high, so people want to increase their saving. Thus a good match between wants and resources at home causes an increase in both saving and investment at home.

To illustrate, imagine a small country that produces output x using human capital h and physical capital k. For a coefficient b, assume we have:

$$x = bh^\alpha k^{1-\alpha}. \tag{24.1}$$

Assume the world is certain, except for occasional shocks, with interest rate r. Human capital is immobile but physical capital is fully mobile, so the small country's residents hold essentially all their physical capital abroad. The return on physical capital is r, but the return on human capital s can differ from r.

$$s = \alpha b(k/h)^{1-\alpha} \tag{24.2}$$

and

$$r = (1 - \alpha)b(h/k)^\alpha. \tag{24.3}$$

Since human capital is immobile, (24.2) defines s. Since physical capital is mobile, (24.3) defines k. People change their human capital investments only gradually to bring s into line with r.

Since local residents hold all their physical capital abroad, income y consists of interest on foreign physical capital w held by local residents, plus their income from human capital.

$$y = rw + sh = rw + \alpha x. \tag{24.4}$$

Assume consumption is constant for everyone in the short run. For the world as a whole, variation in income and output matches variation in saving and investment.

Now imagine a shock λ that multiplies b, h, and k. It represents a change in the match between wants and resources. The change in b is temporary, while the changes in h and k are permanent. We want to figure the initial effect of the shock on income and output.

Because domestic residents own all their physical capital abroad, domestic output goes up by more than domestic income does. Domestic output rises because both human and physical capital rise due to the shock, and because physical capital flows in. Using primes to denote values after the shock, we have:

$$b' = \lambda b, \tag{24.5}$$

$$h' = \lambda h, \tag{24.6}$$

and

$$r = (1 - \alpha)b'(h'/k')^\alpha. \tag{24.7}$$

Combining these equations and solving for k', we have:

$$k' = \lambda^{1+1/\alpha}k. \tag{24.8}$$

The original shock multiplies domestic capital by λ, and the inflow of physical capital multiplies it again by $\lambda^{1/\alpha}$. Similarly, we have:

$$s' = \lambda^{1/\alpha}s, \tag{24.9}$$

$$x' = \lambda^{1+1/\alpha}x, \tag{24.10}$$

and

$$y' = rw + \lambda^{1+1/\alpha}\alpha x. \tag{24.11}$$

Equation (24.10) shows the increase in output, and (24.11) compared to (24.4) shows the increase in income. Output rises more than income because of the inflow of physical capital.

Write f for investment and g for saving. If we define investment as the change in capital and saving as the change in wealth, the effect of the shock is:

$$f = k' - k + h' - h = (\lambda^{1+1/\alpha} - 1)k + (\lambda - 1)h \tag{24.12}$$

and

$$g = h' - h = (\lambda - 1)h. \tag{24.13}$$

Saving and investment both respond to the shock, and investment responds more. The trade deficit spikes up as capital flows in. Thus shocks to the match between wants and resources in a world with immobile human capital can help explain why investment, saving, and the trade deficit move together.

Incomplete Markets

In the standard general equilibrium model, we have markets for all kinds of contingent claims. All trading occurs at the start, but the markets remain open. Prices change as uncertainty is resolved, but people have insured themselves through diversification and hedging as much as they are able to or want to, so they don't continue to trade.

In the real world, people do not diversify fully, even when they have no special views on the future of specific firms or the economy as a whole. They continue to bear risks that they could hedge. Contingent claims markets that might exist do not.

In part, this reflects the costs of opening and operating markets. People would rather bear some risks than the costs of supporting the operation of markets in less important contingencies. In particular, they keep most of their human capital risks, because selling a share of human capital can sharply reduce its value.

Completing markets can be a very important part of an economy's development. The first step is to establish a legal framework for protection of property rights. The next is to free markets in all kinds of risky assets and to remove restrictions on borrowing and lending. Freeing trade and investment with other countries is especially important. The last step is to allow creation of derivatives markets that amount to state-contingent claims.

Completing markets in this way can encourage growth, and can improve the trade-off between variability and income or expected growth. It can reduce uncertainty, especially as seen by an individual, but it can also increase uncertainty when it encourages risk taking.

Thus financial intermediation, defined in a very broad way, reduces the specific risk that each individual bears, and allows those who are less tolerant of risk to shift general risks to those who are more tolerant of risk. It can greatly increase expected utility.

Still, completing markets does not affect the qualitative behavior of the economy. No matter how complete markets are, the match between wants and resources drives business cycles, and people can choose faster expected growth for a given level of political stability only by consuming less or by taking more risk. Permanent and temporary changes in output are highly correlated.

No matter how complete markets are, growth can continue indefinitely because we face no fixed factors for the foreseeable future. Employment will vary more in sectors producing durables than in sectors producing nondurables or services. Vacancies will be procyclical.

In other words, we can explain almost all of our stylized facts equally well in models with varying degrees of market completeness. An incomplete markets equilibrium looks like a complete markets equilibrium, except that people don't go out on a limb so much.

When they can't trade in everything, they don't specialize so much in production or consumption, and they don't make as many investments that take a long time to pay off.

Incomplete markets, which reduce welfare, make prices and quantities *less* volatile than they would otherwise be. Output, unemployment, and asset prices are volatile despite market incompleteness, not because of it.

Money

When I modify the general equilibrium model to include money (Black (1987)) along with conventional securities and to provide a reason for using money, I find that the government must passively supply whatever money the private sector demands. It cannot "print money" without running massive deficits. I find no scope for monetary policy. In other words, money doesn't matter.

I can find no mechanism consistent with general equilibrium by which open market operations can affect the real economy, nominal interest rates, or the price level. Changing the private sector's holdings of currency, reserves, and government bonds simply makes people want to reverse the open market operation. It does not make them want to change their rates of consumption or investment.

When I relax the assumptions of the general equilibrium model a bit, I find that open market operations can have an impact, but not on the level of output or the inflation rate. Rather, the government can affect interest rates, raising some and lowering others, thus changing the shape of the yield curve.

If open market operations are purely domestic, the government engages in "operation twist." For example, suppose the central bank wants to drive down the short rate by offering to lend unlimited amounts at an artificially low rate. Since the rate is low, many banks and other borrowers will take the offer. Money will flow out. To replace this money, the central bank sells some of its longer-term securities, driving their prices down and their yields up. Thus the central bank increases the slope of the yield curve between the artificially low short rate and the artificially high longer rates.

If the central bank holds foreign securities, it can sell those rather than its own longer-term government bonds. Then it raises foreign interest rates. It increases the slope of both domestic and foreign yield curves.

The private sector makes money from this by borrowing at artificially low rates and lending at artificially high rates. The central bank loses a similar amount of money. Since central banks normally make lots of money by issuing liabilities that pay no interest, these losses are not obvious.

By distorting interest rates, central banks also distort forward currency rates. A forward currency rate must, by arbitrage, be roughly equal to the difference between the two domestic interest rates with the same maturity as the forward rate.

Without central bank intervention in domestic money markets, forward currency rates might be closely related to expected spot rates. With intervention, the forward rates are distorted, and need not be related to expected spot rates. Intervention creates opportunities for private sector trading in forward currency markets, as well as opportunities in domestic money markets.

Intervention also distorts domestic forward interest rates. Artificial forward interest rates need not be closely related to expected spot interest rates.

This version of the general equilibrium model, while not very specific, suggests ways of interpreting a variety of studies of the behavior of interest rates and currency rates. It also suggests profit opportunities that will remain so long as central banks persist in distorting interest rates.

Inflation

My version of the general equilibrium model suggests that the overall rate of inflation, for countries with sound tax systems and well-developed financial markets, is unaffected by open market operations and other instruments of monetary policy. By intervening in gold markets, a country can affect its inflation rate, but few countries do that any more. By intervening in foreign currency markets, a country can reduce its inflation rate, but only by increasing another country's inflation rate. In any case, inflation has no special welfare consequences in the general equilibrium model.

When a government prints money to finance most of its spending, it causes hyperinflation. Running the printing presses to finance spending implies a large budget deficit. I think it's the deficit that causes hyperinflation, rather than the money growth itself. An economy with hyperinflation has so many distortions that I think of it as out of equilibrium.

If monetary policy doesn't normally affect inflation, what does?

The inflation rate is indeterminate. That means that it is not directly affected by any of the variables we normally include in our models. It can be whatever people think it will be. (The money supply will passively accommodate whatever the inflation rate turns out to be.)

Here, in fact, is a pure case of self-fulfilling expectations. If people expect a certain inflation rate, that's what they get, because they set prices and wage rates to match their expectations. Monetary policy might even play an indirect role in fixing the inflation rate. If people *think* monetary policy works, and they see signs of a tight monetary policy, they may reduce their inflation expectations. This, in turn, may reduce actual inflation.

But styles in economics change. Sometimes people think that budget deficits have a big influence on inflation; at those times, thinking it may make it so.

Thus my prediction is that the best inflation model will change over time. Whatever theory is currently fashionable, especially in the popular press, will work. We won't find any theory of inflation that works reliably until we can all agree on a macroeconomic model explaining such things as money and business cycles.

In any case, we need not worry about what causes inflation, since inflation doesn't matter, as a first approximation. It starts to matter in an economy with currency only when it becomes negative enough to drive the nominal interest rate near zero. A very negative inflation rate can drive the nominal rate to zero, which implies an artificially high real interest rate. Many will want to lend at that rate, but few will want to borrow. I don't know how the economy can reach equilibrium with the nominal rate stuck at zero.

Fixed and Floating Exchange Rates

Even though monetary policy is passive everywhere, two countries can fix their currency exchange rate by agreeing to exchange each currency for the other without limit at the agreed rate. Or either country alone can do this, so long as the other country doesn't try to set a different fixed rate.

In a world without exchange or capital controls, the cost of this is modest. The intervening country need not maintain significant reserves, since it can always sell assets for currency in the other country. It will earn a competitive return on any assets it holds that are denominated in the other country's currency.

It's important that each country recognize that monetary policy is passive even with floating rates, and that devaluation has no significant impact on the real equilibrium. The only real effect is to help or hurt those who borrow or lend between the two countries. That way neither country has much incentive to devalue, so speculators are unlikely to put pressure on the currency.

In the general equilibrium model, floating rates and fixed rates are equivalent in the sense that the paths of real relative prices are roughly the same under both regimes. Fixed rates with periodic devaluation or revaluation give about the same paths for real relative prices too, but with this regime, intervention can mean that governments lose to speculators when rates change.

I try not to use the phrase "purchasing power parity," because it has so many meanings. Since real relative prices are highly uncertain and are constantly changing, both within and between countries, conventional tests for purchasing power parity will fail to find it. The sense in which I believe it holds, as a first approximation, is that if we were to shift between fixed and floating exchange rate regimes, holding fixed all other government policies including taxes and regulations, we would not change the conditional joint distribution of future relative prices for any pair of goods and services for any measurement time.

Using conventional measures, though, real relative prices seem to vary much more between countries with floating exchange rates than between countries with fixed exchange rates. What does this mean?

I think it means our measures are flawed. What we see between countries with floating exchange rates is the natural level of volatility, and what we see between countries with fixed exchange rates is artificially smoothed. Probably the main reason for the apparent low volatility of the real exchange rate with fixed currency rates is the difference between posted prices and actual transaction prices. Posted prices are smoothed in ways that transaction prices are not.

One way we can see this is by increasing the differencing interval. The apparent difference in variability between fixed and floating rate regimes is greatest at quarterly intervals. It declines as we go to yearly intervals, and it declines further as we go to five-year and ten-year intervals. The longer the interval, the more the natural volatility shows through.

The Great Depression

What caused the Great Depression, which affected so many countries during the 1930s?

The usual culprits, I believe, played a big role. Firms made investments during the 1920s based on their beliefs about what tastes and technology would be, along many dimensions, during the 1930s. Those beliefs turned out to be very wrong, so the investments were not worth much and ability to produce what people wanted was low.

Some bad investments were in agriculture. Some were in consumer durables. Some were in export sectors affected by the Smoot–Hawley tariffs. To find out in more detail which investments went most wrong, we can look at stock price changes by sector and at business publications from the 1920s and 1930s.

But monetary forces played a big role too, and interacted with these real forces. In the process of going back on the gold standard and staying on it, many countries experienced sharp deflation, which drove their nominal interest rates down. Normally, very low nominal rates mean a big demand for currency. In the face of such a big increase in demand, some countries stopped supplying currency passively. This meant a serious breakdown in financial markets.

What's worse, though, is that the deflations forced short-term nominal interest rates to zero in some countries, and would have made these rates negative were it not for the effective floor at zero. This caused disequilibrium in real asset markets. The real interest rate was forced above its natural level. It was a kind of "currency trap."

Longer-term nominal interest rates did not fall to zero, because they reflected the chance that the nominal short rate would bounce back to positive levels. But they were artificially high, so longer-term real rates were artificially high, even more so than short-term real rates.

In this situation, currency and government bonds became very attractive relative to real assets. Real asset prices fell to artificially low levels. Most new investments became unattractive. Saving became more attractive, and consumption became less attractive.

To meet the demand for their nominal liabilities, governments were led to buy private assets or (more ominously) to enter previously private businesses. This amounted to a kind of large-scale open market operation. To cover their losses from this, they raised taxes. Since government businesses often lose money, they raised taxes more.

All these things happened because the nominal interest rate can't fall below zero in a world with currency. And because they happened, they made worse the mismatch between wants and resources. Who could have foreseen, in the 1920s, that nominal short rates would fall to zero in the 1930s, and that both financial and real asset markets would be thrown out of equilibrium?

The gold standard helped cause these problems, but it can also help avoid them. If we use a gold standard with a gold price that is high enough (or increases fast enough) to keep the nominal short rate well above zero, we will not fall into this currency trap. In this limited sense, there is a trade-off between inflation and unemployment, even in a general equilibrium model.

Evidence

My approach to evidence is similar to McCloskey's (1985, 1990) and Summers' (1991). My job, I believe, is to persuade others that my conclusions are sound. I will use an array of devices to do this: theory, stylized facts, time-series data, surveys, appeals to introspection, and so on.

Because it is largely an observational science, economics progresses slowly. There are no decisive experiments that others can verify independently. This makes it especially hard to settle questions of causality, which are often the questions we want most to answer. Correlation does not imply causation, even when we observe the correlated variables at different times. In economics, we often observe the effect before we observe the cause.

Econometrics tells us that an effect can precede its cause, and general economics tells us that a price increase can mean either greater demand or smaller supply. Yet economists continue to look for "predetermined" or "exogenous" macroeconomic variables that allow them to identify a system of equations.

Such variables are very hard to come by, so I think most attempts to use econometrics to settle economic questions are misguided. I'm always looking for the dreaded phrase "identifying restriction." To me, that means an assumption adopted solely to make the researcher's life easier.

In principle, we can use marketing and engineering data to identify supply and demand. In practice, we will find it very costly to gather this information and interpret it.

Econometric models use the language of general equilibrium, but I almost always view them as too specific. They can tell us about correlations, including partial correlations, but they can't tell us what we really want to know.

What kinds of quantitative evidence do I find most reliable?

First of all, I believe in the market values of securities. I think market values tell us about "effective capital," and changes in market value tell us about "economic depreciation."

When market values are not available, I look at gross output and gross income. Since market values are almost never available for human capital, and are not very comprehensive in most countries, I do this often. I think a good first approximation is to assume that a country's effective capital is proportional to its gross output.

Still, I use the history of security returns to estimate expected return and risk. From expected return and risk I estimate an economy's risk tolerance.

I use value-added data to estimate the rental rates for physical and human capital, and thus to estimate the shares of output that go to each. This gives me a rough idea of the relative values of physical and human capital.

I use consumption data to estimate the kind and degree of consumption smoothing. When consumption is very smooth relative to wealth, we need to use slowly declining weights on past consumption in the geometric average in our utility function.

Beyond this, I find myself interested in details. What goods and services did well in the last upturn? What kinds of workers lost jobs in the last downturn, and where did they end up? What kinds of good luck have the fastest growing countries had recently?

Part III

Issues

Here are some issues in the literature, and my responses.

Adjustment costs

As I noted under "aspects of general equilibrium," we can always create a general equilibrium model with no adjustment costs to explain any relation we see involving prices and quantities. In that sense, adjustment costs add nothing to our models of the world.

I'm especially skeptical of the use of adjustment costs in models of business fixed investment spending. Installing new investment goods (or repairing old ones) is costly, but these costs do not differ in any clear way from the other costs of an investment. Thus I don't see why we want to highlight them.

On the other hand, I claim we can't understand growth patterns or business cycles fully without using models that have observable adjustment costs for shifting resources from one area to another. If adjustment costs are zero, the match between wants and resources is unimportant. We can just transform abundant resources into scarce ones.

I don't think a model of the costs of reallocating human and physical capital will look anything like the models of business fixed investment spending.

Aggregate demand

In the most general sort of equilibrium model, I don't know how to define "aggregate demand." Since I can't define it, I can't imagine how shifts in it can contribute to business cycles or fluctuations.

Does aggregate demand mean a weighted sum of demand curves across many different goods and services? I don't see any economic meaning in such a sum.

When people say that they see shifts in aggregate demand, they may mean that they see changes in the match between wants and resources. Thus in a more specific sort of model, high aggregate demand can mean a good match. If this is what "aggregate demand" means, we could also call it "aggregate supply."

In a still more specific model with fixed proportions, changes in the supply of or demand for the binding resource can trigger effects that look like changes in aggregate demand. A model where oil shocks are important may be an example, but we don't expect a single commodity to play this role indefinitely.

Aggregate shocks and allocative shocks

Some people try to classify shocks to the economy as aggregate or allocative. An aggregate shock might be a shock to aggregate demand (for people who believe in aggregate demand), or a technology shock that affects most sectors in the same direction. A change in the political system might be an aggregate shock. An allocative shock might be a shift in tastes, away from one sector and toward another. Sometimes we call it a "sectoral shock."

I don't find this distinction very useful. A shock to tastes or technology will always show up as partly aggregate and partly allocative. The ultimate shocks that drive the economy cannot be classified in this way. And in any given period, we have numerous shocks to both tastes and technology, so we can't identify individual periods with aggregate shocks or allocative shocks.

I am especially puzzled by attempts to count shocks: to say that a certain fraction of them are aggregate, while the rest are allocative. I don't know what to make of the percentages that people come up with.

Aggregation

A collection of diverse people need not behave as if everyone were average. The risk tolerance of a group may differ from the risk tolerance of its members. A group may be more willing to substitute present for future leisure than any member is.

All of these are aggregation problems, but they are all minor compared with the problems we create by assuming a single kind of person consumes a single good that a single kind of firm creates using a single technology. With that assumption, we lose the essential driving force behind business cycles and variation in growth rates: changing expectations that cause a varying match between wants and resources.

For some problems in economics, aggregation of this kind provides a useful abstraction. But for understanding business cycles, unemployment, and growth, I think the details are essential.

Business fixed investment

What do we learn from the literature on business fixed investment spending? Not much, I claim.

This literature emphasizes tangible business assets rather than all business assets. Why should we focus on tangible assets?

It treats investment as determined by Tobin's q, which is like a price. How can we look at a supply curve like this without also looking at the corresponding demand curve?

For the world as a whole, investment equals saving. For a country, investment and saving differ by the trade balance. How can we model a component of investment without thinking about saving, the trade balance, and the other components of investment?

The assumptions that people make in this literature are even more restrictive than usual. When we relax those assumptions, all the results collapse.

Calibration

In general, calibration means adjusting the structure or parameters of a model to match certain stylized facts, especially the means and volatilities of various economic time series. In this sense calibration is a form of estimation.

Unfortunately, many different kinds of models will match the stylized facts that people usually choose. Thus calibration can't tell us much about the structure of the economy. The relation between calibration and structure is like the relation between correlation and causation.

Researchers like Kydland and Prescott (1982) sometimes use "calibration" to refer to estimating a number like risk aversion from one study, and using that number as a restriction in other studies. This is a perilous process.

If we generalize the utility function so that it's time-nonseparable and state-dependent, many studies that allegedly provide estimates of risk aversion collapse. We can still use the expected return on wealth (in excess of the interest rate) to provide evidence on risk aversion, but this is very hard to estimate, partly because it surely changes over time.

There are similar problems with all the other numbers people try to transfer from one study to another. I'd be very cautious about such transfers.

Capital mobility

If both physical and financial capital were perfectly mobile, people would hold much more fully diversified global portfolios of physical assets than they do, and we would see huge flows of financial and physical assets between countries as conditions change.

Even though we have global television (Cable News Network), a global language (English), and a global currency (dollars), people are still largely parochial. They prefer local news, regional dialects, and national currencies. They shop near home and they invest at home. The markets for goods and services are more local than global, and people show a strong home bias in their investments.

For now, at least, capital is not much more mobile than people are. Even financial capital has trouble moving across national boundaries. Thus we should not find it surprising that saving and investment are almost equal across countries and through time, or that consumption levels in different countries are imperfectly correlated.

Cash in advance

Can we tell anything by looking at a model like Lucas and Stokey's (1983) that assumes money is the world's only asset?

I don't think so. Adding capital and bonds completely changes the character of the model. I don't think any significant features of the simpler model generalize to a more complete model with fully developed capital markets and a more or less balanced government budget.

Chronic laziness

Does a theory where taste shifts play a central role rely on chronic laziness to explain business cycles?

Not at all. The activities we class as leisure are just a few of the uses people have for their time and money. A general shift in preference from work to leisure activities will be just one of the innumerable kinds of shift that can occur. In total, taste and technology shifts between different kinds of work or different kinds of leisure will play a far bigger role than shifts between work and leisure.

The movie business provides a good example. The success of a film is very hard to predict. The success of the movie business overall is more certain, but fluctuates substantially with the average popularity of films. Technology, as in the development of the video cassette recorder, plays a big role too. What matters for business cycles is whether people like the films that the industry releases, given the technologies available for viewing them.

In a general equilibrium model, we can even assume that the real interest rate and all other expected returns are constant without changing the model's predictions much. People who rely on shifts of leisure between present and future, though, need such changes to make their models predict business cycles.

Consumption correlations

Some, like Backus, Kehoe, and Kydland (1992) and Devereux, Gregory, and Smith (1992), find it odd that consumption growth in one country and consumption growth in another country are imperfectly correlated.

I think imperfect correlation is natural. We predict perfect correlation only when people diversify their investments completely and consume a single common good. In fact, though, people diversify their physical capital investments very little. They show a strong home bias and keep very little in foreign assets. They don't diversify their human capital investments at all. Add in the fact that people have different preferences among different goods and services, and we expect only modest consumption correlations.

In the short run, errors in measuring consumption in different places make the correlations even lower.

Cost of capital

The cost of capital has two components in an integrated economy: the real interest rate and the price of risk. The price of risk is the extra expected return an investor gets for taking an extra unit of risk. The expected return on capital is a composite of these two. It is the real interest rate plus the product of the price of risk and the average amount of risk in the economy's assets. The expected return and both of its components vary across economies and through time.

Researchers often focus on the real interest rate and neglect the price of risk. Perhaps that's because they feel they can estimate the real interest rate more easily than they can estimate the price of risk. Both are hard to estimate, but it takes decades to get a reasonable estimate of the average price of risk, so it's hard to know how the price of risk changes.

When we are trying to understand business cycles and growth, the average price of risk is probably more important than the average real interest rate. In a sense, the price of risk tells you how much extra unemployment and variation in output you have to bear to have a given added amount of expected growth.

Country growth rates

If we identify growth in wealth (measured at market value) with economic growth in human and physical capital, we can see large differences across countries in realized growth rates. Do these differences imply similar differences in past or future expected growth rates?

That's hard to tell. Countries where the ratio of consumption to wealth is consistently low may have consistently high growth in income for that reason, and countries with consistent trade deficits because they are importing physical capital to take advantage of investment opportunities may have consistently high growth in output. Countries where investors have high risk tolerance may have high expected growth because such investors take more risk.

But estimates of expected return are so imprecise that we are unlikely to find consistent differences along this dimension with just a few decades of data. We even have trouble finding consistent differences in real interest rates, given the problems in estimating expected inflation.

Many or most of the measured differences are just luck: tastes and technology happen to shift in a way that favors one country over another. For example, by the start of the 1980s, Japan had invested heavily in the capacity to produce high-quality cars and consumer electronic products. Demand for such products soared during the 1980s, which helps explain Japan's growth over that period.

Cycles

As a first approximation, such measures of economic activity as capital, output, and consumption follow a geometric random walk. As a second approximation, we can see cycles in output and consumption. Perhaps seasonal cycles are the most obvious.

Output has nonseasonal cycles partly because of durables. Output of durables is more volatile than capital, so the difference between current output and the target implied by capital shows cycles, largely in the form of shocks followed by mean reversion. Durables output also has periodicity: for example, a shock to durables output has "echoes" as the durables are replaced.

Inventories are durable, so they have cycles. The ratio of inventories to wealth falls in good times and rises in bad times.

Consumption has cycles partly because it's more sluggish than wealth. The difference between actual consumption and the target implied by wealth shows both shocks followed by mean reversion and periodicity, for seasonal and other reasons.

Even though I don't think of Tobin's q as related to the cost of installing new capital, we can use it to measure cycles. It shows shocks and then mean reversion as historical cost accounting data catch up with market values.

I think we see cycles most clearly, though, in unemployment and help-wanted ads.

Cycles in labor markets differ in nature and timing from cycles in output and other markets. In all markets, though, the speed of mean reversion is probably related to the depreciation and obsolescence rates for human and physical capital, and to the relation between adjustment costs and the speed with which capital moves from one area to another.

Depreciation

How should we model depreciation in physical capital in trying to understand business investment?

The one thing we cannot do is to assume exponential decay at a constant rate. Expected depreciation is procyclical, and partly or fully offsets procyclical rental rates on capital. Actual depreciation is highly variable, because asset values fluctuate like stock and bond prices. Indeed, it's often negative.

Note that depreciation can occur through use, deterioration, and obsolescence. Knowledge depreciates like any other kind of capital, because it becomes obsolete. Even though we may never forget anything, the value of old knowledge declines as new knowledge accumulates.

Diminishing returns

Why does economic growth continue at a rapid rate? Why isn't it limited by diminishing returns?

Because we are very patient, and because so far we have not encountered any truly fixed factors of production. We add human capital as fast as we add physical capital, and the value of real estate lies mostly in its improvements rather than in the raw value of the underlying land.

Even though we assume a competitive world with convex technology, diminishing returns to each factor need not imply that economic growth will slow down anytime soon. I suspect that growth will slow down more because we become impatient than because the expected returns on human and physical capital decline. When we start attaching a higher value to current consumption and a lower value to future consumption, growth may slow or stop.

Dispersion

Can we use the dispersion across sectors of output or employment growth rates as an indicator of business conditions or labor market conditions?

Not with broadly defined sectors. Davis and Haltiwanger (1990, 1992) find that dispersion of net job creation across establishments increases in bad times, but much of this relation is lost when we aggregate, as Lilien (1982) finds. Sectors producing durables are much more sensitive to general economic conditions than sectors producing services, which means we expect high dispersion among broadly defined sectors in both very good times and very bad times. Dispersion at that level is a poor measure of the match between wants and resources.

Divergence

Lucas (1993) rejects the traditional neoclassical growth model because it implies that countries will converge to a common capital-labor ratio and steady-state growth path. He adds human capital and removes the fixed factor of production, but rejects a constant-returns-to-scale version of the resulting model because he says that small differences among countries will cause their output levels to *diverge*. Instead, he suggests making world human capital a factor of production.

I don't think we need this externality to create a model without divergence. One way to do it is to bring back a partly fixed factor of production. I prefer, though, to assume that people in different countries cooperate in producing things, but always use production processes showing constant returns to scale. This eliminates divergence for most countries, and also helps explain why countries that interact more tend to converge more strongly than countries that interact less.

The most extreme example of a model like this, where people all over the world cooperate in producing a single good, looks very much like the model Lucas prefers. Each worker can take output as depending on his human capital and a weighted geometric average of the human capital of all the other people in the world.

Diversification

Do countries vary in the methods that people can use to diversify away the idiosyncratic risks they face? Do countries with better methods grow faster, because entrepreneurs take more risk?

Yes, to some extent. But I don't think this is a major issue, because the incentive costs of diversifying offset the risk reduction benefits. The owners of a private firm have more incentive to manage it well than the owners of a public firm. We could have a market in shares of human capital, but we don't, because selling a part of your human capital reduces your incentive to work, just as a tax on wage income does.

Countries where diversification is easier tend to be countries with strong property rights. I think the benefits of strong property rights dominate the net benefits of easier diversification.

Echoes

Replacement of durable goods tends to be uneven, since anything that speeds up or slows down replacement causes a similar speedup or slowdown the next time the goods wear out or become obsolete.

This is like the echoes that follow a baby boom. When a generation with many members has babies, it creates a new generation with many members. It's also like the patterns we see in traffic congestion. Congestion at one point tends to create echoes at other points, as people speed up and slow down in response to their local traffic conditions.

These echoes in durable goods replacement can help explain both temporary booms, with lots of overtime work, and layoff unemployment. Firms can see the echoes coming and going, so they use lots of temporary hires and layoffs rather than permanent hires and fires.

Econometrics

I feel that econometric studies of time-series data tell us very little about the economy.

In my view, exogenous variables are not exogenous, pre-determined variables are not predetermined, and identifying restrictions are generally unjustified. The identification problem is unsolvable at the macroeconomic level, so structural equations are not structural.

Econometric studies can tell us about variances and covariances, including autocovariances. They can tell us about correlations, including partial correlations. But they can't tell us anything direct about cause or effect, impact or influence, structure or meaning. We kid ourselves when we say that one variable helps to "explain" another. This sounds like causation, but really means only correlation.

Efficiency units

We are used to thinking of the labor input to production in efficiency units. What becomes of this notion when we use human capital for the labor input?

Shifts in market value reflect changes in the effectiveness of capital. When we decompose capital at market value into units and unit value, unit value measures effectiveness. In other words, to measure human or physical capital in efficiency units, we simply estimate its market value.

Effort

Effort is hard to measure directly. We can measure effort indirectly, in efficiency units, by dividing total wage income by a weighted geometric average of current and past levels of human capital at estimated market value. Effort is unusually high when that ratio is unusually high.

There are many possible weighted geometric averages. We choose one that gives a positive correlation (in an intuitive way) between shifts in effort and shifts in human capital.

Embodied and disembodied technical change

I see no useful distinction between embodied and disembodied technical change. An advancement in knowledge that is freely available to everyone increases either the real market value of human and physical capital, or the expected return on a stock of human and physical capital with given risk. A private investment in research or development increases the stock of capital. A firm that installs a new process learns, which increases its stocks of both human and physical capital.

Expected freely available technical change becomes part of the expected return on capital. Actual freely available technical change becomes part of the actual return on capital. Privately developed technical change becomes part of investment in new capital.

In other words, we can treat all kinds of technical change as simply part of the accumulation of capital. We grow by consuming less than the return on existing capital and investing the difference in new capital. If innovation has no net external benefits for the economy, the kind of capital we buy doesn't matter. A device to reduce wind resistance on a truck may be as good as a new way to splice genes. All become part of the capital stock, measured at market value.

Equity premium puzzle

Mehra and Prescott (1985) use a model with time-separable, state-independent utility to show that consumption seems too smooth in light of the estimated equity risk premium and other facts. Their results show, in my view, why we should move to a model with more general utility. The puzzle falls apart when we do that. Even the idea that consumption smoothness and the equity premium should be related seems strange, and gives us a reason to move to more general utility before we look at any data.

Estimation and testing

"Estimation" suggests a Bayesian approach to data, while "testing" suggests a classical approach. I prefer estimation, since I think researchers who want to test often choose models that are more specific than the economics requires. They talk of adding restrictions for no reason other than making their models easier to reject.

Even those who are inclined to estimate may favor models that are too specific. If we take the full general equilibrium model seriously, we may have trouble finding ways to estimate it or to test it. We may be limited to exploring it.

But if we want to know whether government intervention in business cycles makes sense, that is the place to start. If we can't think of a way to reject the general equilibrium model, then we can't show that government action helps. If we can't estimate the model, then we can't tell whether one government action is better than another.

Pretending we know more than we do will hardly shed light on the matter.

Euler equations

We can derive an interesting Euler equation only by severely restricting utility. For example, we may make it time-separable and state-independent.

With these restrictions, we can derive expressions that depend only on utility and asset returns. They do not depend directly on production or supply conditions. This is odd, since equilibrium usually depends in a symmetric way on both demand and supply conditions. We have, in effect, made identifying restrictions without economic justification.

In a full equilibrium model, I don't see any analogue to conventional macroeconomic Euler equations.

Examples

I view most models as simply *examples* that illustrate some of the forces affecting the economy. Thus I don't think it normally makes sense to *test* a model: we don't think an example correctly describes everything we see. I don't even think it normally makes sense to *estimate* a model. As we add structure to an example, the coefficients we estimate will change, often sharply.

To me, the most interesting use of a model lies in making it part of a sequence of models that make more and more realistic assumptions. As we move to more complex models, we can watch the coefficients and other model features change. In other words, we can *explore* the model.

As always, I think we want to move toward a full general equilibrium model with convex technology before we go outside the standard competitive framework.

Excess volatility

Whenever we look at asset market prices, we are apt to see excess volatility, just as we are apt to see patterns in a random walk.

Market prices are driven by expectations, which are volatile and hard to observe. We see the news, but we don't see the processing that follows it, and we don't see a lot of information that never makes it into the news. Thus we are often unable to explain why prices move as they do.

I believe that the only way to demonstrate excess volatility is to describe a "contrarian" investment strategy that consistently makes money. The strategy should work even if the expected return on the market as a whole is constant. Strategies that we find by "data mining" don't count.

The believers in excess volatility have generally not tried to present strategies like this. If excess volatility is out there, it's hard to see clearly. We certainly don't need it to explain business cycles or variations in growth.

Expectations

I think expectations play a major role in business fluctuations.

People create human and physical capital in forms that reflect their expectations. Good times are when these expectations turn out to be more or less correct along many dimensions. Bad times are when they don't.

In this sense, psychological influences play a major role. But I don't think of these influences as residuals representing things we really don't understand. I think of expectations as observable, at least in principle.

We can see expectations in the career choices people make and in the investments that firms make. We can even find out about expectations by asking people what they think will happen in the future.

Financial intermediation

As a country grows, it invests in more and more elaborate forms of financial intermediation. In effect, its markets become more complete. Its residents can diversify better, or hedge the risks they take, or align ownership and control for the investments they make.

In general, this reduces the price-of-risk part of the cost of capital. It increases the expected payoff for taking more risk, as with added specialization or more roundabout production. Increasing the payoff means the economy takes more risk. Expected growth increases, asset volatility increases, and average unemployment increases.

Financial intermediation improves the terms on which people take risk, but it actually increases the risk we measure in the economy.

Government

Even in a general equilibrium model, the government will have some impact on business cycles.

Unexpected shifts in the composition or total amount of government purchases will act like taste changes. Shifts between war and peace are especially dramatic examples.

Shifts in government regulation of business can act like technology changes. Controlling pollution and waste disposal can be a big part of manufacturing cost in some industries, for example, and can affect the manufacturing methods that firms choose. (We might also view this as a shift in society's taste for a clean environment.)

The government creates much of the unemployment we see using minimum wage laws, child labor and homework laws, laws protecting unions, unemployment benefits, and welfare payments (though that is not the intent of these programs). Changes in these areas can cause large changes in the amount of unemployment.

Price controls can have dramatic effects, as we have seen in the formerly communist countries. Taxes and subsidies can have similar, though usually less dramatic, effects.

Even changes in the overall level of the government's debt can have some effect, since it burdens different generations and people with varying family types differently.

Government consumption

Suppose we add a lump-sum tax to a simple linear model with human and physical capital. Assume that the government uses the proceeds to produce something with no value, or with a value unrelated to the values of private goods and services. Does this cause a change in effort?

As a first approximation, it does not. A lump-sum tax now or a path of expected lump-sum taxes in the future is like a decrease in wealth. But effort does not vary with wealth in this kind of model. Wealth and consumption and both human and physical capital grow indefinitely without causing any change in effort. Thus a decline in wealth caused by a lump-sum tax does not cause a change in effort either. It puts private wealth and income on a permanently lower path, but does not affect expected growth.

If we assume that government consumption is a perfect substitute for current consumption of private goods, but is unrelated to current consumption of leisure or future consumption of private goods, then an unexpected and temporary increase in government consumption will affect effort. But why should we assume that? And why should we assume that the resulting change in leisure is related to business cycles? Leisure is not unemployment, and an increase in effort for this reason does not generally improve welfare.

Moreover, we can analyze the effects of government consumption using conventional linearization around a steady state only in a model with fixed factors. When we have no fixed factors, we do not have the required kind of steady state.

Thus I can see neither technical nor economic reasons for using government consumption as a proxy for poorly understood "aggregate shocks" to the economy. The complex findings of Barro (1981) and Christiano and Eichenbaum (1992) depend on very special and unrealistic assumptions.

Granger causation

One thing "Granger causes" a second if changes in the first consistently precede changes in the second.

In a world where expectations drive asset prices, consumption, and investment decisions, Granger causation has little to do with causation. The things we observe may all be caused by more fundamental things we don't observe. Granger causation is simply a form of correlation. As such, it doesn't tell us much.

Growth accounting

In doing his brand of growth accounting, Denison (1985) distinguishes between actual output and "potential output." The difference tends to be greatest when unemployment is greatest.

I think unemployment signals a difference between actual and potential output only in certain limited senses. If the government stopped subsidizing unemployment, or if people could somehow make better investment decisions for their human and physical capital, then average unemployment would be lower (assuming no change in the aggressiveness of investments) and average output would be higher. Denison, though, thinks better fiscal and monetary policy might do the trick.

Denison uses conventional methods to estimate the capital and labor inputs to production. He attributes much of the variation in output to sources other than inputs, while I prefer to attribute much more of it, or even all of it, to variation in inputs. I don't know what to make of the figures he gives, because he makes so many arbitrary assumptions. For example, he uses years of schooling as his only measure of human capital.

More generally, I am suspicious of all attempts to decompose growth or business cycle fluctuations. Decomposition does not tell us anything direct about causation or structure, and it often diverts our attention from the underlying economics. It can even be deceptive, as when it leads us to see "shocks to technology" or "allocative shocks" in the data.

Habit formation

Ryder and Heal (1973) suggest a form of utility that shows "habit formation" or "habit persistence." Past consumption creates a "floor" for current consumption. Higher past consumption relative to current consumption means higher marginal utility for current consumption. Sundaresan (1989) and Constantinides (1990) use this kind of utility to explain the "equity premium puzzle" and other phenomena.

This kind of utility may make sense for drug addiction and related phenomena, but I resist using it more generally, because it has peculiar features. When we interpret it as utility of a lifetime consumption stream, this kind of utility implies that increasing consumption at one time but leaving it unchanged at all other times can *reduce* utility.

We can explain the "equity premium puzzle" using any kind of utility that makes consumption smoother than wealth. I prefer Greenig's (1986) device, which replaces current consumption in the utility function with a weighted geometric average of current and past levels of consumption.

Utility that captures habit formation and utility that captures consumption smoothing are distinct, and I prefer the consumption-smoothing kind.

Help-wanted ads and labor mobility

Why do we see more help-wanted ads in good times than in bad (Abraham and Katz (1986))? And greater labor mobility (Murphy and Topel (1987))?

The normal career path involves many job changes — some within a single firm, and some between firms. Even job changes within a firm may involve help-wanted ads, as the firm checks the market before promoting from within.

Careers advance faster in good times than in bad, as investments in human capital, particularly through learning by doing, pay off. Thus both mobility and the associated help-wanted ads are higher in good times.

Also, help-wanted ads reflect a search for temporary workers in temporarily good times. For example, when demand for durables is high because we are restocking inventories, makers of durables may hire temporarily at all levels.

Hodrick–Prescott filters

Hodrick and Prescott (1981) describe a family of statistical decompositions of an economic series into "trend" and "deviation from trend" components. They apply this, for example, to a decomposition of the path of output into growth and business cycle components.

This method may separate variation in utilization from variation in output at normal levels of utilization, as least roughly. I'd prefer, though, to use a method that relates output to direct measures of utilization and to smoothed levels of composite capital at estimated market value. Such a method would put more emphasis on economics and less on statistics.

Hog cycles

Suppose the supply of hogs falls or the demand for them rises. The price rises. We expect the price to be high for a long time.

What is the hog farmer to do? He can slaughter more sows to take advantage of the high prices, or he can slaughter fewer sows so he can produce more hogs during the next breeding period. If most farmers make the second choice, the price will rise even more in the short run. In other words, small disturbances in demand or supply can create large changes in price and quantity.

Similar things happen in many other areas. When a firm introduces new cost-saving machines, it may have to use the first few to train operators rather than to reduce costs. When a firm hires a skilled manager, he may spend much of his time training other managers rather than managing.

This can even apply to a large sector. If people use lots of human capital in creating new human capital, an imbalance in human capital relative to physical capital may become worse before it improves, since some of an inadequate stock of human capital must be diverted to production of new human capital.

Thus hog cycles and their kin cause periodic business cycles as distinct from mean-reverting cycles. They act like durable goods.

Home bias

Even when barriers to investing across national boundaries are low, people seem to prefer to invest at home. Thus they own physical capital mostly in the country where they live.

This is partly out of ignorance, though people can avoid information costs by hiring agents. This ignorance of foreign countries and foreign assets will decline over time. It is partly because of taxes on cross-border investments, though people can avoid most such taxes by using derivatives. It is partly because of exchange risk, though people can avoid that by hedging, and partly because of actual or possible exchange controls.

I think the biggest factor, though, is just tastes: people care where their capital is located.

As Baxter and Jermann (1993) point out, this bias is especially striking when we consider the high correlation between the returns on human and physical capital. Human capital is mainly domestic, so anyone who has no bias toward domestic physical capital can improve his diversification by favoring foreign assets.

Because people favor domestic assets (and for other reasons spelled out above), investment and saving move together, both across countries and through time.

Imperfect competition

What role does imperfect competition play in a general equilibrium model?

The standard model assumes perfect competition in one sense, but in another sense it already has imperfect competition. Once in place, specific human and physical capital earns rents that vary with the state of the world. Because of adjustment costs (in one version of the model), entry of new capital reduces these rents only gradually, while shocks to tastes or technology can change them sharply in either direction.

Thus I don't see how adding imperfect competition can change the character of the general equilibrium approach.

Intertemporal substitution

In a world with many dimensions, temporary shifts of consumption or leisure between the present and the future don't matter much. We can explain most of what we see in a model with no intertemporal substitution at all, so long as we use a utility function that disconnects risk aversion and the intertemporal elasticity of substitution.

People shift between working and waiting for recall, or between working and job hunting. They do not generally shift leisure from the future to the present and call it "job hunting."

Investment

Why is measured investment more volatile than output, while both are more volatile than consumption?

Output and consumption both behave like smoothed composite capital, but consumption is smoothed more than output. If we define investment as output less consumption, this means it will be more volatile than both output and consumption.

Moreover, businesses and individuals consume the services of durables. When demand for those services changes, output of durables changes sharply. The more durable the goods, the sharper the changes. Thus a simple accelerator effect explains these relative volatilities in a general equilibrium model.

Finally, on-the-job learning creates unmeasured investment in human capital which is highly procyclical. Total investment, including both measured and unmeasured investment, is even more volatile than measured investment.

Irreversible investments

Do irreversible investments, as in Bernanke (1983), play a role in business cycles?

In a very basic sense, as noted above under "aspects of general equilibrium," irreversibility cannot be a central feature of a general equilibrium model, since we can always create a version that explains prices and quantities even though all investments are reversible. In the kind of model where irreversibility matters, it does not matter primarily because varying levels of exogenous uncertainty cause the option values in investments to vary. Instead, irreversible investments play a big role in the match between wants and resources. If investments are fully reversible so we can switch them from one form to another with no adjustment cost, then the match can't get very far out of line, and resources will generally be fully employed.

In fact, we can identify the degree of irreversibility with the extent of our use of roundabout production methods and with the degree of specialization in human and physical capital. While exogenous increases in uncertainty do indeed cause people to choose more reversible investments, the primary causal relation is in the other direction. When people become more tolerant of risk (perhaps because they become wealthier), or when opportunities improve at each level of risk, they will choose more specialized investments. They will take on more risk through less reversible investments so they can have higher rates of expected growth.

"Island" economy
Lucas (1972) and others have proposed a simple model to explain some portion of economic fluctuations. In this model, people live on economic "islands" with limited communication. They see their own monetary shocks, but not those of the inhabitants of other islands.

I don't think this model survives generalization to a world where people hold capital as well as money. Moreover, if some enterprising soul did surveys of monetary shocks in different places and published the results, the remaining uncertainty would likely be very minor.

Job search and matching
Sometimes people create models where a single kind of worker is either employed or unemployed, with given transition probabilities. He becomes employed when he thinks he finds a good match between skills and job. These models do not spell out the dimensions of the match.

I don't think we learn much from this kind of model. In the labor market, the match between wants and available skills is crucial, but we need the details. Only then can we understand how shifts in tastes and technology make the match better or worse, and thus drive business cycles and variation in growth.

Knowledge
Arrow (1962), Romer (Paul, 1986), and Hercowitz and Sampson (1991) assume that knowledge, which makes labor more productive, grows in proportion to capital, which represents the economy's accumulated investment. We learn by investing, and what anyone learns is then freely available to all. Knowledge is thus external to both firms and workers.

I prefer to assume that knowledge is private (though it has both public and private aspects), partly because I see the cost of transmitting it to a new person as large compared to the cost of creating it. I find this assumption especially natural for what a worker learns on the job, which I think is most of the knowledge he uses on the job. We do learn by investing, but mostly by investing in human capital rather than in physical capital.

Knowledge has some features of a "nonrival input" to production or consumption (Romer (Paul, 1990a)). A worker can often pass on what he knows at lower cost than a new worker can learn it for himself. Scientific facts are typically much easier to use than to discover. A newspaper sells for a price that is infinitesimal compared to its publishing cost. Offsetting this, though, is the effect that new knowledge has on the value of old knowledge. New knowledge "steals the market" from old knowledge and reduces its productivity.

As a first approximation, then, we can treat knowledge as similar to all other forms of capital. We can assume it is costly and productive, and plays a role in a convex production process.

Labor hoarding

"Labor hoarding" implies variation in the intensity of work. Counter-cyclical labor hoarding is variation in effort per hour of work, which is one form of variation in utilization of human capital.

Why focus on effort per hour? I like to think about all forms of utilization of human capital together. Higher utilization can also take the form of more hours per worker, moves from unemployment to employment, and moves into the labor force. And if we talk about utilization of human capital, I think we should also talk about utilization of physical capital.

When I see a statement about labor hoarding, I usually translate it into a statement about utilization of human and physical capital. That can cause a dramatic change in its content.

Labor input

The labor input has two parts: human capital and effort. We often measure human capital at a "book value" that depends on years of schooling or job experience, and we often measure effort by adding hours across workers.

I prefer to measure both parts of the labor input in efficiency units. Since changes in market value reflect changes in effectiveness, we can measure human capital in efficiency units by estimating its market value.

The market value of human capital is the present value of future wages, net of direct spending for schooling or training. It's what all the shares in a person's future income net of schooling costs would be worth if a few shares traded in the market. As a first approximation, we can assume that returns on total human and physical capital, figured from market values, are identical.

To measure effort in efficiency units, we can divide total wages by a weighted geometric average of current and past levels of human capital at estimated market value. A complete measure of total wages includes additions to human capital. Effort is high when this ratio is high. Note that this measure of effort goes beyond just weighting hours by average compensation, and it goes far beyond weighting hours by years of schooling or experience.

Labor market sorting

As Williamson (1990) notes, sectoral shifts can disrupt the sorting of workers into job types. More generally, a shift in tastes or technology can change the value of knowledge about the fit between workers and jobs along many dimensions. This is one reason why shocks change the match between wants and resources.

Labor productivity

How should we define "labor productivity?"

Output per worker or output per worker-hour depends largely on human and physical capital. If we want a measure of composite capital, why don't we call it that, rather than calling it "labor productivity?" Assigning weights to workers or worker-hours based on their estimated levels of human capital does not solve this problem: we still end up with a measure of composite capital, modified by utilization.

Composite capital modified by utilization sounds like total output. If we want a measure that applies to labor but not to physical capital, we should use human capital modified by effort. That means that the only meaningful definition of "labor productivity" is total wages per person. We count both measured and unmeasured wages, and we count people who are unemployed or out of the labor force along with workers.

Law of large numbers

People sometimes say that the law of large numbers makes an equilibrium model of business cycles improbable. They believe that a large collection of small shocks should have a negligible effect on the whole economy.

I think this misses the point for several reasons. First, shocks can occur along many dimensions. A shock along a given dimension (exporting firms, firms that use computers, firms that create nuclear waste, for example) is not independent from firm to firm. So it can have a substantial aggregate effect.

Second, individual shocks are not small. The variance of fractional changes in income can be large for individuals and for small firms.

Third, and most important, the shocks in a general equilibrium model are not comparable. In a world where the islands are places that receive independent monetary shocks, the individual shocks are comparable. But where the islands are jobs or firms that differ along many dimensions, the shocks are not comparable. A series of relative price or quantity shocks to lots of islands of this kind will generally have a substantial aggregate effect.

By studying detailed statistics on economic activity along many dimensions, by reading newspapers and magazines, and by analyzing firms' engineering and marketing data, we can find out (after the fact) what these shocks were in any given period.

Learning by doing

This may be the most important way to invest in human capital. You earn less as a junior employee (in part) because you are learning so fast on the job. In effect, your employer pays part of your compensation in the form of training. Part of what you learn you can take with you when you leave, so that forms part of your total compensation.

You learn by investing in human capital more than by investing in physical capital. In fact, learning *is* investing in human capital.

Learning by doing does not involve any externalities or other effects inconsistent with general equilibrium.

It happens that in many countries, this kind of investment in human capital has tax advantages. Since you pay for it through lower current wages, you are, in effect, paying with pretax dollars. This does not mean such investments are untaxed, since your tax bracket may be lower when you are investing than when you are cashing in. Still, it may be one reason why we see more human capital than physical capital.

Leisure

Not many people, I believe, think of unemployment as leisure. Those who are laid off and are waiting for recall, or who are training or hunting for new jobs, experience stress rather than relaxation.

Thus I find it hard to think of intertemporal substitution of leisure as a key to business cycles. The activities we find in recessions occur because equilibrium wages in specific jobs fall so far that people would rather not work than work at those wages. Thus firms dismiss them or lay them off. The people who keep their old jobs are the ones whose equilibrium wages do not fall so far.

We can explain business cycles using a model with no leisure at all, or one where consumption of leisure is inelastic. In fact, I think we are very willing to shift leisure across time in the short run, but in the medium and long run, I think we smooth leisure the way we smooth consumption. We tend to set a pattern and stick to it.

Market stealing

A firm that uses advertising to take market share from another firm whose outputs have similar quality is "stealing the market." Since this activity is costly, we can imagine making everyone better off by eliminating it. The trouble is, no one has found a way to reduce this cost without introducing other, bigger costs. Fighting for market share creates costs that are unintended but unavoidable consequences of competition.

Similarly, new knowledge damages old knowledge. Even though we don't forget what we knew before, its value in production is reduced because it is partly obsolete. This external cost offsets the external benefits that come from the use and reuse (at low cost) of new knowledge.

Natural rate of unemployment

My first impulse is to define the "natural rate of unemployment" as whatever the rate currently is. It depends on everything: tastes and technology defined along many dimensions, plus things like political stability and strength of property rights.

Still, many changes in the unemployment rate seem temporary, so we may want to define the "natural rate" as the target rate that the actual rate moves toward. Unfortunately, it's hard to make this notion precise. The actual rate may vary around a short-run target rate, which varies around a medium-run target rate, which varies around a long-run target rate. We can probably put as many levels into this kind of decomposition as we want.

That takes me back to my original definition. The natural rate is the current rate. It is subject to various temporary shocks, which are correlated and take varying amounts of time to decay, plus an occasional more or less permanent shock.

New entrants

How will the behavior of new entrants, just starting their careers, differ from that of those whose careers are well established or nearing an end?

The new entrants should shift their job choices much more in response to taste and technology shocks than those with established careers. Since some human capital is very durable, changes will come much more often at the start than at the middle or end of a career. Those with a lot of human capital who are out of work or "underemployed" are likely to wait for the shift in the flow of new entrants to increase the relative demand for their services.

Overidentifying restrictions

I am suspicious of all restrictions in econometric models, since I think researchers put them in more often for their own convenience than for economic reasons. I am especially wary of overidentifying restrictions, since the researcher must put in many restrictions to make his model overidentified. The most natural case, at the macroeconomic level, is an unidentified model.

We can identify a model, in principle, by using firm and industry data on technology (including very detailed information on staffing, inventory policy, marketing, and the like) and relating this information to price and sales data. Or we can use similar data on individual tastes. I call this "identification at the microeconomic level." It's so costly that I doubt we will actually do it.

Moreover, the whole idea of overidentification makes more sense in classical statistics than in Bayesian statistics. My preference for a Bayesian approach also inclines me against the testing of overidentifying restrictions.

Overlapping generations

Some people die without children or other relatives they care for. Others do not want to make significant gifts or leave bequests to the next generation. Because of these people, an economy's consumption rate is higher than it would otherwise be and its growth rate is lower.

Still, most private wealth is held by people who do care about the future, and the government transfers resources to the next generation, partly by subsidizing education. This is probably why most countries have shown continuing growth.

I think we capture these two influences by assuming a world where people live forever but have an intermediate degree of impatience to spend. I don't see that we learn much by assuming a world where people have finite lives and no bequest motives. This world is hard to analyze, because we must decide how to weight the utilities of people of different ages.

In fact, an overlapping-generations model sometimes tempts us to maximize the utility of the representative person in the indefinite future. I can't imagine what would lead a society or an individual to make decisions using that criterion. There is no way of weighting the utilities of people currently alive that leads to that rule.

I think conventional overlapping-generations models are more likely to lead us astray than to teach us something, so I don't use them.

Part-time work

Part-time work pays much less per hour than full-time work. The main reason for this is that full-time workers maintain higher levels of human capital than part-time workers. Extra hours per day means more learning by doing, and thus greater human capital at each stage of a person's career.

But there are other reasons, too. For example, it is due partly to the start-up costs of beginning work each day, and to the cost of maintaining a place for an extra worker (physical space, accounting, regulatory costs, and potential lawsuits, for example). It is due partly to extra coordination costs, including extra managers, when a firm uses more workers to do a given job.

It is also due to the team nature of much of the production process. In many lines of work, each member of the team is far more productive when the other members are present. (Assembly lines and securities trading come to mind.) The very term "full-time work" suggests a process where a team works together for a standard day. And the "team" may include members from many firms. It includes competitors, customers, and suppliers.

For all these reasons, those who work only part time receive less per hour than those who work full time.

Permanent income

For many individuals, permanent income is much smoother than periodic income. To some degree, they gear their consumption to permanent income, and to some degree they gear it to things like take-home pay. But what *is* permanent income?

For the economy as a whole, we can think of permanent income as following a geometric random walk, like the market value of wealth. Measured income is smoothed permanent income plus transitory components. Consumption is smoother (in the medium term) than measured income, partly because people smooth out the transitory components, and partly because people simply *like* smooth consumption.

Perpetual growth

Do we expect growth to continue forever?

That's not reasonable. Someday, we will encounter limiting resources of one sort or another. Science helps us substitute away from inputs that limit us, but only for a while.

We can postpone the end of life as we know it, but not indefinitely. If we don't run out of oxygen or carbon or sunlight, we may be smashed by a meteorite. Jumping to another solar system is a long shot.

Thus a model with no fixed factors is only an approximation. A better model has fixed factors, though they play a small role. The exponent on reproducible factors in the production function is less than one, though we may not be able to detect the difference from one right now.

Similarly, our willingness to save is affected by the physical environment. We can grow only if we consume less than our income. As the limits to growth or the threats to life become more apparent, we will become less patient. Growth will stop because of a combination of falling expected return and rising consumption.

Persistence

A good match (or a poor match) between wants and resources tends to persist. A good match persists because tastes generally change slowly, and because technology that's good now will usually be good in the future too. A poor match persists because it takes time and effort to shift resources to new areas. This kind of persistence makes the average duration of business cycles several years, and magnifies the variation in country growth rates.

In Long and Plosser (1983), "persistence" refers to the permanent changes in quantities related to capital or wealth. Even when all goods are seemingly perishable, a change in wealth is associated with a change in expected consumption in every future period. This kind of persistence causes many economic variables to follow an approximate geometric random walk.

Political stability

Investing in political stability is delicate, because either too little or too much stability can reduce expected return and growth.

With too little political stability, we may see riot, revolution, and government or private theft of property, which means little incentive to save or invest, and a significant chance of losing the principal of any investment we make. With too much political stability, we may see debilitating tax-and-transfer schemes, plus a large government sector, which guarantees that we will lose a fraction of the return on any investment we make, especially if it succeeds.

In my view, the government's most important role is finding the right level (and the right form) of political stability.

Price and marginal cost

In competitive equilibrium, price equals both short-run and long-run marginal cost, measured along all the margins that a producer controls. I see prices changing sharply as conditions change, as when firms vary their use of discounts and special terms. To me, this means that the factors affecting marginal cost also affect price. Only enterprises heavily controlled by the government, directly or through unions or through entry restrictions, show clear evidence of a difference between price and marginal cost.

I believe that firms know more about their costs than economists do. When economists claim that prices are more or less procyclical than costs, I suspect this is due to mismeasurement of prices or costs or (most likely) both. I have a similar reaction when economists claim to see a difference between short-run and long-run marginal cost.

As Alchian (1959) shows, firms can vary output along many margins. We may find special exceptions, but in general I think they are setting price equal to cost along all of these margins at once.

Price of capital
Some researchers assume that the price of a unit of capital is constant, as when they assume that capital and consumption goods are identical. Some assume that the price of a unit of capital can differ from the price of a unit of consumption goods only by an adjustment cost that makes Tobin's q differ from 1.0.

I assume that the price of a unit of capital follows a geometric random walk with (varying) drift. The drift varies with the expected return on capital and inversely with capital's rental rate. In good times, when rental rates are temporarily high, the drift may be temporarily *low*.

Prices and quantities
In a general equilibrium model, prices and quantities are symmetrical. Either can fluctuate more than the other. In particular, hours can fluctuate more than wages.

Procyclical productivity
When people divide output by the number of hours worked, they understate the variation in the marginal product of labor. They ignore changes in the marginal product of workers who move into or out of the work force, and they understate the impact of those who begin or end overtime work. They ignore changes in the rate at which workers accumulate new human capital.

When properly measured, hours worked and the marginal return to working are strongly correlated, as the general equilibrium approach predicts.

Production smoothing
Some, including Blinder and Maccini (1991), still feel that inventories are a mystery. They ask, "If firms use inventories to smooth production, why is production more variable than sales?"

But firms *don't* use inventories just to smooth production. They use inventories to smooth production *and* to avoid stockouts *and* to speed delivery to customers. Sometimes they use inventories to *concentrate* production, as when a publisher produces a book. More generally, firms sometimes use inventories to be able to offer a wide range of products with immediate or fast delivery.

In other words, firms use inventories to reduce cost or to improve service. When we add the fact that inventories are durable and the fact that many changes in sales rates are permanent, we find that inventories are no longer a mystery. Similarly, it is not a puzzle that production is more variable than sales for some measurement intervals.

Blinder and Maccini note that the ratio of inventories to sales has been trendless for 40 years. To me, that means that the benefits from using computers to track inventories have been offset by added diversity in the products offered to customers.

Productivity
When does an economy become more productive? When its technology improves? When output per worker or per hour of work rises?

Technology helps only when it is relevant. I don't know how to estimate an aggregate technology factor, and I don't know how to measure its relevance, so I don't see how to take that route in defining "productivity." Solow residuals combine tastes and technology, and they change completely when we define the inputs to production correctly.

I don't feel right adding workers or worker-hours, and I don't see the sense in dividing output by a measure of only one of the factors of production. That eliminates the second route.

Why not just use output per person to measure productivity? Then we can call labor's part of output "labor productivity," and capital's part of output "capital productivity." The two parts add up to total productivity.

Purchasing power parity
To me, purchasing power parity means that relative prices vary within and between countries, and change over time, in a way that is independent of inflation rates and exchange rate regimes. It means that the real equilibrium is independent of anything nominal.

It means that devaluations and revaluations, between countries or relative to a standard like gold, have real effects only on borrowers and lenders using currency-fixed claims. It does not mean that relative prices are constant, or that a good in one location sells for the same price as a similar good in another location. Similar goods sell for very different prices even within the same city. The differences are greater across locations that have different languages, different populations, and different customs.

In particular, purchasing power parity does not mean that the relative price of two regions' consumption baskets should remain fixed, in the short run or in the long run. Even when individual relative prices show mean reversion, changing quantity weights means that price indexes need not. Even in the long run, the relative price of two countries' consumption baskets follows something like a geometric random walk. This can be true even when purchasing power parity, in my sense, holds.

Quits and layoffs
Why do quits fall in a recession, while layoffs rise? Doesn't an equilibrium theory predict that quits will rise with layoffs?

I don't think so, for reasons laid out by Hall (1980). In a general equilibrium model with complete markets, everything that will happen (contingent on the future state of the world) is arranged in advance. People have contracts covering all contingencies. Some of these contracts provide that workers and firms will separate in bad times. Whether it's a quit or a layoff doesn't matter to either party, as a first approximation.

As a second approximation, though, it may matter. For example, layoffs may entitle workers to unemployment insurance, while quits do not. For reasons like this, we adopt the convention that most separations in a recession will take the form of layoffs.

Moreover, the label may signal the type of separation. As in Becker, Landes, and Michael (1977, p. 1145, n. 4), a quit may signal better opportunities elsewhere, while a layoff may signal worse opportunities with the current employer. A quit may signal a move along a career path, while a layoff may signal a job move to a new career path. A quit may signal a job change without intervening unemployment, while a layoff may signal one with intervening unemployment (especially when the label qualifies the worker for unemployment benefits). Or, as in McLaughlin (1991), the label may simply signal who first discovers that the current match between worker and job is inefficient.

Random walks

Both human and physical capital (measured at market value) seem to follow a geometric random walk with varying drift.

Assuming that output and income are roughly constant as fractions of wealth, they will also look like random walks. Indeed, as Nelson and Plosser (1987) and Campbell and Mankiw (1987a, 1987b) show, shocks to GNP are largely permanent.

This means that the economy keeps some of its gains when the match between wants and resources is good. When the match is poor, some losses are permanent. Permanent gains and losses imply random walks.

Real interest rates

In some models, real interest rates play a key role. They set the terms on which we exchange current and future consumption. A productivity shock operates partly through its effect on current and future real wages, and partly through its effect on real interest rates.

In general equilibrium models, real interest rates play only a minor role. For one thing, risk premia are at least as important as interest rates in relating current and future opportunities (though we can observe interest rates more easily). For another thing, taste shocks are as important as technology shocks, and a taste for the present instead of the future covers only one of the many relevant dimensions.

Real interest rates are so unimportant that we can assume they are constant without changing the properties of our models significantly.

Real wages

What is a country's real wage, and how does it change?

If we figure the real wage by dividing total wages by total hours worked, it doesn't vary much. Wages and hours are almost equally procyclical. But this ratio makes little sense to me, since it assumes we can combine hours of different people.

If we substitute weighted total hours for total hours, where we use a person's wage or total pay to compute this weight, the ratio makes more sense, and it's more procyclical. But this number is an average wage, and real wage sounds marginal to me.

If we figure an average marginal real wage over everyone in the economy, we assign zero to people who are unemployed and overtime wages to people on extra shifts. We add in unmeasured wages in the form of human capital accumulation. This measure of the real wage is strongly procyclical. Isn't it the one we want?

Reallocation shocks

Can we say that reallocation shocks account for a certain fraction of total unemployment or of the variation in unemployment, while aggregate shocks account for the rest? Can we assign shares to reallocation and aggregate shocks in specific recessions?

We can assign them arbitrarily, but I don't see a natural way to do it. Even if the shocks are just unexpected shifts in tastes and technology, they can look like aggregate shocks to those who believe in aggregate shocks. For example, suppose we have two shocks: the first leads to temporary layoffs and some job changes along various dimensions, while the second simply reverses the first. After the second shock, unemployment falls, help-wanted advertising and career growth pick up, and wealth rises. It looks like an aggregate shock, but in fact it's just a reallocation shock.

Reallocation timing

Davis (1987b) and others suggest that people may change jobs more (with a spell of unemployment) in recessions, because the cost of doing so is lower then.

To me, this is a piece, but only a small piece, of the full general equilibrium story. I think a person switches jobs mainly because a new career path looks better than the old one, enough better to offset the cost of moving. He may decide to move because the cost of moving changes, but he is more likely to be motivated by a change in the relative value of the two career paths.

We have bad times when wants and resources are mismatched. Thus people gain a lot from transferring resources and improving the match. Reallocation speeds up in bad times more because the benefits are higher than because the costs are lower.

Recessions

What are recessions? In a conventional real business cycle model, we model a recession as a form of technical regress. This doesn't seem convincing, even though technical regress might be shorthand for a more complex and more realistic change.

In my model, the shocks that lead to a recession involve a shift in tastes plus a shift in technology that leave the match between wants and resources worse than before. The poor match causes depreciation in human and physical capital, which looks somewhat like technical regress. But it's the match that counts. We may have invested in very efficient ways to produce lots of goods and services that people turn out not to want. In engineering terms, this is progress. In economic terms, it's regress.

Recessions and productivity

Is a recession a time when firms and individuals invest in ways that enhance future productivity? Does this unmeasured investment mean that recessions are not as bad as they seem?

If we look at the economy in enough detail, I imagine we can find a few investments that are consistently countercyclical. For example, we might view changing careers with intervening unemployment as an investment, and that activity is certainly countercyclical.

In general, though, almost all investments are procyclical. The biggest unmeasured investments are investments in human capital associated with career advancement, which are strongly procyclical. They swamp unmeasured investments in reallocation of human and physical capital in bad times.

In my view, all investments add to productivity, by adding to the stock of human and physical capital. As a first approximation, there are no special productivity-enhancing investments. In general, investments are strongly procyclical.

Rents

In some models, "rents" imply economies of scale or monopoly power. A competitive firm that hires all the factors of production may pay out everything it receives to the factors, leaving no profits for the firm.

I think of a rent as the payment to a factor of production. A factor in short supply can earn high rents for a time, but if ownership of the factor is dispersed, this is perfectly consistent with competition.

Replacement cost

How can we estimate the replacement cost for an asset, or for all the assets in the economy?

One possible definition for replacement cost is market value. We can sometimes replace an asset by buying its equivalent in the market. When an asset doesn't trade in the market, we can estimate its market value by comparing it to similar assets that do trade.

We have many choices in replacing an asset. We can replace it brick by brick, but that's usually so costly that no one would do it. We can replace its functions, but we get a different number for each way of defining its functions. Normally, quick replacement costs more than slow replacement, so we have a different replacement cost for each completion time. Alchian (1959) shows several of the relevant dimensions.

When economists estimate replacement cost for the whole economy (or for the economy's physical assets), as when they estimate Tobin's q, they usually use accounting numbers. I am unable to persuade myself that these numbers tell us about economic replacement cost. They tell us more about historical cost.

To me, "replacement cost" is a synonym for "market value," and Tobin's q as a measure of their ratio is identically one.

Representative agent
For some purposes, assuming a representative agent makes sense. A model with identical individuals is easier to understand and modify than one with more diversity. For business cycles, though, I think this assumption does more harm than good. It encourages us to describe unemployment as leisure, and to focus on intertemporal substitution as a key process in business cycles.

In a modern economy, people live on "islands" only in the sense that they are specialized in skills and knowledge. Specialized people cannot easily substitute for one another, so they are subject to random fluctuations in tastes and technology that increase or decrease their human capital values. To create a realistic general equilibrium model that explains both business cycles and growth, I think we must give up assuming a representative agent who has a single skill and consumes a single good.

Roundabout production
People can increase the expected payoffs from their investments by using roundabout production methods. An investment this year may have no payoff by itself, but makes next year's investment more productive, and so on.

For example, a farmer may let a field lie fallow this year so it will produce more next year. A college graduate may take an internship at very low wages to gain experience that will help him in future jobs where he will gain still more experience. A cosmetics marketer may test a new hair spray on a small scale, so he can change his formulation or his marketing strategy, if necessary, before spending a lot on national distribution.

A roundabout production method is usually more efficient, but carries high risk. By the time the sequence of investments pays off, conditions may have deteriorated so much that the results are meager, or they are abundant in things that people don't want.

A person using a roundabout method must forecast tastes and technology far into the future. Such forecasts are uncertain in the near future; they are very uncertain in the distant future. Incorrect forecasts can mean low investment returns, high adjustment costs for reallocating resources, and high unemployment.

Thus roundabout production, like specialization, increases both risk and expected return. People will choose interdependent sequential investments only to the extent that the added expected efficiency compensates for the added risk.

Kydland and Prescott (1982) start to analyze the influence of time in production. Long and Plosser (1983, 1987) add multiple sectors. There is also an entire literature on sequential investment from a micro point of view; for example, see Dixit and Pindyck (1994), especially pp. 319–356. But none of these approaches encompasses anything like the full impact of roundabout production.

Schooling and growth

When he looks at growth over many countries and many years, Barro (1991) finds that countries with relatively low output — holding schooling fixed — grow faster than others, while countries with relatively low levels of schooling — holding output fixed — grow more slowly than others. What does this mean?

Some say that investments in schooling pay off big for a society, perhaps because schooling has external benefits. Some say better schooling increases the rate at which an economy can adopt new technology. My explanation is simpler than these.

I think production is symmetric: it uses human and physical capital in similar ways. I think schooling is a signal of an economy's level of human capital, even though most human capital comes from other sources, especially on-the-job learning. Thus countries with relatively low output *or* relatively high levels of schooling — holding the other fixed — have an imbalance: they have too little physical capital for their level of human capital.

Since physical capital is more mobile than people, it flows into those countries. That inflow causes relative output to grow faster than usual.

Sectoral shifts

Overall, movement between jobs, or between narrowly or broadly defined sectors, is more common in good times than in bad times. Most such moves are promotions or sideways moves along generally advancing career paths. The cost of moving is lower in good times, because many sectors have temporary openings that a person trying to switch sectors can use to gain experience.

In bad times, though, more people move between sectors with a spell of unemployment between jobs. The cost of moving is higher in bad times, and includes the cost of extra job hunting. The people who move in bad times are usually restarting careers, because they have found their accumulated human capital to have little value.

In good times, most narrowly defined sectors and almost all broadly defined sectors do well. In bad times, most narrowly defined sectors and almost all broadly defined sectors do badly. The dispersion in performance among narrowly defined sectors shows a strong countercyclical pattern, while among broadly defined sectors it shows a mild countercyclical pattern.

All of this is consistent with the general equilibrium approach. A good match between wants and resources means faster career advancement and more moves between sectors without intervening unemployment. Only crude sectoral models predict that all labor mobility will be countercyclical.

Seniority

The largest shifts in job flows occur for entry-level jobs among workers who are just starting out. The next largest source of volatility is among junior workers who have low seniority.

Low seniority means little human capital, especially firm-specific human capital. Thus it's natural that when conditions change, these workers leave before workers with more seniority.

The monopoly power of unions may express itself, in part, through seniority rules, but we expect seniority to be important even where we find no unions.

Separations

In general equilibrium, as a first approximation, it doesn't matter who initiates a separation. If the worker finds out he's better placed elsewhere, he tells the firm. If the firm finds out, it tells the worker. Quits and terminations are equivalent.

As a second approximation, it does matter. The firm may wait to tell the worker until it finds a replacement. The worker may wait to tell the firm until he finds another job, so he can maintain his pay and his experience as long as possible.

In practice, a change in employment conditions may not lead to a separation. The worker's pay or job may change without a switch to another firm. This possibility may also cause one side to defer telling the other. The worker may wait to give bad news about the value of his skills to the firm, and the firm may wait to give good news.

Also, government policies that subsidize unemployment more when it starts with a termination than when it starts with a quit will influence the form of the separation.

All these second approximations are consistent with general equilibrium.

Solow residuals

The conventional measure of the Solow residual is the percentage change in output less the percentage change in capital (measured by cumulating investment less depreciation) weighted by capital's fractional share of output, and less the percentage change in labor (measured by aggregate hours) weighted by labor's fractional share of output.

In no sense does the Solow residual measured this way reflect changes in technology rather than taste changes. Mostly, it reflects omitted factors like human capital, changes in the effectiveness of human and physical capital, and changes in the utilization of human and physical capital.

Specialization

Much of what we call "progress" seems to involve ever-increasing specialization in both production and consumption. In other words, both the inputs to and the outputs of the production process become more specialized.

More specialized tools are more efficient at one job, but are less efficient at somewhat different jobs. More specialized services are more satisfying if they fit your preferences, but cost more than generic services.

As specialization increases, the economy's ability to give us what we want when times are good increases, but so does the chance of a mismatch between wants and resources along one dimension or another. It's largely because we can choose more or less specialization at a given time (and because we can make production more or less roundabout) that we face a trade-off between business cycle severity and the level of output or its growth rate.

Why doesn't ever-increasing specialization mean ever-increasing business cycle severity? Because more specialization can mean more diversification at the same time. A mismatch in a subsector is less important than a mismatch in a sector. But even if the average degree of mismatch does not vary much, more specialization can mean a higher average level of unemployment as resources are shifted from one subsector to another. We face the usual trade-off, but in another form.

Moreover, the degree of diversification is limited. Sectors and subsectors are not independent. We make common assumptions when we invest in human and physical capital across many subsectors. When these assumptions are wrong, we can face losses in many areas at once.

Stock prices
Stock prices respond quickly to changes in expectations, so they can tell us about the shifting match between wants and resources that underlies growth and business cycles. The simplest way to find out which particular bad investments led to a recession is to look at the sectors with the worst stock market (and bond market) returns going into the recession.

We can also use stock prices to identify the most relevant dimensions along which tastes and technology change. We can use principal components analysis to suggest important dimensions.

We can use stock index returns to estimate changes in the market value of physical capital and even human capital. By conditioning output changes on current and past stock returns, we can separate them into temporary and smoothed permanent components.

Some researchers even use dispersion in stock prices as a measure of unpleasant surprise. Loungani, Rush, and Tave (1990, 1991) relate dispersion and several real variables, including unemployment.

Structural relations
Structural relations are causal relations.

We can use econometrics to tell us about structural relations only when correlation tells us about causation. Even with lags and sophisticated techniques like vector autoregression, econometrics tells us directly only about correlations. This is one reason it's very hard to test theories by studying data.

Tastes

Tastes play two distinct roles in the general equilibrium approach.

Even when they are known and constant, they can affect the economy's behavior. For example, a taste for smooth consumption can make consumption smoother than output and investment more volatile. Impatience, even when it is constant, plays a big role in explaining growth.

But uncertainty in tastes may play an even bigger role. Uncertainty in both tastes and technology makes investments risky, and gives us a frontier of choices among different combinations of expected payoff and risk. High risk investments also have high levels of expected unemployment for both physical capital and labor.

Introducing tastes does not make the theory into a black box, though, since tastes are largely observable. We can estimate them with surveys, introspection, and detailed marketing and engineering data.

Tastes and technology

Tastes and technology are parallel in several respects.

They are observable to roughly the same degree. Estimating supply curves is as difficult as estimating demand curves. It's as easy to see what and how much a person or a household or a community will buy at given prices as it is to see how much a plant or an office or a machine will make at given prices. We can study tastes by reading popular magazines and marketing studies. We can study technology by reading engineering magazines and journal articles.

Both tastes and technology are uncertain before the fact, but are largely observable after the fact. The more finely we categorize the world, the more changes we see. Moreover, these uncertainties are correlated across people and firms and sectors. People investing in human and physical capital at a given time tend to make common assumptions. If those assumptions turn out to be largely correct, we'll have a match between wants and resources that is temporarily better than average. Since the assumptions are common, wealth or capital and such variables as consumption, income, wages, and investment are all high in most broadly defined sectors at the same time.

Uncertain tastes and uncertain technology should be about equally important in business cycles. If uncertain tastes were less important, we could create more varied products and services with little risk, while holding fixed the specialization of our production methods. Thus the attempt to balance risk and return in our real investments tends to equalize the importance of these two kinds of shocks at the margin.

Team production

As Hall (1991) points out, it can pay for a firm or a worker to be active just because other firms or workers are active at the same time. Production uses teams. Sometimes a relay team is fine and production steps are sequential, but sometimes all team members must be active at once for greatest efficiency.

Through written and unwritten rules, firms coordinate the activity of their workers, suppliers, and customers. The pattern may be somewhat arbitrary, but once established, takes on a life of its own. Almost everyone finds it pays to conform.

This is one reason why firms decide when to lay off or fire workers (rather than reducing their pay and letting the workers decide to quit). When a firm cuts back production, it cuts back the whole team. No need for a finisher when the metal cutter isn't working.

These "thick-market effects" (or perhaps "fixed-proportions effects") also help explain why fluctuations affect many kinds of businesses at once. They help account for daily, weekly, seasonal, and cyclical fluctuations in general equilibrium. They can occur even when production is convex.

The consumption side of the market can work the same way, but I imagine that fixed-proportions effects are more common in production than in consumption.

Technical regress

Can we ever have technical regress? Or does science always move ahead, building new knowledge on the foundation of old knowledge?

We can imagine a world where the frontier of production possibilities always moves out, because we never forget what we know, though we may lose capital to wars, natural disasters, depletion, and depreciation. In a world like that, we can have no technical regress in an engineering sense.

Even in that world, though, we can have technical regress in the economic sense. We call it "obsolescence." We still know as much as before, but some of it is always becoming irrelevant. In aggregate economic models, then, we can have both expected and unexpected technical regress.

Technology adoption

Parente and Prescott (1994) say that barriers to technology adoption are crucial to understanding variation in growth across countries or through time. For example, workers sometimes destroy new capital equipment that they find threatening to their jobs. More generally, those who will be hurt by a reallocation of resources in the face of shifts in tastes or technology may try to slow the reallocation, perhaps through government regulation or subsidies to traditional activities.

These barriers matter a lot. Political stability may depend on having some of these barriers in place, and political stability helps, up to a point. These barriers themselves, though, reduce output and expected return and growth when there are no fixed factors.

But I think barriers to technology adoption are like taxes, where the tax revenues are redistributed. Tax distortions reduce output and usually reduce growth.

I see technology adoption as an investment like any other. In a model with no fixed factors, penalizing investment in human or physical capital is like taxing the stock of human or physical capital. A tax like that can have big effects on growth rates.

Temporary and permanent shocks

Permanent shocks are what any series with random walk elements has. For example, capital, output, and consumption all look roughly like geometric random walks. Even smoothed random walks have permanent shocks.

Temporary shocks can vanish without a trace, but they generally have cyclical aftereffects or revert gradually toward a mean.

Most economic series that show permanent shocks also have correlated temporary shocks. Clark (1987), Stock and Watson (1988), and Quah (1992) show it is not easy to identify this correlation using statistical analysis on a single series, but we can identify it by understanding the economics behind the series, and by relating several series whose shocks have common causes.

Time to build

What can "time to build" an investment, as in Kydland and Prescott (1982), add to a general equilibrium model of business cycles?

It's a start toward modelling the impact of roundabout production methods on the equilibrium. In a sense, we can take all of capital to be part of a giant incomplete investment project. To make sense of business cycles and variations in growth, though, we need to include many production periods and many sectors.

Tobin's q

Tobin's q, which is supposed to measure the ratio of capital's market value to its replacement cost, seems to lose its meaning in a general equilibrium model. I don't know any reasonable definition of replacement cost other than market value, where market value exists. Thus the ratio of market value to replacement cost is identically one.

We incur adjustment costs when we shift resources from one area to another, but I don't know when in this process to start measuring the adjustment cost. I also don't know how to allocate these costs between the declining area and the growing area, or how to aggregate them to use them as a basis for an overall measure of q.

Conventional measures of Tobin's q use the perpetual inventory method applied to historical cost in estimating replacement cost. These measures show cycles, because they move up in good times and down in bad times, but keep returning toward a target value. Since I don't think the usual perpetual inventory method gives numbers with economic meaning, I don't think these measures of Tobin's q have economic meaning either.

Trade balance

Why is a country's trade deficit generally procyclical?

Suppose the country finds a good match between its wants and its resources. Its income, consumption, and investment are all high. It imports lots of foreign consumption goods to go with its high level of domestic consumption.

Meanwhile, it also has a good match between the demand for and supply of its workers' skills. Employment is high and unemployment is low. More work, and more effective work, mean that the return to and demand for physical capital are high. The country imports physical capital, or imports consumption goods and diverts domestic output from consumption goods to investment goods.

For these reasons, imports rise or exports fall (or both) in good times. The trade deficit is procyclical.

Inventories and stocks of consumer durables play a role too. As its desired levels of these durables rise, the country can import them to reach its targets quickly, rather than waiting to save what it needs.

Uncertainty

Some models (like Lucas (1975)) emphasize uncertainty about the present state of the world. Take away that uncertainty, and the model's cyclical behavior vanishes.

The general equilibrium model emphasizes uncertainty about the future. Even when markets are complete, this uncertainty has a big impact on resource allocation. It is automatically resolved when the future becomes the present.

Unemployment turnover

Davis (1987a) finds that in recessions, high unemployment is accompanied by a high rate of attachment of unemployed people to new jobs. In other words, unemployment turnover is high in recessions, although job turnover is high in booms.

This fits easily into a general equilibrium model, where a large part of the new unemployment in a recession is people changing career paths. (As Davis notes, only a small fraction of the added unemployed are people laid off who are destined to be rehired.) There is a core of long-term unemployed, including people who are not seriously searching for work, so as more people become unemployed in the process of finding new work, the rate at which unemployed people find jobs goes up.

Utilization

How should we measure utilization of composite capital? Or effort, which is utilization of human capital? Or utilization of physical capital?

Effort varies in ways we can't clearly see. To define utilization of physical capital in the usual way, we must define its "capacity." Yet the capacity of a piece of capital seems to depend on the other factors of production that we use with it. Thus I don't see any way to build up a micro-based measure of utilization.

Instead, I think we need to infer utilization from the behavior of output. Roughly, utilization is high when output is temporarily high. One approach to measuring utilization is to divide output by a weighted geometric average of current and past levels of composite capital at estimated market value.

Vacancies

Vacancies, as measured by help-wanted ads, reflect in part a search for *temporary* workers in temporarily good times. Thus it's natural that vacancies rise in good times and fall in bad times.

In a sense, vacancies are the mirror image of layoff unemployment. In good times, firms hire temporarily, and in bad times, they fire temporarily.

Vacancies also occur when people are moving up their career ladders rapidly, since such moves create job openings. These vacancies too are procyclical.

War

Measured output and employment usually rise when a country enters a war. Should we attribute this to increased government purchases, which raise the real interest rate and induce a shift of leisure to the future?

I think not. I prefer to think of the government as an agent of the people, even though officials' private interests sometimes influence their behavior. The country goes to war because the people want war (perhaps to defend against an invasion).

We can always model preferences as depending on world events, so that an unexpected event causes the move to war. But I find it simpler to start by thinking of the cause as a taste change. Though we don't like to use an "epidemic of laziness" to explain employment declines, perhaps we can use an "epidemic of patriotism" to explain war.

When we take either world events or a taste change as the cause, we do not expect the real interest rate or the market risk premium to rise. We can explain the production changes in wartime without appealing to changes in interest rates or risk premia at all.

Most countries spend large amounts on the military even in peacetime. They prepare for possible war. This is like investing in the belief that war will probably occur (or in the hope that preparation will prevent it). If war comes or is prevented, the investment was justified. If not, it was largely wasted.

In general, we have booms when the events we plan for occur and busts when they do not. Thus war is associated with a boom, even though overall welfare may fall in wartime (through death, injury, and loss of property).

Weighted geometric averages

A weighted geometric average of current and past values, or of current and future values, is a product of powers of the values, where the exponents sum to one. We might also call it "a geometric distributed lag." I use weighted geometric averages repeatedly: in defining utilization of composite capital, in relating consumption to wealth, and in capturing the utility that leads to consumption smoothing.

Worker-specific firm capital

Just as a worker has firm-specific human capital, a firm has worker-specific capital, much of which lies in the knowledge that his coworkers have of him. This is one reason that firms show a high ratio of employees to output in a recession. If a worker leaves, the firm loses some of its worker-specific capital.

Readings

Here are some comments on the literature in light of the concepts described above.

Abel (1990) tries to explain the "equity premium puzzle" using utility that allows for either consumption smoothing or relative consumption ("catching up with the Joneses"). Neither gives good results in his model. I like his version of consumption smoothing: it's a special case of Greenig's (1986). Utility is a discounted sum of products of powers of consumption at adjacent times. But he assumes that perishable consumption is exogenous, where percentage changes in consumption are independent and identically distributed. This simplifies his computations, but makes his model irrelevant to the "equity premium puzzle," since the reason for the puzzle is that consumption is smoothed relative to a geometric random walk. If he starts with a consumption series showing an appropriate amount of positive serial correlation in adjacent percentage changes, and if he adds powers of several leading and lagging consumption levels to his utility terms, I think he'll find that he can explain the puzzle easily.

Abel (1991) surveys the literature on the "equity premium puzzle." After mentioning many possible variations on the consumption-based capital asset pricing model, he notes that either "catching up with the Joneses" (Abel (1990)) or "habit formation" (Constantinides (1990)) can easily resolve the puzzle. Both of these are ways of making utility state-dependent. He says that growth and real business cycle theories need to take account of these modifications (p. 13). I say, in contrast, that we need similar modifications both to explain the equity premium and to explain business cycles. Going to a full general equilibrium model solves both problems at once!

Abel and Eberly (1994) extend the conventional model of investment under uncertainty (the model that makes use of Tobin's q) to incorporate fixed costs of investment, a wedge between the purchase price and sale price of capital, and potential irreversibility of investment. In particular, they question the relevance of Pindyck's (1993) argument that adjustment costs are not relevant with perfect competition and constant returns to scale. Although they extend the conventional model, they continue to assume that the firm has only a single type of capital that depreciates at a known rate. In fact, I believe the firm's crucial decisions involve what kinds of capital to acquire, rather than how much to acquire. The relevant adjustment costs are those involving changes in the composition of the capital stock, and they apply more to an industry or the economy than to an individual firm. Thus Tobin's q becomes only a "reduced form" measure of the wisdom of the economy's recent decisions about the allocation of capital — a measure of the match between wants and resources.

Abraham (1987) looks at the relation between help-wanted ads (as an indication of job vacancies) and unemployment, for the U.S. and for many states, from 1951 to 1985. She notes that the negative relation between help-wanted ads and unemployment shifted outward over this period. It shifted outward less for individual states than for the U.S., and the dispersion in employment growth among states increased over the period. Thus the results are consistent with a sectoral explanation for the shift in the curve, where we assign workers to sectors along the "location" dimension.

Abraham (1990) tries to interpret the Davis and Haltiwanger (1990) evidence on job creation and destruction, and to relate it to the more sectoral studies of Lilien (1982) and Abraham and Katz (1986). She describes unemployment and vacancies as stocks, and job creation and destruction as flows. She wonders whether "aggregate shocks" can be causing the Davis and Haltiwanger results. I have difficulty reacting to her discussion, since I don't know what an aggregate shock is in general equilibrium (other than a big shift in tastes or technologies along one or more dimensions). The Davis and Haltiwanger correlations show how hard it is to sort out general and specific shocks.

Abraham and Katz (1986) show that vacancies, as measured by help-wanted ads, are negatively related to the dispersion of employment growth rates across 11 major sectors from 1949 to 1980. They say that this shows that aggregate shocks play a bigger role in business cycles than sectoral shocks. I believe that what Abraham and Katz call "aggregate" and "sectoral" shocks are both the result of underlying shocks to tastes and technology across many dimensions. The general equilibrium approach explains counter-cyclical unemployment and procyclical vacancies, so it is entirely consistent with the evidence they cite.

Abramovitz (1989) takes a broad view of economic growth. He notes the importance of social climate (like secularism, egalitar-ianism, and nationalism) and the interactions between growth in technology and growth in the inputs to production. He points out that "learning by doing" is more than just "learning by investing in physical capital." He emphasizes the inadequacy of quantitative growth accounting, partly because it doesn't fully recognize growth in human capital and gains from specialization. In fact, he says that at least some kinds of investment in technology are qualitatively identical to investment in general (p. 35). His views seem broadly consistent with mine, except that he doesn't put as much emphasis on "luck" as a factor explaining differences in the growth experiences of different regions, and he puts more emphasis on economies of scale. He does not tie the factors explaining growth to those explaining business cycles as closely as I do.

Aghion and Howitt (1992) write down a simple model of endogenous growth where vertical innovations create temporary monopoly power but destroy the value of earlier innovations. Research is costly and competitive. The equilibrium amount of research can be either too high or too low. While we cannot presume that a competitive equilibrium is optimal in a model like this, we also cannot predict what kinds of government intervention will improve welfare. Aghion and Howitt end by suggesting that we integrate the study of technical change (as in their model) with the study of business cycles. This is exactly what the general equilibrium approach tries to do!

Aghion and Howitt (1994) study the relation between growth and unemployment in a model with creative destruction, where new technologies require labor reallocation. Thus faster growth through faster innovation means higher unemployment. This is exactly the sort of trade-off that I feel we face. They look at other cases that I consider less relevant, where faster growth can give lower unemployment. They even look at a form of endogenous growth that can give multiple equilibria in their model.

Aghion and Saint-Paul (1993) explore some causal relations between productivity growth and economic fluctuations, using mostly noncompetitive models. They even claim that recessions can improve productivity: by eliminating inefficient firms, by creating low-cost times for reorganization or training, by disciplining (through bankruptcy) firms that don't reorganize, and by making it easier for workers to tell the difference between good and bad firms. They conclude that the structure of the business cycle can affect long-term growth, but they can't say which mechanism will dominate. They also look at cycles in models designed to illuminate growth, especially the Cheng and Dinopoulos (1991) model, where fluctuations in the monopoly profits in a patent race can generate cycles in the form of "Schumpeterian waves." They seem to want to find models that can be "empirically tested," but I think that goal is illusory. I agree that we want to find theories that explain both growth and fluctuations, but I look for deeper causal factors than the ones they mention. For example, variation in political stability and in the degree of specialization in an economy can explain variation in both business cycles and expected growth, even in a competitive model.

Aiyagari (1994) suggests an alternative to conventional real business cycle methods for estimating the contribution of technology shocks to business cycles. He pays special attention to the correlations between productivity and labor input, the variability of labor input relative to output, and the share of labor income in GNP. He notes that even his methods require assumptions about external economies of scale, monopolistic competition, wage schedules for straight and overtime labor, and errors in measuring output and labor input. His criticisms of conventional procedures are refreshing, but I think we can criticize his procedures on similar grounds: restrictive assumptions, omitted variables, and errors in measuring everything. I am especially troubled by his assumption that the labor input varies over the cycle, while the capital input does not. I think properly measured physical and human capital and utilization behave (and are compensated) in very similar ways, which is why we can think of labor's share of output as a constant fraction. I like his willingness to call some shocks "nontechnology shocks," without identifying them with something like monetary or fiscal policy. I think the most important nontechnology shocks are taste shocks (along many dimensions). In the end, I don't think it's meaningful to ask for a numerical estimate of the contribution of technology shocks to business cycles.

Alchian (1959) studies the relation between costs and outputs. He defines the cost of a production program as a present value rather than a rate. He relates cost to (1) the output rate, (2) the total volume to be produced, and (3) the starting date for production. (More generally, it depends on the detailed pattern of planned production.) He notes that increasing the output rate (holding volume and starting date fixed) increases cost at an increasing rate; while increasing volume (holding output rate and starting date fixed) increases cost at a decreasing rate. Increasing volume while holding the other two fixed reduces the cost per unit. In many cases, people who see "economies of scale" are simply seeing the effect of higher volume of production on unit cost. We might even call this "Alchian's Q." In Alchian's examples, production is always convex, so this effect does not disrupt the competitive equilibrium. He notes that delaying the start of production reduces cost, partly because it allows more time to plan. He notes that there is no distinction between "short-run" and "long-run" marginal cost: once we lay out the dimensions of the production plan, each dimension has only one marginal cost. Still, we can see how each marginal cost varies with the starting date of the production plan: total, average, and marginal cost all decrease as we delay the start of production, other things equal. Finally, he says that as volume increases, the cost of *future* output declines. This is the "learning curve." I have used these ideas repeatedly, especially in thinking about the cost-reducing impact of "roundabout production."

Alesina, Özler, Roubini, and Swagel (1993) use varied regressions on 113 countries for the period 1950–1982 to show a positive relation between political stability and economic growth. They recognize that causation flows in both directions and that common factors can affect both stability and growth. They note that political stability is closely related to security of property rights and to the relative absence of rent-seeking behavior. They find no systematic tie, in theory or data, between democracy and growth. The correlations they explore are related to the effects that sometimes give a negative relation between volatility and expected growth, even though individuals can generally increase income and expected growth in wealth by taking more risk.

Ambler and Paquet (1994) introduce exogenous "depreciation shocks" into a conventional real business cycle model to help explain the volatility of hours worked and the apparent low correlation between hours worked and average labor productivity. I like the idea of stochastic depreciation since it's a step toward valuing capital at market, but because they have a fixed factor they say that destruction of capital *increases* its marginal product. In my models, a decline in the value of human and physical capital is generally associated with a decline in capital's rental rate. Moreover, I think properly measured labor compensation is highly variable and highly procyclical, so there is no "business cycle puzzle" to explain.

Ando (1983) criticizes equilibrium business cycle theory as proposed by Lucas (1972) and Sargent (1976). He finds these theories inconsistent with true equilibrium, and too simple to explain the richness of economic fluctuations. I agree. Ando's alternative is a large-scale econometric model, though, while mine is a large-scale general equilibrium model (if we must have a detailed model).

Andolfatto and MacDonald (1993) create a model of Schumpeterian innovation and imitation where knowledge spreads largely beyond the control of the innovator. They try to match features of the U.S. economy with their model, even though it has the usual defects of the neoclassical model, including the absence of human capital as a factor of production. They find that allowing imitation improves steady-state welfare, even though it weakens property rights. They try to assess the relative contribution of technical change and capital formation in generating growth, and claim that technical change gives the vast bulk of it. I think their conclusions are highly model-specific. If they include human capital and omit any fixed factors of production, they may not even be able to ask about the relative importance of technical change and capital formation. The growth of knowledge and the growth of human capital are probably inseparable.

Ashenfelter (1984) looks at both macro and micro studies of labor supply. All the studies, including his own, fail to find a high elasticity of labor supply in response to temporary or permanent changes in real wages. He notes many difficulties in these studies, including measurement error, aggregation bias, and especially the fact that supply is fluctuating along with demand; but he thinks the fact that hours seem to fluctuate more than real wages is a puzzle. If he figures an average marginal real wage over everyone with human capital, and if he includes unmeasured additions to human capital, I think he'll find that "the" real wage is strongly procyclical, so the puzzle vanishes.

Atkeson and Kehoe (1993) create a growth model that emphasizes information about the match between managers and plants or between managers and technology. Their model has constant returns to scale in production and a competitive equilibrium. They "calibrate" it using both micro and macro data from several countries, and conclude that a certain kind of economic reform can lead to a decade of recession and a five-year pause in physical investment before the benefits of reform are realized. I like their use of a "match" as a part of the growth process, but their match bears little resemblance to the match between wants and resources that I think lies behind business cycles. I like their example of information as capital, but I think match information in their sense is probably not a big part of information capital. Indeed, I think technology, which they treat as exogenous and smoothly growing, is by far the biggest part of information capital. Their model has micro uncertainty but no macro uncertainty, and omits more key features of the economy than it includes, so I am amazed that they try to fit it to quantitative aspects of U.S., Japanese, and European economic experience. Since it is so limited, I have no faith in their exact description of the costs of the transition following large-scale economic reform. Their model has a steady state, which makes it inappropriate for analyzing a world with no fixed factors. What surprises me most, though, is their view that "spillovers" account for most of the gains from reform. I think it's just the opposite! I think the gains come from more clearly defined property rights applied to all kinds of property, including knowledge. Thus I think the gains come from *reducing* spillovers.

Backus, Kehoe, and Kydland (1994) use a conventional real business cycle model, extended to two countries and two goods, to explore such features of the global economy as countercyclical movements in net exports and the tendency of the trade balance to be negatively correlated with current and future movements in the terms of trade, but positively correlated with past movements. They call this shape of the cross-correlation function for net exports and the terms of trade the "S-curve." They choose a version of their model that matches a number of apparent features of the data, but are unable to match the large variability in the terms of trade, and the fact that output seems more highly correlated across countries than consumption. Because they use models with fixed factors but no human capital; with technology shocks but no taste shocks; with capital inputs measured at book value; with two countries but only one sector per country; and with leisure but no unemployment as such; I don't know what to make of either their successes or their failures in matching the data. I think fixing these defects has higher priority than explaining the two anomalies they identify. In fact, when they eliminate fixed factors, they will have to change the way they do their analysis, since they will no longer be able to look at deviations from a steady state. Even in a model with a single composite capital good, it's easy to create high output correlations across countries, and consumption smoothing is apt to make consumption correlations lower. In fact, I think the puzzle about their model is not that output correlations are lower than consumption correlations; rather, it is that output correlations are unreasonably low. When people in different countries use common assumptions about future tastes and technology in making their investments, output fluctuations will naturally be highly correlated. Moreover, with many sectors arrayed along many dimensions, where each sector has its own distinct good or service and where people care about an array of things in ways that shift over time as much as technology does, large variability in relative prices is natural.

Backus, Kehoe, and Kydland (1995) review recent work comparing properties of international business cycles with those of conventional real business cycle models as extended to a global setting. They focus on two "anomalies": in the data, the correlations across countries of output fluctuations exceed the corresponding consumption and productivity correlations, while the reverse is true in these models; and the standard deviation of the relative price of imports and exports is larger in the data than in these models. They consider changing elasticities, adding variation in government purchases, making utility of consumption and leisure nonseparable, increasing the correlations of productivity shocks across countries, adding transport costs, adding multiple consumption goods and nontraded goods, restricting trade in risky assets, adding money, making competition imperfect, and adding preference shocks. None of these changes seems to explain the two anomalies without creating new anomalies. Perhaps this means that conventional real business cycle theory is flawed! When we eliminate fixed factors; add human capital; make utility and production nonseparable across time, goods, and countries; measure physical capital at market value rather than book value; and allow shocks to both tastes and technology across many sectors common to different countries in many dimensions, I think we'll find that these two anomalies do not arise in the first place. The problem with conventional real business cycle models is that they are heavily restricted in arbitrary ways. One clue is the use of "first order conditions" that depend on utility and production functions which are separable in particular ways. In the authors' models, these first order conditions create a tie between price volatility and quantity volatility. In full general equilibrium models, we know that there is no definite relation between price and quantity volatility: either can vary more than the other. In fact, we can create versions where either prices or quantities are nonstochastic.

Baily (1981) argues that the measured decline in labor productivity growth between 1968 or 1973 and 1979 was due mostly to a decline in the services of capital and labor relative to measured quantities of these units. He says the decline in the services of capital was signalled by a decline in market value, or in Tobin's q. He creates a model of vintage capital where market value precisely measures the services of capital. In analyzing the data, though, he finds he only needs to give one-third weight to market value to fully account for the slowdown. He even spells out the structural changes that contributed to the obsolescence of capital, including especially the increased cost of energy. His entire approach to physical capital is consistent with mine. I only wish he had applied the same logic to human capital. For example, both workers and plants in the automobile industry were affected by the oil price change; both suffered obsolescence; and both experienced a decline in marginal product. He doesn't need the effects on labor to account for the slowdown, but the logic is the same.

Bak, Chen, Scheinkman, and Woodford (1993) combine local supply interaction between production units and severely nonconvex technology to create a model where many small, independent sectoral shocks can give fluctuations in aggregate economic activity. In their model, neither feature alone is sufficient. I think local supply interaction between production units is indeed important in understanding business fluctuations, and their lattice diagram helps in understanding the workings of a complete general equilibrium model. In such a model, though, we don't need their nonconvexities. Partly this is because shocks to tastes and technology are not all small and independent: look at the disruptions to U.S. military production caused by the breakup of the Soviet Union. Partly it's because "team production" and fixed proportions technologies have some of the same effects as nonconvexities. In other words, I think they'll find that as they relax the restrictions in their model they don't need nonconvexities. The "production smoothing puzzle" is especially easy to handle in a general equilibrium model: variation in the sales rates for consumer durables can give much larger variation in production for retail inventories, especially when each sales rate follows a process that looks like a random walk in the short run.

Barro (1981) suggests that government purchases may affect output through changes in the equilibrium real interest rate. He thinks temporary changes should have bigger effects than permanent ones. As he shows, this logic is very model-dependent. Changing from lump-sum taxes to distorting taxes can reverse the sign of the effect on output. Moving to a model with no fixed factors can eliminate the effect. Moreover, in a general equilibrium model, we don't care much what the effect on output is. We do care about the effect on welfare. For that, the composition of government purchases matters more than the amount. His logic seems especially inappropriate for war, which is the case he emphasizes. If we take war to come from a shift in world events or from a change in tastes, the effect on output is direct, rather than working through the real interest rate (plus the market risk premium). I don't know what to make of his empirical work, since he claims to find causation in the coefficients of a conventional econometric model.

Barro (1989) tells why researchers have largely dropped money from their new classical business cycle models. He mentions that (1) informational lags do not seem very important; (2) the predicted positive effect of surprise money on output and employment is not truly consistent with a symmetric equilibrium model; (3) monetary aggregates do much better than the price level in "explaining" output; (4) broad monetary aggregates are more closely correlated with output than narrow ones; and (5) the theory cannot generate procyclical real wages easily from monetary shocks. To these I would add, as in Black (1987), that I know of no microeconomic theory for a world with developed financial markets that gives an equilibrium mechanism by which money changes affect the economy. I don't even see how changes in monetary policy can affect the price level.

Barro (1990a) explores the relation between government spending and growth in a model with constant returns to a combination of human and physical capital and the amount of public services provided to each household producer. With lump-sum taxation, the economy's growth rate maximizes utility, but with income taxation, growth is too slow. His discussion of empirical results assumes, among other things, a world with no uncertainty and with independence across countries between overall productivity and the productivity of public services relative to private services. I have little confidence in his interpretation of these results.

Barro (1990b) finds that stock returns predict changes in investment better than conventional measures of Tobin's q, although changes in q are dominated by stock returns, largely because the change in q involves a first difference of an annual average. He finds that stock returns predict output changes very well. For the period from 1891 to 1987, omitting the two world wars, he estimates an R^2 of .67 for investment changes and .56 for output changes. (He also finds that U.S. stock returns predict Canadian investment changes better than Canadian stock returns do.) In other words, the stock market is a very good predictor of business cycles and fluctuations as measured by output and real fixed nonresidential private domestic investment. My only question is why he seems to take seriously the idea that q measures the ratio of market value to replacement cost for some class of assets. His results seem perfectly consistent with a general equilibrium approach.

Barro (1991) looks at economic growth between 1960 and 1985 in a cross-section of countries. The simple correlation between *per capita* growth (1960–1985) and the 1960 level of *per capita* GDP is close to zero, but the correlation is negative if we hold fixed initial school-enrollment rates (as signals of human capital). Given initial GDP, the growth rate is positively related to starting school enrollment. He also finds that countries with high school enrollment have low fertility rates and high ratios of physical investment to GDP. Finally, he looks at measures of government consumption, public investment, political stability, and price distortions. Cross-sectional regressions like this are tricky: perhaps certain types of countries were just lucky over the period, and the regression tells us which types. Correlations of outcomes by type destroy any simple significance tests. Still, I accept the idea that school enrollment signals human capital, even though most human capital comes from parents and jobs. In a model where output (ignoring variation in utilization) depends on human and physical capital, and where physical capital is more mobile than human capital, I think we expect exactly these results. Low output for given human capital and high human capital for given output both signal a low ratio of physical to human capital. This should lead to high investment in physical capital to bring the two kinds of capital into balance, and thus rapid growth in output.

Barro and King (1984) point out that separable utility in a conventional one-good real business cycle model implies that changes in future prospects don't affect current effort. Monetary disturbances, even if imperfectly perceived, don't either. Temporary and permanent changes in government purchases have the same impact. They note that positive comovement in production, employment, investment, and consumption can come only from current productivity shocks (or taste shocks for the present over the future). I take this as showing that we don't want to use such a model, except possibly as a reduced form. If it is a reduced form, then a "technology shift" can stand for a complex change to both tastes and technology in the full model, so we need not take it literally.

Barro and Lee (1994) study the relations among GDP growth rates and measures of initial GDP, schooling, health, investment, black market premia, terms of trade, political instability, freedom, and tariffs. For reasons that I don't understand, they especially emphasize education and health. They mention most of the econometric problems in the kinds of regressions they do, but I think these problems are more severe than they say. Surely we don't need more than one significant digit in regression coefficients when the problems are so great. I like their use of initial income to represent initial capital in their regressions: income varies in about the way that capital at market value probably varies. The biggest problem they have is in trying to infer causation from coincident or lagged correlation. Perhaps their second biggest problem is in choosing between levels and first differences. Growth rates are first differences, yet they use levels for most of their other variables. They justify this by saying that they are trying to explain the steady-state growth path for income. Yet another major problem is in their "tests" of significance. Omitted variables, which they acknowledge, can affect significance levels as well as coefficient estimates. And they don't try to adjust for data mining. In sum, I don't see how we can interpret these regression coefficients even when we can measure them without bias.

Barro, Mankiw, and Sala-i-Martin (1992) discuss the influence of capital mobility on conditional and unconditional convergence of countries and states. They see unconditional convergence in homogeneous groups of countries, in that poor countries grow faster than rich ones. They see conditional convergence among all countries, in that economies grow faster if they start out below where they should be, as judged by some indicator of potential output. The neoclassical growth model with human capital but with "raw labor" as a fixed factor fails to fit the facts when they assume full capital mobility. They try to fix it by assuming that a country can use foreign debt to finance only a portion of its capital (perhaps its physical capital). We can fix it more easily by assuming away the fixed factor of production entirely, and by assuming that "homogeneous groups of countries" produce many things jointly. The authors make so many arbitrary modelling assumptions that I don't take their numerical predictions seriously; I'm especially puzzled by their attempt to use a model with no uncertainty to match a world that is plagued by uncertainty. For example, the real interest rate in their model is the return to capital, while the real interest rate in the world is only the borrowing and lending rate. We can easily match the same facts using a model with uncertainty and joint production but no fixed factors and no restrictions on movements of physical or financial capital.

Barro and Sala-i-Martin (1990) study expected real interest rates and investment-GDP ratios for a "world" consisting of ten OECD countries. They find a strong relation between expected real interest rates and prior stock returns; for example, expected real interest rates and world stock returns were both high in the 1980s. I find this correlation very interesting, though I don't know how to interpret it. One explanation, which they do not discuss, is that unexpected increases in wealth make people more tolerant of risk, which reduces required market risk premia and increases expected real interest rates. In their theory, they speak of the expected real interest rate as the price that moves to equate the demand for investment and the supply of saving. I think this is incomplete at best, since the price of risk is at least as important as the expected real interest rate in balancing saving and investment. Moreover, we should distinguish between high and low risk investments. They argue that expected real interest rates should be positive or only slightly negative, but I don't think low risk investments with near-positive real returns exist. Finally, their evidence suggests that by two measures — stock returns and expected real interest rates — productivity was very high in the 1980s. The "productivity slowdown" in the U.S. was limited to the output-per-worker measure of productivity.

Basu (1993) looks at two explanations for measured procyclical productivity: that utilization of capital and labor varies, and that firms have overhead capital and labor costs. He finds both explanations valid, using a conventional production function with conventional capital and labor inputs plus materials. He cannot find any clear evidence of imperfect competition. I don't put much weight on his numerical estimates, since his asymmetric production function is so conventional. I like his conclusion, but I think cyclical utilization and overhead inputs (at the plant level) are two aspects of the same thing, so I don't see why he claims to be able to separate them. In particular, if he is able to identify permanent demand shocks, I don't see why overhead inputs mean they should cause a permanent change in the ratio of materials to other inputs. In my models, overhead inputs are simply inputs you commit early in the production process, and cyclical utilization is simply cyclical utilization of the overhead inputs. Even without labor hoarding, variation in hours represents variation in the utilization of human and physical capital: adding labor hoarding just increases this variation.

Baxter and Crucini (1993a) use an extension of the King, Plosser, and Rebelo (1988a) model to show that we can have a high correlation between saving and investment even when capital is highly mobile, and even when we also have a strong relation between investment and a country's trade deficit. In their model, the correlation between saving and investment is higher for large countries and the relation between investment and trade deficit is stronger for small countries. They assume a cost that increases with the rate of investment in a country, as with Tobin's q, while I would prefer costs associated with moving physical capital between countries (similar to the costs of moving it between sectors). Since investors in most countries hold most of their capital at home, I don't see where the puzzle is. (Baxter and Jermann (1993) discuss this "home bias.") The home bias automatically gives a high correlation between saving and investment. Some physical capital does move between countries, though, which gives the positive relation between investment and a country's trade deficit. People simply do not behave as if physical capital were highly mobile. The home bias is partly a matter of tastes, and partly a matter of ignorance, which will decline over time.

Baxter and Crucini (1993b) use an extension of the King, Plosser, and Rebelo (1988a) model to explore the relation between global asset market linkages and business cycles. They find that banning risk transfer between countries matters in some models but not in others. In particular, when shocks in different countries are correlated and largely permanent, banning risk transfer reverses the average relative values of output correlations and consumption correlations. These differences seem largely driven by wealth effects rather than interest rate or wage effects. I especially like their emphasis on general equilibrium models, and on the sensitivity of their results to the specific assumptions they make. I wish they had extended this sensitivity analysis to more of the assumptions in conventional real business cycle models. They assume that people want to share risks across borders, so that banning such trades is suboptimal; I think that the "home bias" means people don't want to trade risks with foreigners, so the resulting equilibrium may still be close to optimal. They talk about why people don't share labor market risks across borders, but I think this is for the same reason that people don't trade human capital claims inside countries: for example, governments fail to enforce claims to a part of someone's human capital, and preempt the market with mandatory unemployment and poverty insurance. They note that changing the definitions of the capital and labor inputs to production can matter, but they don't consider the extremes of physical and human capital at market value, possibly modified by utilization. Finally, they miss a major general equilibrium effect of allowing borrowing and lending between countries but banning risk transfers: other things equal, countries that lend a lot tend to be more tolerant of risk at home and thus to have more risk, and higher market risk premia, than countries that borrow a lot.

Baxter and Jermann (1993) explore a model where the returns to human and physical capital in a given country are highly correlated. They show that it pays for a resident of a country to hold a short position in that country's physical assets, since that helps to hedge his human capital risk. Thus they deepen the "international diversification puzzle," wherein residents of all countries actually seem to specialize in holding domestic physical assets, thereby showing a "home bias." They treat returns from human and physical capital as arising from technology shocks, but we can easily modify their model to give taste shocks equal billing, and to allow for parallel investment in human and physical capital. They define the value of each kind of capital as the present value of rents net of future investment, which is consistent with a general equilibrium view.

Becker and Murphy (1992) model the division of labor with coordination costs and human capital. In their model, coordination costs, such as free riding and bargaining about the division of gains, rather than the extent of the market, limit the degree of specialization. Knowledge makes specialization more profitable, and specialization makes learning more profitable. In effect, they have a growth model with no externalities, no fixed factors, and many dimensions. I think if we add uncertainty in tastes and technology to their model, we'll have a good model of business cycles and stochastic growth. We will also have another force limiting the degree of specialization: risk. I think that greater specialization means higher income and expected growth, but also greater uncertainty about income and growth. The balance between these helps fix the degree of specialization at any moment.

Bencivenga, Smith, and Starr (1994) use a conventional overlapping-generations model to explore the effects of varying secondary-market transaction costs on assets with different gestation periods. They find that the effects of transaction costs on steady-state capital and welfare depend on the degree to which long-lived and short-lived assets substitute for one another in production. They suggest using their model to look at the impact of government intervention to change the slope of the yield curve on bonds. I don't believe their results generalize to more realistic models, and I don't think they capture the effects of more efficient financial intermediation. People in an overlapping-generations world would not vote to maximize steady-state wealth or welfare, so I don't know why we look at that criterion. In the authors' certainty model, the "term structure of yields" means the expected returns on assets with different gestation periods: I see almost no connection between that term structure and the yield curve for government bonds. I like their emphasis on gestation periods for investments, but I don't think the degree to which long-lived and short-lived assets substitute for one another in production will matter much in a fuller model. Good financial intermediation helps by improving the allocation of resources along many dimensions, not just the gestation period dimension. I doubt they will find in a fuller model that better intermediation can sometimes hurt welfare. Finally, I think the efficiency of intermediation in their sense is not a crucial development issue. Far more important are such issues as political stability, clearly defined property rights, size of the government sector, level of capital taxation, and openness to international trade and investment.

Benhabib and Jovanovic (1991) show that growth patterns across countries and through time are consistent with the conventional Solow growth model, expanded to include uncertainty and knowledge, but with no externalities. In particular, they look at Romer's (Paul, 1987a) data and find no evidence of externalities associated with investment of physical capital or with increased variety in intermediate investments. They assume (like Romer) that knowledge is disembodied and they measure labor input in hours, so it is especially convincing that they find no externalities. The basic argument for externalities is that a change in output is associated with a roughly equal percentage change in capital input, at least over long periods, whereas the Solow model says an increase in capital input should give a percentage increase in output about a third as big, since capital's share of output is about a third. The simplest way to explain this is to assume a linear model with no fixed factors, where human capital grows along with physical capital. Then we don't need Benhabib and Jovanovic's elaborate machinery. They say that in Romer's model, growth in capital causes growth in knowledge (or in the availability of specialized inputs), whereas in their model, growth in knowledge causes growth in physical capital. I find both notions strange. I think growth in capital and growth in knowledge have common causes. One of the causes is patience. I agree fully, though, with Benhabib and Jovanovic's main conclusion: we don't need externalities to explain the facts of growth.

Benhabib, Rogerson, and Wright (1991) introduce home production into a conventional real business cycle model with shocks to productivity. They say that a two-sector version of the conventional model has the odd feature that in good times, labor flows out of consumption goods production into investment goods production. When they add home production, they can make market output of both consumption and investment goods procyclical, and they make the conventional model more realistic in other ways as well. Going to a general equilibrium model solves those problems in a different way. We don't literally need home production to create realistic business cycles, but it is surely part of a detailed model. If I were adding home production, I would probably start by modelling the process of changing jobs as a form of home production.

Bental and Eden (1993) use a competitive model to explain the behavior of inventories and the prices of inventoried goods. They assume that buyers of different types (like tourists and business travelers buying airline tickets) arrive in batches with uncertain size and timing. It is a general equilibrium model that helps explain the frequent occurrence of stockouts. In their model, output can be more volatile than sales even without serial correlation in demand or large supply shocks.

Bergman (1985) shows that time-separable and state-independent utility is necessary for Breeden's (1979) consumption-based capital asset pricing model. It is not necessary, though, for Merton's (1973) intertemporal capital asset pricing model. He considers utility generalized by the linear Koopmans aggregator, and he notes that Merton's results hold up for the most general von Neumann–Morgenstern (1946) utility function.

Bernanke (1983) uses the irreversibility of specific investments to help explain why "recessions are felt so disproportionately in durable goods" (p. 104). He says the "accelerator" plays a role (I think it's the bigger role), but that when investments are irreversible, varying uncertainty causes firms to vary their waiting time before committing to specific projects. Greater uncertainty increases the

value of the option to change your mind about how to invest. I agree
with his point, but I think he is ignoring the most important effects of
irreversibility (or adjustment costs). In a world where investments
vary along many dimensions, shifts in tastes and technology change
the match between wants and resources, which changes asset prices
and the types and amounts of unemployed resources. This gives a
business cycle much like the one we see even when the degree of
uncertainty is constant through time. He mainly assumes that
uncertainty is exogenous; his reference to uncertainty that is
generated within the system involves confusion between transitory
variation in aggregate demand and permanent variation in tastes and
technology (p. 104). A far more important source of endogenous
uncertainty, in my view, comes from the role of risk tolerance in
choosing among investments at different levels of risk and expected
payoff. Indeed, I think a society with high risk tolerance creates
both uncertainty and high expected growth by making more
irreversible investments.

Bernanke (1993) seems to be persuaded by Eichengreen (1992) that
the Great Depression was caused in large part by a slavish adherence
to the gold standard in many countries. He says that, assuming
Eichengreen's work holds up, "contemporary classical theories that
give no weight (or almost no weight) to monetary factors, such as
the real business cycle theory, will have the most trouble accommo-
dating a new 'money-based' consensus on the Depression" (p. 266).
Bernanke pays special attention to the impact of deflation on
borrowers, but ignores the equal and opposite impact on lenders.
My view is that common and unexpected shifts in tastes and
technology across many countries played a major role in the
Depression, but that the deflation, caused in part by the use of a
gold standard with unchanging parity, played a big role too. Not
because wages and prices were inflexible, but because a zero nominal
interest rate can lead to disequilibrium in the asset market, and
because very low nominal interest rates can lead to a breakdown in
financial markets if the government fails to meet the resulting large
increase in demand for currency — in other words, if the government
stops supplying money passively.

Bernanke and Gertler (1989) add to a conventional real business
cycle model the notion of overlapping generations of entrepreneurs
who suffer from excess leverage when asset values fall. Lower
entrepreneurial wealth raises the agency costs associated with capital

finance, which reduces the net return to investment. Thus we see a kind of feedback where bad times create worse times and good times create better times. This feedback can certainly play a role in a general equilibrium story, though I doubt that it plays a big role. For firms that have common stock outstanding, the agency costs that Bernanke and Gertler discuss, together with other agency costs, imply an optimal capital structure. Large changes in asset values move firms away from their optimum debt-equity ratios, and restoring the ratios may take time and money. But this large-firm version of their story does not accelerate business cycles symmetrically, since it implies costs for large moves in either direction. We can create another variant of their story that does accelerate business cycles by focusing on entrepreneurs as relatively tolerant of risk. A decline in asset values shifts wealth from those who are more tolerant of risk to those who are less tolerant, and thus increases the "cost of capital." A rise in asset values does the reverse. Again, we can have feedback, so that bad times create worse times and good times create better times.

Bernanke and Parkinson (1991) find that average labor productivity was about as procyclical from 1923 to 1939 as it was after 1945. They think that technology shocks did not play much of a role in cyclical fluctuations during the 1930s, so they interpret this as evidence against real business cycle theory. I, on the other hand, think this provides evidence that the general equilibrium approach works about as well in the 1930s as in any other period. They discuss technology shocks, true increasing returns, and labor hoarding as possible explanations for procyclical labor productivity. My general equilibrium explanation differs a bit from all of these. I have shocks to both tastes and technology, along many dimensions, affecting human and physical capital in similar ways. So labor compensation is higher in booms than in recessions.

Bertola and Caballero (1994) create a model of aggregate investment based on unsynchronized irreversible investment decisions by heterogeneous firms. In their model, some uncertainty is common to all firms and some is idiosyncratic. I like their emphasis on heterogeneous firms, but I think they can make the model more realistic by putting in many kinds of sectoral uncertainty as well. I don't think irreversibility is key to their model, since we can create an analogous model, observationally identical to theirs, where investments are fully reversible but firms don't want to reverse them.

To do this we just assume that the price process (which is endogenous in their model) is given exogenously by tastes or technology. They use the model to look at conventional data series on things like output and investment. I think this is premature: their model is too restrictive and the data are too arbitrary. For example, depreciation, in both the model and the data, is at a constant known rate.

Beveridge and Nelson (1981) suggest a way to decompose a nonstationary series into permanent and transitory parts, where the permanent part is an arithmetic or geometric random walk with drift, and the transitory or cyclical part is stationary with zero mean. They can decompose a series in "real time," since their method uses only past data. Their dating of U.S. economic cycles between 1947 and 1977 tends to lead the traditional NBER dating. I like the idea of a decomposition that recognizes the random walk elements in output, but I don't think we should force the "trend" in output to be a strict random walk. I like to think of smoothed output as what output would be at normal levels of utilization of human and physical capital and technology. Because it takes time — often a long time — for the economy to adjust to taste and technology shocks, permanent shocks to the market value of composite capital may show up only gradually in output. To reflect this, we can use a simple generalization of the Beveridge and Nelson approach that allows the trend in output to be a weighted geometric average of current and past levels of a geometric random walk with drift. This also allows us to reverse an unusual feature of their decomposition: they define the cyclical component of output as positive when output is *below* trend. This makes sense when output is below trend because it takes time to install new technology, but not when output is below trend because utilization of composite capital is low.

Bils (1987) says that average marginal cost is very procyclical, while average price is countercyclical. He thinks imperfections in goods markets play a primary role in the cycle. He recognizes costs of shifting employment and the fact that reported wages differ from total compensation, yet he boldly tries to estimate averages for marginal cost and price over many two-digit industries at once. He recognizes an important role for overtime pay in compensation, but does not try to include all the costs the firm faces in setting prices. I interpret his findings as saying simply that labor compensation is procyclical, but as not saying anything special about the relation between price and marginal cost. In my image of general equilibrium, prices are somewhat procyclical (when we account for sales and special deals) and labor compensation is more so (when we add in all forms of compensation), but we can assume the overall price level is constant without changing the character of the model.

Blanchard (1993) uses vector autoregression methods to analyze the recession of 1990–1991. He looks at real GNP and its components, like consumption of nondurables and services, and net exports. He makes, but does not justify, two identifying assumptions: within the quarter, the components of GNP depend on each other only through GNP; and the government spending residual is exogenous. He finds that consumption shocks had a major and long-lasting effect on output, operating partly through a noneconomic decline in consumer confidence. I don't think methods like this can tell us about causation, so all we know is that consumption declined by an unusual amount relative to other things. I doubt we can understand this without a detailed look at the components of consumption. My version of Blanchard's hypothesis is that this recession was caused more by a shift in tastes (across many dimensions) than by a shift in technology. We can't test this hypothesis using macro data alone.

Blanchard and Diamond (1989) look at the "Beveridge curve," which shows unemployment and vacancies moving in opposite directions in the short and medium run, but which generally shifts toward higher unemployment for given vacancies from 1952 to 1982, with a partial reversal to 1988. They imagine a world where all jobs and all workers are the same, and where the chance that a worker finds a job depends on a Cobb–Douglas function of both unemployment and vacancies. Using a range of models, they attribute the creation and destruction of jobs to innovations in aggregate activity, reallocation, and labor supply. They define an "aggregate activity shock" as one that causes unemployment and vacancies to move in opposite directions, and a "reallocation shock" as one that causes them to move in the same direction. They conclude that short- and medium-term fluctuations in unemployment have been due mainly to aggregate activity shocks, rather than to changes in the degree of reallocation intensity. I agree, but I think the phrase "aggregate activity shock" is misleading. The underlying shocks affect tastes and technology in detail along many dimensions; when these shocks change the match between wants and resources, we see what Blanchard and Diamond call an "aggregate activity shock" most of the time and a "reallocation shock" some of the time. But resources are reallocated all of the time. An aggregate activity shock is like a drawing from a distribution, while a change in the degree of reallocation intensity is like a change in the shape of the joint distribution from which we draw innovations to tastes and technology. Blanchard and Diamond recognize that their matching function hides "a complex reality," but do not recognize that it hides the underlying causes of unemployment and vacancies. We can't see those causes in a model that talks about matching but treats all jobs and workers as identical. They say that causal relations can run from dependent to independent variables in their regressions, but they don't say that the true causes are shocks to variables that they do not examine. They repeatedly use the language of causation to describe correlations. They try to exclude layoff unemployment from their measure of unemployment, but do not try to exclude temporary jobs from their measure of vacancies. More generally, they treat unemployment and vacancies as symmetric; but if we exclude temporary unemployment and temporary vacancies, I don't think they are symmetric at all. The unemployed are most often changing career paths, while vacancies are most often associated with movements along a career path. In general, the Beveridge curve data they present seem perfectly consistent with a general equilibrium approach to unemployment and related phenomena, but the models they present don't add much to our understanding of the factors that cause movements along the Beveridge curve or shifts of the curve.

Blanchard and Wyplosz (1981) create an econometric model relating such things as income, investment, interest rates, physical capital, human capital, and Tobin's q. They say it is a structural model of aggregate demand. They try to create a structure that is policy-invariant, and they say they avoid data mining by reporting all their regressions (except mistakes). They use standard NBER quarterly data from 1952 to 1978, but without questioning the numbers. They claim to be able to test potential instruments, though they give reasons why such tests may not be valid. Using the concepts in this book, we can question almost every step of their argument. Econometric models, even sophisticated ones like theirs, tell us about correlation rather than causation or structure. Aggregate demand is undefinable. Money is endogenous — even passive — rather than exogenous. Tobin's q is identically one.

Blanchard and Wyplosz even assume the earnings-price ratio measures expected return on stocks. I am most puzzled, perhaps, by their examples of "aggregate supply" factors, which include the price level, the government budget constraint, the link between investment and capital, and the role of expectations (p. 25). Or by their statement that output may change sharply without warning only when prices are inflexible (p. 26). In a general equilibrium model, output and prices can both vary a lot.

Blinder (1986) asks if the production smoothing model of inventory behavior can be "saved." He thinks it odd, in the light of that model, that the variance of detrended production exceeds the variance of detrended sales. He feels we must introduce cost shocks and a difference between what the firm knows and what the researcher knows to save the model. He defines long-run production smoothing as having lower production variance than sales variance, and short-run production smoothing as having a lower production response to a sales shock with inventories than without. I don't understand either definition. Production and sales both have random walk elements, so their unconditional variances don't exist; and the variance of production is naturally greater with inventories, because a permanent sales shock causes a matching production shock plus an extra shock in the same direction to adjust inventories. I define production smoothing as what a firm does when it faces costs related to changes in its output rate. These costs may be small, and the firm is optimizing along many margins, as in Alchian (1959), so production smoothing in this sense implies only that production will be smoother than it would be if these costs were zero.

Blinder and Maccini (1991) review the literature on inventories. They note that inventories can be held to improve production scheduling, to smooth production in the face of fluctuating sales, to minimize stockout costs, to reduce purchasing costs by buying in quantity, to shorten delivery lags, and for other reasons (p. 78). Yet most of their discussion emphasizes only one or two of these reasons. They continue to believe that the volatility of production relative to sales and the positive correlation between inventory changes and sales changes are puzzles. They do not emphasize the fact that aggregate sales and production both show permanent shocks as well as temporary shocks, or the fact that almost any micro model of a firm's inventory behavior will give target aggregate inventories that are roughly proportional to sales. When sales rates have permanent shocks, production is always more volatile than sales at some differencing intervals, though production smoothing can make production less volatile than sales at very short intervals, at least for individual firms. They claim that the economies of large production runs are inconsistent with a conventional neoclassical model (p. 92, for example), though Alchian (1959) shows otherwise. They claim that inventories should be lower when real interest rates are higher; but that looks at only one side of a supply-demand relation. Similarly, they claim to be puzzled by the fact that the ratio of inventories to sales has been steady over a period when technology has greatly improved a firm's control over its inventories (p. 75). I explain that fact by noting that over the same period, firms have vastly increased the diversity of the products they stock.

Blomström, Lipsey, and Zejan (1993) look at correlations among growth and many other factors, across countries and across time, including especially lagged, coincident, and leading levels of fixed investment, using Summers and Heston data from 1965 to 1985. Because fixed investment lags growth more consistently than it leads growth, no matter what they control for, they conclude that they find no evidence that fixed investment is the key to economic growth. They mention a number of factors as important in growth, such as the efficiency of government, the degree of corruption, the level of violence, the attitude toward individual enterprise, and the extent of controls on trade and investment. I agree that these factors are important, but I doubt that the authors' correlations tell us much about causation. Thus I question their evidence, along with that of De Long and Summers (1991, 1992), who argue that fixed investment does play a causal role in growth. Blomström et al. end by downplaying the importance of saving and investment generally; but I think that's going too far. We can't have growth, I believe, without the patience that causes saving and investment.

Boeri (1994) looks at job turnover across establishments within ten OECD countries. While movements between broadly defined sectors seem countercyclical, establishment-based movements do not. At all stages of the business cycle, as Davis and Haltiwanger (1992) show for the U.S., the growth and decline of new and small establishments account for a large amount of turnover. He suggests that changes in specialized consumer preferences account for a lot of the job turnover, especially when firms use workers of similar skills to produce a range of products and services, and finds some empirical support for this view. All this is consistent with the general equilibrium approach, especially the idea that we must look at tastes and technology defined in great detail along many dimensions. If he extends his analysis to job changes within firms, I think he will find that turnover is clearly procyclical. And if he extends his analysis of worker skills to a much greater level of detail, I think he will find that shifting demand for different kinds of workers acts much like shifting consumer demand for different kinds of products and services.

Boldrin (1991) notes that even with certainty, a conventional two-sector model with capital and consumption goods outputs can give very complex, even chaotic, paths for macroeconomic variables. He emphasizes intersectoral substitution rather than intertemporal substitution, while I think inability to substitute along either dimension gives more insight into business fluctuations than easy substitution. I think the two-sector models he discusses have strange and special properties, as illustrated by the Rybczynski theorem. With more general production technology, these properties vanish. In particular, it helps to think of labor as a form of capital rather than a fixed factor.

Bosworth (1975) discusses the relation between the stock market and the economy. He assumes that stock prices sometimes move in ways that are obviously irrational, and that monetary and fiscal policy work by affecting "aggregate demand." He treats investment by firms as a component of aggregate demand. In discussing the results of empirical work, he assumes that correlation can tell us about causation. None of this is consistent with general equilibrium as I define it.

Boyd and Smith (1994) look at the impact of credit market imperfections in a multicountry overlapping generations model where some young people have access to investment projects and some don't. They assume conventional asymmetric production using labor and capital. State verification is costly, so the credit market is somewhat inefficient. They find multiple steady states. In the stable steady states, differences in income are permanent, and open economies oscillate around their steady states. Steady-state welfare comparisons are ambiguous. I don't understand why they choose this kind of model or why they look at steady-state welfare. I prefer a model with permanent growth where human and physical capital are symmetric inputs in production. Differences in income in this model are permanent in autarky, but we can have convergence if the economies are open, because they will produce some things with inputs from both countries. There is only one equilibrium. Trade and investment improve welfare in both countries because they can use more specialized production. Costly credit hurts welfare, but has no other notable effects. People in countries with unstable governments will lend abroad to escape expropriation of wealth. Lending from unstable poor countries to rich countries thus improves welfare by keeping assets away from politicians: it is not perverse. Indeed, I think it may be more important for a developing country to allow capital outflow than to allow capital inflow. Capital that flows in sometimes goes mostly to the politicians, which is a problem worse than costly state verification.

Brainard and Cutler (1993) try to measure the relative impact of sectoral reallocation and aggregate shocks on U.S. employment. Like Loungani, Rush, and Tave (1990, 1991), they use the cross-sectional variation of stock returns to measure reallocation shocks. They say that reallocation accounts for 40% of aggregate unemployment but a smaller percentage of the variation of unemployment through time. I don't know what to make of their classification of shocks into "aggregate" and "sectoral," since shocks to tastes and technology along many dimensions can give both kinds of employment movements, especially when we use broadly defined sectors. They say that the Beveridge curve posits a negative relation between unemployment and vacancies in response to aggregate shocks; but a general equilibrium model with human capital, careers, and varying utilization of human and physical capital suggests a similar relation in response to taste and technology shocks of all kinds.

Brainard, Shapiro, and Shoven (1991) explore the notion of "fundamental value" and the correlations among "fundamental return," market return, and individual stock return for a sample of nonfinancial, nonextractive firms from 1962 through 1985. They define fundamental return as corporate profits from the national income and product accounts (with capital consumption and inventory valuation adjustments) divided by total assets of the corporate sector from the flow of funds accounts. In essence, they use book value of corporate assets for fundamental value. They find that fundamental value is far less volatile than market value, and that fundamental returns are almost uncorrelated with stock and bond returns. I think that's because fundamental value doesn't measure anything of economic significance. Also, I think profits measure value more than change in value, so the ratio of profits to book value is like a scaled ratio of values, rather than something analogous to a security return. I don't think they have defined a measure of fundamental value that adds information to estimated market value.

Bresnahan and Ramey (1993) study inventory-sales ratios, capacity utilization, and shifts in plant capacity for several auto size categories in response to the oil shocks of the 1970s. They show the delays (and by implication, the costs) in capacity reallocation. Their example is a model of the process by which micro shocks have macro effects. The oil shocks were relatively large scale "demand" shocks. I think most of the action is at a finer level of sectoral detail and involves both demand and supply shocks.

Brock (1982) has a multisector stochastic growth model that generalizes the single-sector model of Brock and Mirman (1972, 1973). If we add nonseparable utility, adjustment costs for moving capital from one sector to another, human capital, and a few other features, we will have a model of the kind I favor.

Burnside, Eichenbaum, and Rebelo (1993) say that conventional real business cycle theories overestimate the importance of technology shocks, because "labor hoarding" means that effort per hour of work is procyclical. They use "indivisible labor" to explain variation in employment, and take shocks to government consumption as a major economic force. They treat government consumption as a perfect substitute for current private consumption but unrelated to future private consumption, and they say that shocks to government consumption and technology should be uncorrelated. They think it's a virtue to have a model that produces a near-zero correlation between average productivity and hours. In other words, their model has all the defects of the conventional real business cycle model, plus some extra unmotivated assumptions. Their assumptions about government consumption seem especially odd to me. For example, I think technology shocks and shocks to government consumption should be correlated, since both are correlated with income. I think measured Solow residuals reflect all kinds of shocks to tastes and technology along many dimensions, so I don't see why we want to treat them as depending only on aggregate technology shocks and aggregate effort. Putting effort per hour into the production function is a step in the right direction, but a bigger step would be adding human capital and (as they note) utilization of physical capital. I think they are aiming at the wrong target for the correlation between average productivity and hours, since correctly measured average productivity is procyclical. I don't think we can use an imperfect model like theirs to fit data in quantitative detail, but we can learn that variation in effort per hour is one reason for variation in the measured Solow residual.

Caballé and Santos (1993) model endogenous growth with physical and human capital. They analyze cases where the ratios of physical capital to human capital to consumption are constant. Since they have no fixed factors, growth can continue without limit. They use a certainty model, so they do not look at the tie between business cycles and growth. They think of human capital as arising mostly from schooling rather than experience. They choose very special production functions for human capital, so they sometimes find the paradoxical result that higher physical capital leads ultimately to a growth path with lower physical capital, because it increases the opportunity cost of schooling. If Caballé and Santos move to a model where human and physical capital are symmetric (except that we accumulate human capital by working), I think they will find that their "paradoxical" cases vanish.

Caballero (1993) shows that the lumpiness of durable goods purchases can help explain their sluggish response to changes in income or wealth. He is able to analyze a model with a continuum of individuals, each making an independent decision on replacing his durable. I view this as one way to move toward a model with enough diversity and structure to explain business cycles in a general equilibrium context. Waves of replacement of durables may account for a significant fraction of layoff unemployment. I tend to think other factors are more important in explaining the "excess smoothness puzzle," though. Perhaps the most important is simply a preference for smooth consumption, as in Greenig (1986). If we start with utility that is time-nonseparable and state-dependent, the puzzle doesn't arise in the first place.

Caballero and Engel (1991) model the aggregate dynamic behavior of an economy where individual units adjust their positions only when they reach upper or lower bounds. Their examples include menu costs that make firms change prices infrequently, costs of adjusting cash balances, infrequent technology updates, lumpy purchases of durable consumer goods, and discrete capital stock adjustments by firms. Their model allows for only a single common factor, but they show that with enough heterogeneity, the lumpiness can appear smooth in the aggregate. I don't think lumpiness matters much for the character of business cycles, but I think heterogeneity matters a great deal. They show one way to model heterogeneity.

Caballero, Engel, and Haltiwanger (1994) study data on employment changes and hours per production worker for about 10,000 plants over a nine-year period. They estimate a distribution of differences between actual and target employment for each quarter, and an employment readjustment for each region of that distribution. They find that the fractional employment readjustment increases with the degree to which a plant is out of equilibrium as measured by the difference between actual and desired employment. They also find that aggregate employment fluctuation is associated more with changes in the cross-section of disequilibrium than with changes in the readjustment conditional on the degree of disequilibrium. When they classify periods into those with aggregate shocks and those with reallocation shocks, and when they look at the interplay between the cross-section, conditional readjustment, and the kind of period, they conclude that very little of the fluctuation in the cross-section that is associated with aggregate employment fluctuation is associated with reallocation shocks. Actually, they conclude more than that, because they use words that imply causation rather than just association. I don't know what to make of their detailed conclusions, since I think their classifications are arbitrary. I don't even think the classification of shocks into "aggregate" and "reallocation" is meaningful. Their results are consistent with a general equilibrium view of employment fluctuation. We know that because plants use team production, and because teams have an optimal size, employment changes are apt to be lumpy; and we know that when hours per worker are high, firms are likely to add new shifts or new plants that will bring down average hours per worker. The authors put numbers on these facts. Indeed, they give us a striking new stylized fact: overall, employment changes and hours changes are positively correlated; but for a given plant, employment changes and hours changes are negatively correlated.

Caballero and Hammour (1994) discuss variation over the business cycle in the rate of creation and destruction of production units. They use a vintage model of an industry subject to exogenous technical progress and demand shocks. A new production unit embodies the leading technology when it is created, but does not gain from further technical improvements. It is destroyed when its costs exceed its revenues. Because creation is costly, a decline in demand shows up partly as a decline in creation and partly as a rise in destruction. When demand follows a sine wave pattern, a model of this form can show a stronger cyclical pattern in destruction than in creation. They refer to destruction as "cleansing" because the least efficient production units are destroyed in a recession. I think their model fails to capture the reasons for the relatively large cyclical moves in destruction. Variation in efficiency across production units is minor compared to variation in the exact nature of a unit's inputs and outputs. Caballero and Hammour have a certainty model, so they do not capture the uncertainty in tastes and technology that drives business cycles. They do not mention durables, which account for the periodic nature of demand in certain industries. Any model with procyclical net growth of establishments and countercyclical dispersion in growth rates will have greater cyclical movements in destruction than in creation. This model has those features, but I don't think it has the right underlying structure.

Campbell (Jeffrey, 1994) creates a vintage capital model of technical change, where only new plants have access to the leading technology, but the "scrap capital" from existing plants goes into the new plants. He uses a standard asymmetric production function and the calibration methods from conventional real business cycle models. He claims to be able to explain the behavior of the Solow residual, even though in his model it represents changes in the leading edge technology that are available to new plants only. I like the fact that a vintage capital model recognizes the time dimension in production and the diversity of inputs, but I think diversity in productivity has only minor effects on economic behavior. When we measure capital at market value and recognize the effects of new technology on the market values of old plants, we can think of the new technology as applying to all capital vintages. It's far more important to bring in diversity in the kinds of capital used in different plants (or teams that produce services) and in the goods and services produced. I don't know why Campbell tries so hard to match the statistical behavior of the measured Solow residual. If we bring in human capital at market value and allow for changing utilization of composite capital, the Solow residual can vanish entirely. His identifying restrictions are arbitrary, as when he claims that various measurement errors are independent of one another; but this problem is minor compared to the structural defects in the model he uses. I don't think we have good enough models to start trying to match the statistics of the U.S. economy.

Campbell (John, 1994) suggests "inspecting the mechanism" behind the conventional stochastic growth model. He looks at linear approximations to deviations from steady-state growth. He looks at the model's sensitivity to the elasticity of the labor supply, the intertemporal elasticity of consumption, the persistence of technology shocks, and the permanence of shocks to government spending. I like his willingness to explore the implications of each of the conventional model's assumptions; he has moved beyond the notion that only a model's predictions matter. In general, I think his analysis shows clearly some of the peculiarities of the conventional stochastic growth model: labor is a fixed factor; people do not choose technology; capital grows smoothly; there's no human capital; leisure variation is key to output variation; a single kind of worker produces a single good for a single consumer; and utility is separable in time and independent of economic conditions. In the end, when we use a model with no fixed factors and time-nonseparable utility, even if we don't model roundabout production in a world with highly differentiated inputs and outputs, we cannot use the solution method that Campbell recommends. Euler equations collapse in such a world, and there is no steady-state growth path.

Campbell and Mankiw (1987b) use the unemployment rate to separate the cyclical and trend components of real GNP. They assume that the two components are uncorrelated, and that the trend component is that part of GNP uncorrelated with unemployment, either currently or with leads and lags. They find that fluctuations associated with the business cycle are not obviously more trend-reverting than other fluctuations in output. I question both of their assumptions. To justify them, they say only "one usually thinks of trend and cycle as having a low or zero correlation" (p. 114). My approach is almost the opposite of theirs. I assume that temporary and permanent shocks are correlated, but not perfectly correlated, and I assume that without changes in utilization, output would look like a smoothed geometric random walk. I like conditioning on other variables, though I'm inclined to use capital at market value along with the unemployment rate.

Campbell and Mankiw (1989) look at a model where half of the people consume their permanent income, and half consume their current income. People in the second half use a "rule of thumb." The authors say this helps explain predictability in the consumption series, independence of consumption and expected real interest rates, and the fact that periods when consumption is high relative to current income are typically followed by rapid growth in income. I agree that many people use such rules of thumb, and that this helps us understand consumption figures. They identify the permanent income hypothesis with separable utility and the Euler equation, but I don't know why they take any of those things seriously. They say that even their model fails to explain such things as the equity premium, but that moving to nonseparable utility or changing tastes may rescue it (p. 211). In other words, a full general equilibrium model with general von Neumann–Morgenstern utility fits the data.

Cardia (1991) simulates a real business cycle model for a small open economy. She concludes that persistent productivity shocks can explain such things as the high correlation between national saving and investment, and that monetary and fiscal shocks play a minor role. While I like her conclusions, I question her methods. Cash-in-advance models don't generalize to a world with developed capital markets. Unexpected budget deficits seem unlikely to explain business cycles, though they may explain shifts in saving and investment. In a general equilibrium model, an improvement in the productivity of human and physical capital in one country seems likely to attract physical capital (and people) to that country, so it affects saving and investment differently. She uses estimated Solow residuals for productivity shocks, and I don't see any good way to define or interpret these residuals. We can see one of the problems by looking at her stylized facts for the U.S. and Germany in Tables 2 and 3 (pp. 425–426). She finds a negative correlation between the capital stock and GNP for both countries. If we use estimated market values for the capital stock, I'm sure these correlations will turn positive.

Carroll and Weil (1994) study the relation between saving and growth. Using both aggregate and panel data, they find that high growth leads high saving, and that young households that should expect rapid income growth save more than other households. They question the strength of the "mechanical link" between saving and growth. They feel that a combination of habit formation and responses to uncertainty can explain some of their findings. I find their analysis very specific to the rather narrow set of models they examine. For example, they do not make full use of "first order uncertainty" in wealth and income, or of the notion that consumption measures "true income" or "permanent income" better than direct measures. They do not consider including growth in human capital as part of income and saving, and they do not consider the implications of variation in work effort on both labor income and additions to human capital through "learning by doing." They use a form of "habit formation" where past consumption has a consistent negative impact on current utility, while a more natural preference for consumption smoothing implies the opposite. We can understand all their results easily in a fully general equilibrium model. With first order uncertainty and consumption smoothing, an increase in human and physical wealth (assuming no change in discount rates) leads to an increase in saving because of consumption smoothing. Young people who save a lot in physical and human capital naturally expect rapid income growth through the "mechanical link." In a classical model, the mechanical link holds by definition, so long as we keep the right things fixed. Their question about that causal relation makes sense only in a Keynesian model. They consider a special effect of discount rate changes on human capital, but I think such changes affect physical capital in similar ways. They speak of the interest rate as the discount rate, but I think the price of risk varies as much as the interest rate. They insist on using growth models with fixed factors, even though we see no evidence of diminishing returns to total world capital. They treat growth and saving as comparable variables, though in a model with first order uncertainty, growth is the first difference of a stock, while saving is a flow.

Cheng and Dinopoulos (1991) explore a "Schumpeterian" model of economic growth and fluctuations. They assume a firm that wins an R&D "race" enjoys monopoly profits for a time. They consider this as a possible complete model of business fluctuations, including varying unemployment through variations in the work-leisure trade-off. I like the fact that they include many "industries," but I don't think we need monopoly power to explain fluctuations. I don't know why we want to focus on R&D investments, or for that matter, on technical change. In my view, *all* investments interact with uncertainty in both tastes and technology to give substantial and realistic cycles, even in a fully competitive model. But I agree that assuming unique investments earn "rents" for a time adds realism to the model.

Cheng and Dinopoulos (1992) consider R&D breakthroughs and improvements in a world with imperfect competition to be central to both growth and fluctuations. They find aggregate technology shocks neither necessary nor sufficient. I, in turn, find R&D and imperfect competition to be neither necessary nor sufficient. In the general equilibrium approach, competition is close to perfect, and investments in R&D differ very little from investments in any other kind of capital.

Chirinko (1993) divides models of business fixed investment spending into those with "implicit" dynamics and those based on "explicit" dynamics, including more equations capturing optimizing behavior and rational expectations. He favors the second group, though they are not now used much in policy studies, because they make it easier to combine the results of different econometric studies, and because they use theory that is more correct. Even though the micro studies he cites seem to give better results than the macro studies, he favors the latter. He even says that macro equations and data are likely to be better than corresponding micro equations and data. I think the opposite is true. As he notes, almost all the models he surveys assume putty–putty capital and constant geometric depreciation. I think these assumptions are fatal. Capital fluctuates in value because it takes specific forms, and depreciation (or appreciation) is highly erratic because capital fluctuates in value. Indeed, these studies all assume that we can find a sensible measure of capital other than its market value. I think we can divide total productive capital into units and unit value, but I think the total matters more than the components. Chirinko treats the correlation between output and investment as troubling (given price and other variables), yet to others (including me) that is a key fact. Only by detailed micro analysis can we hope to illuminate the underlying shifts that affect output and investment through price. In general, I don't see that adjustment costs, other than those inherent in the specific nature of all investments, have much of a role to play. As a first approximation, adjustment costs simply mean a lower overall return on marginal investments of any kind. They do not have the qualitative effects implied by almost all these models when we move to general equilibrium.

Christiano (1987) has a model that uses a serially correlated productivity "shock" to make consumption smoother than income, even though utility is time-separable and state-independent. He starts by saying his goal is to bring in substitution effects by letting the interest rate vary, but in his simulations he finds a smooth consumption series without a significantly changing interest rate. He has mixed success using his model to match real data. Since the model is quite simple, I don't know why he looks at real data in any detail. It's possible that the details of the process driving tastes and technology help explain consumption smoothing, but I suspect other factors, especially nonseparable utility, are more important.

Christiano and Eichenbaum (1992) add government consumption to a conventional real business cycle model to explain the apparent low correlation between hours worked and return to working in U.S. data. Thus they find a role for "aggregate demand shocks" of a certain kind, though they assume that shifts in government consumption are unrelated to developments in the economy. They use a conventional real business cycle model, with all of its problems, including especially the idea that leisure and unemployment are identical. In their model, government consumption reduces the marginal utility of private consumption in the same period, but has no effect on its marginal utility in other periods. Thus temporary shifts in government consumption induce people to shift both consumption and leisure between the present and the future. This gives fluctuations in output through fluctuations in "effort." Can this really be a significant cause of business cycles? This result is specific to their model, and does not generalize to a model with no fixed factors, or to a model where taxes are distorting, or to a model where government "consumption" includes payments to people who don't work. Indeed, their whole method of analysis, which relies on deviations around a steady state, collapses when we assume a model with no fixed factors. In a sense, I agree with their alternate explanation wherein we "abandon one-shock models of aggregate fluctuations and suppose that the business cycle is generated by a variety of impulses" (p. 431). But I don't want to assume that shocks to labor supply are very important. So my deeper explanation is that they (and others) have mismeasured the return to working. In bad times, the return to working is lower, largely because the value of added human capital is lower. The marginal return to working varies more than the average, because some people become unemployed and others lose their overtime. Using "average productivity" or output per worker understates the variation, because it omits nonworkers who would like to work. Workers clearly have higher total compensation in good times, including on-the-job gains in experience, than in bad times. If the statistics show otherwise, we should find new kinds of statistics.

Clark (1987) decomposes industrial production and real GNP from 1947 through 1985 into independent "nonstationary trend" and "stationary cycle" components. Shocks to the nonstationary trend are permanent, while shocks to the stationary cycle are temporary. Assuming that shocks to one are independent of shocks to the other, he estimates that shocks to GNP are half permanent and half temporary, while shocks to industrial production are one-third permanent and two-thirds temporary. For reasons I don't understand, he says that independence and perfect correlation are the only plausible assumptions for the two shocks, and he argues that independence is more plausible. I think that an intermediate case is more reasonable, and that the correlation is probably high; also, I like treating the trend as a smoothed geometric random walk. Clark acknowledges that his results are only suggestive, and that a range of hypotheses may be consistent with his findings.

Cochrane (1991) describes a production-based asset pricing model analogous to the consumption-based asset pricing model. He defines an "investment return" that depends on investment, the capital stock, adjustment costs, and the marginal product of capital. Under certain assumptions, investment return and stock return should be equal. Using conventional data, he finds that forecasts of investment return match forecasts of stock return, and that stock and investment returns make the same forecasts of subsequent economic activity. Cochrane makes some unmotivated assumptions (like choosing specific functional forms as he moves from his general model to models for production and capital accumulation), but I find even his "general" model too specific. After carrying state-dependence through most of his derivation, he suddenly writes a capital accumulation equation that is state-independent (p. 215). To me, this is analogous to assuming time-separable, state-independent utility in the consumption-based model.

Cochrane (1994) finds, using data from 1Q1947 to 3Q1989, that consumption is nearly a random walk (looking back two quarters), that the ratio of GNP to consumption is stationary, and that changes in GNP given consumption tend to be transitory. I interpret this as meaning that consumption reflects mostly business fluctuations following a geometric random walk, while the part of GNP not explained by consumption represents business cycles. I think he would find, if he looked over many quarters, that consumption is smoother than a geometric random walk.

Cochrane (1995) finds the shocks that drive economic fluctuations somewhat mysterious. Using a conventional production function and a lot of vector autoregressions, he concludes that they are neither technology shocks in the traditional real business cycle sense; nor money shocks; nor oil price shocks; nor shocks to financial intermediation. He suggests shocks that reflect private news about future economic conditions, acting in part through consumption. He talks a lot about specification error and econometric problems, so I don't know why he shows us so many quantitative exercises. In my view, the problems he mentions are overwhelming. I like his emphasis on news, though I'd expand his concept to include news about both tastes and technology along many dimensions. I don't know why he insists that the news is "unobservable": I think it's just costly to observe, so we don't bother. And I don't know why he picks on consumption, since both news of changes and actual changes in tastes and technology affect all the economic variables we think about.

Constantinides (1990), like Sundaresan (1989), uses "habit formation" to explain the "equity premium puzzle." His example follows Sundaresan in using a "floor level of consumption," as in Ryder and Heal (1973). While this device does smooth consumption, it has the feature that higher consumption today, holding future consumption fixed, can reduce utility. That may be a good way to describe drug addiction, but I don't think it explains consumption smoothing. I prefer a model like Greenig's (1986). In any case, if we start with general time-nonseparable utility, the equity premium puzzle does not arise.

Cook and Hahn (1990) analyze the evidence on the relation between the yield curve slope and expected short-term interest rates. They attribute the weak relation between forward rates and expected spot rates to the detailed operation of monetary policy. Their explanation is close to mine, but they suggest that a rise in short rates is accompanied by a smaller rise in long rates (holding expected inflation fixed), while I think it is accompanied by a fall in long rates (other things equal), as the central bank uses cash it receives from artificially high short rates to buy long bonds.

Cooley, Greenwood, and Yorukoglu (1993) revisit the vintage capital question in a model with skilled and unskilled labor plus physical capital of various vintages. They find an equilibrium mix of vintages and a balanced growth path. With no taxes, their competitive equilibrium would be optimal. They find that an investment tax credit paid for by taxes on physical capital and labor income can improve welfare. I believe their conclusions are highly model-specific. The model I prefer has no fixed factors (like unskilled labor) and no special technology for producing human or physical capital. We can use several kinds of human and physical capital in production, but the optimal tax scheme treats them all the same. If effort is inelastic, we should probably replace capital taxes by consumption taxes, but we should neither tax nor subsidize investment in a specific kind of capital.

Cooley and Prescott (1995) summarize their current version of the conventional real business cycle model. They call it an "empirical model" because they fit it to certain aspects of U.S. data. They say it is "fully specified" and that it includes all forms of capital, even though they have only a single "productivity shock" and they omit human capital, which probably exceeds the forms of capital they include. They ignore variation in utilization and its associated variation in expected depreciation. They continue to treat unemployment as a form of leisure. They figure an "interest rate" from capital's part of output (net of depreciation) rather than from securities markets. They decompose the path of output into cyclical and trend components without trying to make the trend component follow a geometric random walk with drift. I think many of their "facts" come mostly from measurement problems: for example, because they don't try to measure physical capital in efficiency units, they say that capital fluctuates much less than output and is largely uncorrelated with it; and because they mismeasure both wages and productivity, they say that wages vary less than productivity. They roughly decompose secular growth as one-third due to changes in capital and two-thirds due to changes in productivity, while I would attribute all of it to changes in efficiency units of composite capital;

and they decompose the business cycle as two-thirds due to changes in labor and one-third due to changes in productivity, while I would attribute part to changes in efficiency units of composite capital and part to changes in utilization. They speak of their decomposition as causal, while mine is only an arbitrary accounting. I think the causal factors are deep, and do not show up explicitly in any aggregate model. Given the structural problems with their model, I am amazed that they conclude that much, but not all, of the variation in output is "accounted for" by technology shocks.

Cooper and Haltiwanger (1990) explore possible reasons for serially correlated output movements and positive comovement in output across sectors of a multisector economy. They consider variants of the Long and Plosser (1983, 1987) model where a technology shock in one sector leads to added output in that sector, some of which is used for producing other commodities in the next period. They feel that common shocks to different sectors in that model cannot explain the patterns they see; so we must use a version of the Long–Plosser model with strong technical complementarities. Cooper and Haltiwanger's alternate approach stresses linkages across sectors from the demand for consumption goods in a world with imperfect competition. Because sellers have market power, an underemployment equilibrium is likely. Shocks to one sector spill over to others through the inventories that some agents hold. In general, they are engaged in a hazardous enterprise: using correlations to infer the structure of the economy. If they take inventories to be just one of the many kinds of durables used in production, if they add human capital and allow utilization of both human and physical capital to vary, and if they allow people to wait for recall or search for new careers when not working full time, I think they will find that a number of general equilibrium models can explain their stylized facts. In fact, Davis and Haltiwanger's (1990, 1992) results provide a key part of the story: when people change jobs, they usually do so across narrowly defined sectors but within broadly defined sectors.

Cooper and Haltiwanger (1993a) look at the empirical implications of "strategic complementarity," which roughly means, "If others work harder so will I." They treat strategic complementarity and aggregate shocks to tastes or technology as competing views in explaining positive comovement, synchronization of discrete choices, and magnification and propagation. They conclude that models with strategic complementarities are consistent with the data, though in many cases other models are too. I claim that the general equilibrium approach outlined above provides a third view that can explain all these facts. A shifting match between wants and resources at the microsector level can explain positive comovement between broadly defined sectors, negative comovement between narrowly defined sectors, and smaller negative comovement in good times than in bad times. Team production with constant returns to scale can explain synchronization. Durables can explain magnification and propagation. I am especially troubled by their claim that calibration of a conventional real business cycle model modified to allow contemporaneous and lagged spillovers supports the idea of production externalities. The basic model has so many flaws that I don't know what to make of this exercise.

Cooper and Haltiwanger (1993b) discuss the replacement of obsolete machines. In their model, productivity and the associated employment decline as a machine ages. The natural replacement cycle creates natural fluctuations in employment. The authors feel this may be one source of business cycles. Replacement occurs in their model during downturns, when resource costs are low. Independent producers synchronize machine replacement because they face common variations in the environment or because of strategic complementarities. In the auto industry, which they use as an example, model changeovers often do coincide with vacation periods. More generally, though, investment (including machine replacement) is strongly procyclical. Team production can explain both coordinated replacement and "spillovers" to other areas of the economy. I feel a conventional general equilibrium model can explain all the phenomena they describe.

Cowen and Kroszner (1992) discuss early twentieth-century German-language analyses of economies with credit systems that make monetary policy passive. These German writers hold views of money very similar to my views.

Cromwell (1991) analyzes the regional distribution of job losses in various recessions. He finds sharp differences among regions and across recessions. In the 1990–1991 recession, he finds that 59% of the job losses were in states where the first quintile of the working population lives (ranked by severity of job loss), while the fourth and fifth quintiles had no significant job losses at all. I believe that geographical dimensions are among the most important ones in a general equilibrium approach to business fluctuations.

Cummins, Hassett, and Hubbard (1994) use tax reforms as "natural experiments" to estimate the fixed investment behavior of firms, using conventional models involving Tobin's q or the "user cost of capital." They find significant effects of tax reform surprises, and their estimated adjustment costs are more reasonable than those from other studies. In a general equilibrium context, this whole line of research on business fixed investment seems very peculiar. It uses certainty models with many structural problems and inputs estimated from book values rather than market values. It pretends that identification is possible. And I don't know why we want to estimate investment behavior in the first place. Is it because a large response by firms implies a large welfare loss when the government taxes different forms of capital differently? In my models Tobin's q is identically one and adjustment costs are zero (at the margin). If I wanted to estimate the elasticity of business fixed investment, I would use the ratio of that form of investment to total investment rather than the ratio of that form of investment to business fixed capital. Of course, my ratio is hard to estimate, because it involves investments in intangible physical capital, residential real estate, consumer durables, and especially human capital. I would relate my ratio to a measure of the differential taxation of business fixed capital, and I would not distinguish between expected and unexpected changes in differential taxation.

Danthine and Donaldson (1993) review methodological and empirical issues in real business cycle theory. They argue that this theory's main contribution is in fact its methodology: construction of "computable" general equilibrium models whose characteristic statistics match those of the data. While I like the idea of using small models, I think computable models are premature: I don't think we are close enough to the right theoretical structure. Where Danthine and Donaldson see puzzles, I see the natural workings of a multidimensional general equilibrium. In particular, they claim that the essence of the "employment variability puzzle" is the fact that "quantities bear the brunt of the adjustment to fluctuations whereas Walrasian theory predicts that prices (and wages) should serve this function." But general equilibrium theory treats prices and quantities symmetrically. Either can fluctuate more than the other. Again, I fail to see the puzzle.

Davis (1987a) discusses the role of "allocative disturbances" in aggregate economic fluctuations. He sees them as both cause and effect of the shocks that give us business cycles. He allows for both allocative sectoral shocks and aggregate shocks, which he describes in one place as "cross-sectoral average marginal product disturbances." I don't know what aggregate shocks are in a general equilibrium model, unless they are just descriptive measures of changes in economic activity. I would omit them. Davis discusses "reverse reallocation," which occurs when an allocative shock reverses the effects of previous shocks. He notes that "unemployment turnover" is countercyclical (though job turnover, usually without a spell of unemployment, is procyclical). His work is broadly consistent with the general equilibrium approach.

Davis (1987b) discusses three hypotheses that people use in explaining unemployment rate fluctuations: (1) the sectoral shifts hypothesis, which says (unlike most search models of unemployment) that information about the desired labor force allocation arrives unevenly; (2) the normal business cycle hypothesis, which says that sectoral moves are a side effect of cyclical aggregate shocks, so variation in the pace of reallocation is not very important; and (3) the reallocation-timing hypothesis, which says that reallocation of specialized resources speeds up in recessions, since it's less costly then. He extends Lilien's (1982) work by showing that covariances among sectoral growth figures matter along with the variances that Lilien discusses. He shows that history matters: a shock that largely reverses an earlier shock, such as the end of World War II, does not give much unemployment. He emphasizes the reallocation-timing hypothesis, but that doesn't play a major role in my models. I think people change sectors more because they are moving to better career paths than because the cost of doing so is temporarily low. He says (pp. 350–353) that Abraham and Katz (1986) put too much emphasis on the "stock" of vacancies (as measured by help-wanted ads) and not enough on the flow (including jobs filled with a zero vacancy duration). I don't think this point is relevant, since I think even the flow of vacancies is procyclical. I think help-wanted ads are more closely associated with career moves in good times (and temporary adds to staff) than shifts to new careers, which we see more in bad times. I don't understand why Davis emphasizes the uneven arrival of information about sectoral reallocation: even information that arrives evenly has very different implications about reallocation at different times. (Consider, for example, his point about the end of World War II.)

Davis and Haltiwanger (1992) look at a huge databank of manufacturing plants, giving size, SIC code, and location in each quarter from 1972 through 1986. They find large size changes so common that gross job creation and destruction, measured by size changes, runs at about 10% per year and (even more dramatically) 5% per quarter. This is not workers moving into and out of a static pool of jobs: it is movement of jobs from plant to plant at a very high rate. They find a strong relation (negative) between gross reallocation and net job growth, and (positive) between gross reallocation and unemployment. They find that intense reallocation shocks lead to quick job destruction and then delayed job creation. Job creation and destruction are largely permanent. Davis and Haltiwanger try to classify shocks as aggregate, sectoral, and idiosyncratic, but in a multidimensional general equilibrium model I suspect this classification collapses. All shocks are sector-specific, but some shocks affect more firms than others. Overall, I view their findings as consistent with a general equilibrium approach to business fluctuations. In particular, their data help explain how countercyclical unemployment can be related to dispersion in performance of narrowly defined sectors, even though broadly defined sectors usually move together. Thus we don't need the noncompetitive "strategic complementarities" that Cooper and Haltiwanger (1993a) explore to explain these facts.

Davis and Haltiwanger (1994) try to tease the relative impact of aggregate and allocative shocks out of their data on job creation and destruction. They (refreshingly) explore a range of identifying assumptions, and look at both specification and estimation error. They use a "structural" vector autoregression method. They find that they can't pin down the relative importance of aggregate and allocative shocks; that aggregate shocks, if dominant, must cause asymmetric contemporaneous job creation and destruction responses; that allocative shocks drive shifts in job reallocation intensity; that aggregate shocks have short-lived effects on job creation and destruction; that allocative shocks cause a sharp increase in job destruction that quickly diminishes, but a long-lasting impact on job creation that peaks at about four quarters; and that oil and credit shocks do not look like either aggregate or allocative shocks. In effect, they are classifying shocks in terms of their impact on job creation and destruction, both now and in the future. I'm not sure how useful their classification is, because shocks to tastes or technology can show up as either "aggregate" or "allocative." For example, a shock that leads to a poor match between wants and resources can cause immediate job destruction and a slowdown in job creation, followed eventually by a return to more normal levels for both. Both layoffs and career changes look like this. In fact, I find the Davis and Haltiwanger data perfectly consistent with a general equilibrium approach to business cycles where the shocks cannot be classified as aggregate or allocative in any meaningful way.

De Long (1991) attributes the severity of the Great Depression to "collective insanity." He notes that people who owned bonds prospered as prices fell. He also notes, in a review of Eichengreen and Hatton's (1988) book, that countries on the gold standard had much more severe depressions than those not on it (De Long (1990)). I conclude that the gold standard, interacting with the zero floor on nominal interest rates, contributed more than collective insanity to the Great Depression. De Long says that the gold standard played a role in other recessions after 1890 too. Finally, he shows the huge variation in railroad construction in the late 1900s. This illustrates the instability we can have in a sector producing durables, though De Long seems to think the waves of optimism and pessimism driving these cycles may have been unjustified. Railroad construction also illustrates the large but temporary role that a particular sector can play as a limiting factor for the economy.

Denison (1985) gives one in a series of studies decomposing output growth into components like "changes in the amount of work done and the composition of workers (except for their education)," "advances in technical, managerial, and organizational knowledge," "the increase in private capital," "the increase in education of employed persons," "economies of scale," "improved allocation of labor among uses," "reductions in output per unit of input deriving from pollution and safety regulations and crime against business," and "other output determinants" (p. xvi). He creates index numbers for each input, weighting by that input's part of total output as an estimate of marginal product. He computes potential output from actual output, assuming unemployment falls to 4% and conditions are otherwise normal. He could have made assumptions that differ enormously from the ones he made, so I don't know what to make of the figures he gives. For example, I don't know how we can justify a split between knowledge and private capital, the omission of human capital (except through education), or an exact estimate for economies of scale. If I were to try to decompose growth, I would assume that all of it is from a change in the smoothed market value of capital, and I might decompose composite capital into a units series and a unit-value series.

Detemple and Selden (1992) show that with "recursive utility," as in Epstein and Zin (1989), risk and time preferences are no more separable than they are with conventional von Neumann–Morgenstern utility. That separation, then, is not a reason to abandon the traditional general equilibrium utility function.

Detemple and Zapatero (1991) generalize the habit formation model of Sundarasen (1989) and Constantinides (1990). Their model can explain consumption smoothing, but it is restricted to the use of utility that depends on a weighted average of past consumption. Utility cannot depend on products of powers of past consumption, as in Greenig (1986). They derive "testable" consequences from their model only because they restrict its form. I don't understand why we want to test a model that is still as restricted as theirs.

Díaz-Giménez, Prescott, Fitzgerald, and Alvarez (1992) simulate a "computable general equilibrium economy" with costly interme-diation, reserve requirements, and a government-controlled bill rate that can depend on the state of the economy. They calibrate their model to various aspects of the U.S. economy, and measure the welfare impact of policy changes using the "compensation principle" and summing over households alive today. (I think their welfare measure is far better than one based on the utility of individuals in steady state.) They find large gains from lower inflation, but they find that a procyclical real interest rate policy neither stabilizes the economy nor significantly improves welfare. As usual, I feel that calibration doesn't help our understanding unless we have a model's structure right. I believe the government can control the inflation rate by using a gold standard with a varying price of gold, but cannot control the bill rate (as a first approximation) in a world with fully developed capital markets. The direct reason is that the bill rate must equal the nominal return on riskless capital, or the interest rate part of the cost of capital in a world with risky capital. They don't have this equation, because they assume that no one can hold both capital and bills. Because of this structural problem with their model, I feel the effort they put into calibration was wasted.

Donaldson and Mehra (1983, 1984) analyze an abstract discrete-time model with capital, consumption, and investment. They use a state of the world that describes current production conditions. They can model a changing risk premium and a changing interest rate, but I claim we can understand growth and business cycles using simpler models where the interest rate and the risk premium are constant. Donaldson and Mehra use time-separable utility, so they don't use preferences to explain consumption smoothing. Their model generalizes simple real business cycle models by allowing correlated "technology shocks."

Donaldson and Selden (1981) show that we can't tell whether tastes do or don't change in a general model by looking at demand behavior. Marketing studies, though, look at *potential* demand behavior, so they can tell us when tastes change.

Dotsey and King (1987, 1988) survey rational expectations business cycle models with and without money. They favor restricted models, since they say that "unrestricted models of expectations preclude a systematic inquiry into business fluctuations" (1988, p. 3). I disagree. I favor unrestricted general equilibrium models, partly because I think expectations are largely observable. Shocks have lasting effects in the models they discuss because people accumulate capital to smooth consumption, and because changes in exogenous productivity tend to persist. In my models, shocks have lasting effects because a match or mismatch between tastes and technology tends to persist, and because capital (including human capital) is durable. In the models they discuss, investment is volatile because it is a residual (p. 5). In my models, investment is volatile largely because investment goods are more durable, on average, than consumption goods and services. They discuss the use of nonseparable but recursive preferences (p. 5), while I favor nonseparable but nonrecursive preferences to maintain the general equilibrium framework. They talk about using nonconvex production to go from hours variation to employment variation, while I favor using "team production" to do the same thing. They talk a lot about monetary features of the business cycle; I find them less interesting since I think monetary policy is largely passive. Finally, they note the Nelson and Plosser (1987) findings that many economic quantities are close to a geometric random walk. They think this has implications for both business cycles and growth, because it implies that fixed factors are unimportant, and that temporary shocks to the economy's production possibilities can have permanent effects. It's also true that permanent shocks can have temporary effects.

Dynarski and Sheffrin (1987) use retrospective labor force experience data from the 1982–1983 Panel Study of Income Dynamics to investigate the duration of unemployment spells. They find that completed durations are on average shorter when the unemployment rate is higher. They take this as evidence in favor of an equilibrium view of unemployment. In my view, it simply means that in bad times, the newly unemployed tend to be recalled or to find new jobs relatively quickly.

Easterly (1993) explores the effects of differential taxes on two kinds of capital in a growth model with no fixed factors. He finds that differential taxes reduce growth, just as taxing capital rather than consumption does. The effects on growth and welfare are greatest when the two kinds of capital are poor substitutes. He also tries to relate measures of input distortions to growth rates, and seems to find the negative relation we expect over the 1970–1985 period for a number of countries. All the variants he tries give the same results.

Easterly, Kremer, Pritchett, and Summers (1993) note that country growth rates are highly unstable, with a correlation across decades of .1 to .3, while country characteristics are stable, with cross-decade correlations of .6 to .9. This means that much of a country's growth is due to factors we can describe as "luck." They claim that terms-of-trade shocks are among those factors because they find a significant correlation between actual growth and changes in a country's terms of trade. I don't see why they refer to a price as a causal factor; I think the factors affecting actual growth also affect the terms of trade. The importance of luck, though, is a central element of the general equilibrium approach to macroeconomics.

Easterly and Rebelo (1993) explore the ties in both directions between fiscal policy and growth. They find that poor countries use international trade taxes, while rich countries use income taxes; that public investment is correlated with growth; that high-population countries use income taxes more, while spending more on defense and less on transport and communication; and that the correlations between income tax rates and growth are fragile. They are refreshingly candid about the implications of correlation for causation, but they think they can find instrumental variables, and they don't talk much about data mining as an explanation for some of their findings. A great many researchers have now processed the Summers and Heston (1991) data using related methods.

Eden (1990) shows that Hall's (1988c) findings are consistent with a competitive market where firms invest in capacity before they know what final demand will be. In other words, Hall underestimated marginal cost. Eden uses a model where markets open as new groups of buyers arrive, but he shows in an appendix that we can model the same thing in an Arrow–Debreu model with contingent contracts. "Investing in capacity" is the early part of "roundabout production."

Eden and Griliches (1993) show that when we take account of optimal investment in "capacity," we cannot reject the hypothesis that firms set price equal to marginal cost. We can, therefore, reject Hall's (1988c) argument that firms set price higher than that.

Eichenbaum (1991) notes that people working with conventional real business cycle theories claim that technology shocks account for most of the variability in aggregate U.S. output. He argues that the data and methods these people use are almost completely uninformative about the role of technology shocks. In particular, he finds that the Kydland and Prescott (1991b) claim that technology shocks account for 70% of fluctuations is very sensitive to their measurement period and the details of their model. The figure could also be 5% or even 200%. For example, when he divides their 1955–1984 period into two subsamples and adds labor hoarding or indivisible labor, he finds that the figure falls by 60%. He also feels that "calibration" is not a useful way to decide which impulses have been the major sources of postwar fluctuations in output. I agree with all these points, but my conclusion is different: he favors the traditional view that shocks to "aggregate demand," perhaps through monetary policy, are the key impulses to business cycles, while I feel that shifts in tastes and technology along many dimensions are the key impulses.

Eichenbaum, Hansen, and Singleton (1988) investigate a model that allows time-nonseparable utility of consumption and leisure, using monthly data on consumption, leisure, real wages, and the real interest rate from 1959 through 1978. Their estimates imply that leisure today decreases leisure services in the future, which is the opposite of what Kydland and Prescott (1982) assume. They rule out shocks to preferences so they can estimate consumers' aggregate utility, and they limit time-nonseparability so they can use an extended Euler equation. Most important, they use a model that abstracts from the detail that I think is crucial to understanding business cycles. I don't know why they bother to estimate or test such a restricted model.

Eichenbaum and Singleton (1986) find that money shocks do not "Granger cause" output changes in the 1949–1983 period. They view this as moderately strong evidence against an important role for monetary policy in a macroeconomic model. I see little connection between "Granger causality" and "causality," so even though I like the Eichenbaum–Singleton conclusions, I feel their evidence is weak. They favor adding "identifying restrictions" to a model so it will have "refutable implications" (p. 97). I am baffled by this. I would use only restrictions that make strong economic sense.

Eichengreen (1992) says that the interwar gold standard was less stable than the nineteenth-century gold standard. Indeed, he thinks that trying to stay on the gold standard helped to precipitate and magnify the Great Depression. He says that restrictive monetary policy in the U.S. during 1928 and 1929 triggered the downturn, and that attempts to maintain the gold standard in many countries allowed this impulse to propagate. In other words, the breakup of the gold standard did not contribute at all to financial and economic instability. Rather, it allowed the recovery to begin. He feels that government monetary and fiscal policy can have big effects. He thinks inflation causes expansion and deflation causes contraction. He thinks that government spending and deficits are expansionary, and that government rescue of failing banks helps to slow or reverse a decline. I agree that the gold standard helped cause the Great Depression, but only in countries where the nominal short-term interest rate approached zero. When expected deflation made the real rate high because the nominal interest rate can't fall below zero, lots of people wanted to lend but few wanted to borrow. Moreover, the decline in interest rates caused demand for currency to expand rapidly. If the government failed to meet this demand, financial markets could collapse. Thus I agree with Eichengreen's main point, but I wholly disagree with his reasons.

Epstein and Zin (1989, 1991) analyze a generalization of conventional time-additive expected utility. An agent forms a certainty equivalent of random future utility using his risk preferences, and then combines this with current consumption using an aggregator function to figure his current utility. This allows them to separate intertemporal substitution and risk aversion. But why not retain all the nice properties of von Neumann–Morgenstern intertemporal utility by just relaxing the conventional assumption that utility is time-separable and state-independent? They don't tell us why they don't follow this path. They say that one reason for their choice was "empirical tractability" (1991, p. 284). To me, that means they chose a model for their own convenience, rather than for economic reasons.

Epstein and Zin (1990) use a recursive utility function where the risk premium for a small gamble is proportional to the standard deviation rather than the variance. They say they can explain the "equity premium puzzle" this way. They say that nonexpected utility lets them maintain constant relative risk aversion; but with fully general nonseparable expected utility we can choose many functions with constant relative risk aversion that allow us to explain a volatile asset market with high expected return together with smooth consumption. They say that Constantinides (1990) must assume negative time preference to explain these facts (p. 389). My reading of Constantinides, however, suggests that habit formation alone is sufficient. In any case, we do not need to give up the nice properties of expected utility to explain the "equity premium puzzle" with constant relative risk aversion. All we need is a preference for smooth consumption.

Fair (1988) uses a U.S. econometric model to estimate the quantitative importance of various sources of output variability. He says he finds "demand shocks" much more important than "supply shocks," even looking ahead two years. He finds many sources of variability, but says Kydland and Prescott (1982) and Lilien (1982) have only a few sources in their models. (He does find only a few sources of variability for the GNP deflator, though.) Since he uses a conventional econometric model, I don't know what to make of his results. He talks about "effects" and "explanations" and "exogenous variables" and "structural equations," but I think he offers only volatilities and correlations. I feel his results are perfectly consistent with a general equilibrium model of the economy that has no scope for the kinds of fiscal and monetary policy he claims to be analyzing.

Fama and Schwert (1977) find a weak relation between stock returns and a measure of human capital. They define the total payoff on human capital as wage and salary disbursements plus proprietors' income (p. 97). Thus they do not include capital gains and losses associated with expected future wages. If they did, I think they would find a strong relation between the returns to human and physical capital. Going to five- or ten-year differencing intervals would be one way to investigate this.

Feldstein and Bacchetta (1991) update the Feldstein-Horioka (1980) study of the relation between national saving and international investment. They continue to find a strong relation between domestic saving and domestic investment. The relation is weaker than it was, especially for the EEC countries, presumably because capital mobility has increased. Their explanation sounds like my "home bias" explanation: for example, they say that many nonfinancial corporations "choose to avoid net foreign exchange exposure as a matter of policy" (p. 203). They continue to measure saving using what Baxter and Crucini (1993a) call "basic saving," which is output less the sum of private and government consumption. (True saving is *income* less consumption.) This causes them to overstate the relation between saving and investment. They conclude that domestic saving increases a nation's capital stock and thus the productivity of its work force. I would restate that as: domestic saving increases a nation's stock of both human and physical capital.

Fischer and Merton (1984) discuss the role of the stock market in reflecting changes that cause business fluctuations. They show that the stock market is the best "single" predictor of several economic series. They show the difficulty in estimating the cost of capital when the expected return on equity can move somewhat independently of interest rates, especially after-tax real interest rates. They show the difficulty of using data on any series *other* than stock market values; in particular, they show that Tobin's q is hard to estimate in any meaningful way. They give several examples of the difficulties of "identifying" economic models. In other words, the market value of capital, as measured by changing levels of the stock market, is one of the few reliable numbers we have in analyzing business cycles. While stock prices may sometimes react to irrational forces, they give us more reliable numbers than any other economic time series.

Fisher (1930) favors a utility function defined on the entire consumption program. Thus he rejects time-separability in the utility of consumption. He does not, though, go all the way to the most general utility function that fits the standard general equilibrium model.

Flavin (1993) shows that "excess sensitivity" of consumption to current income implies "excess smoothness" of consumption relative to permanent income, even when current income and permanent income are equally volatile. Thus consumption may appear smooth even without a specific preference for smoother consumption.

Freeman and Polasky (1992) model knowledge-based growth. They assume that people obtain knowledge by studying, and that knowledge can be owned and sold. They see positive externalities because an agent's stock of knowledge is undiminished when he sells it to someone else, and because we cannot fully observe the transfer of knowledge. They ignore the negative externalities in "market stealing" or "creative destruction," as in Aghion and Howitt (1992). Thus I continue to believe we can ignore all externalities in the creation of knowledge, at least as a first approximation. Similarly, I think their analysis of the gains from specialization in research carries over to similar gains from specialization in all other economic activities.

Garber and King (1983) show that Euler equation methods, even though we assume rational expectations, are subject to traditional identification problems. We must make special assumptions to disentangle taste shocks (which they call "shifts in agents' objectives") and technology shocks. I agree that these problems exist and are hard to solve, but I think Euler equation methods have problems even when identification is possible, since they assume (with no justification) time-separable utility.

Gort and Wall (1993) question the measurement of capital and labor inputs to production. They feel that obsolescence is a major part of depreciation, and that embodied technical change explains much of the output increase that some attribute to disembodied technical change via the Solow residual. With their quality adjustments, the estimated Solow residual often becomes negative. Their corrections are in the right direction, but I think we must use market values to estimate quality change and economic depreciation. The numbers we generate by using conventional measures of the human and physical capital inputs to production are not worth much.

Greenig (1986) explores time-nonseparable utility as a way of separating risk tolerance and elasticity of intertemporal substitution, and as a way of explaining things like the "equity premium puzzle." He introduces exactly the utility function I favor for capturing consumption smoothing (p. 30). In his model, local utility depends on a weighted geometric average of current and past levels of consumption. He finds that a version of this utility function with just one lag does not succeed in fitting the data. With enough lags, though, I think it will do fine.

Greenwood, Hercowitz, and Huffman (1988) create a real business cycle model where shocks affect the productivity of new capital but not old capital. A positive shock reduces the cost of using old capital, so capital utilization rises. Higher utilization implies faster depreciation. With this model, unlike more traditional models, a reduction in the price of new capital can increase both consumption and traditionally defined labor productivity. They can match the moments of U.S. data without relying much on intertemporal substitution. I like their emphasis on utilization of physical capital. It's a step in the right direction, but I'd like to see them continue by introducing human capital and by treating hours and effort as utilization of human capital. Then they can allow the relevance of old human and physical capital to change, which can bring random walk elements into their model. They have so many steps to take that I'm surprised they worry about matching the moments of U.S. data.

Greenwood, Hercowitz, and Krusell (1994) note that the relative price of equipment has declined sharply in the U.S. for the period after World War II, while the measured ratio of equipment to GNP has risen; and that the correlation (in quarterly data) between the detrended quality-adjusted relative price of new equipment and detrended new equipment investment is quite negative. They build and "calibrate" a competitive model where both "neutral" technical change and "investment-specific technical change" (which helps the economy only after people have used the new technology in capital goods) cause economic growth. In the calibrated model, investment-specific technical change accounts for about two-thirds of postwar economic growth and about a quarter of our economic fluctuations. After accounting for this kind of technical change, they find the "productivity slowdown" that started in the 1970s even more striking. While they construct a new series for quality-adjusted equipment, they use a conventional asymmetric neoclassical production function with a fixed factor where technical change is the only force driving the economy, so I don't take their growth decomposition seriously. In my models, either freely available technical change or investment in private R&D, along with investment in new manufacturing capacity, can cause the declining price of new equipment (and of the services it provides). I believe technical change is always investment-specific. We can assume away all "neutral" technical progress without affecting the predictions of our models. Finally, I prefer to measure the "equipment" input to production at market value, to avoid the strange notion that the ratio of equipment to GNP is continually rising, and to emphasize the fact that meaningful aggregation of capital requires prices.

Greenwood and Huffman (1991) analyze the effect of a "stabilizing" output subsidy in a traditional real business cycle model of the sort given in Greenwood, Hercowitz, and Huffman (1988) with constant distorting taxes on labor and capital but no government services. They find the benefit of the stabilizing subsidy is small. They compare welfare of the representative person across steady states; and as they note, looking at welfare change along a single path following a policy change may give very different results. What's equally serious is that this kind of business cycle model has properties that I doubt will generalize when we move to a model with human capital where utilization of human and physical capital vary together, and where depreciation includes changes in the price of capital associated with changes in the state of the world. I grow nervous when people use heavily restricted models to suggest the answers to major policy questions.

Greenwood and Jovanovic (1990) model the relations among financial development, growth, and the distribution of income. They find that investments in financial development and growth feed on one another, and that the distribution of income can first widen and then narrow as a country develops. The gains from financial development come partly from better knowledge of where the best investments lie and partly from better diversification. They model better knowledge as foreknowledge of the payoff from an aggregate shock, so financial development sometimes reduces risk in their model. If better knowledge simply improves the risk-return trade-off, I think we'll find that financial development always increases aggregate risk, as it does when it improves diversification. On the other hand, *political* development that creates a safer society with more stable property rights can both increase income or growth and reduce aggregate risk.

Griliches (1994) says that we don't understand "the residual" very well, partly because we don't put enough care and money into data collection. He thinks the recent apparent decline in the growth rate of productivity may be an illusion, only partly because we mismeasure quality change and shifts to less costly substitutes for goods and services that earn high rents for their creators. He hints at changes in the way we look at the data too: he would focus on disequilibria and the measurement of "knowledge and other externalities." He suggests thinking about organizational quality, the work ethic, and the strength of property rights as factors in growth. He even notes that we measure human and physical capital at "book values," and suggests using measures that reflect obsolescence, as from energy price shocks and the melting away of monopoly rents due to international competition. I agree with all these points, but I would emphasize data problems less and conceptual problems more. If we go all the way to market value in thinking about both physical and human capital, we see that the obsolescence we experienced in the 1970s was more than reversed in the 1980s and early 1990s. I think this is more relevant than conventional measures of productivity growth.

Grossman and Helpman (1991a) add "product cycles" involving both innovation and imitation to Aghion and Howitt's model of quality ladders and creative destruction. They imagine that firms in the North race to bring out the next generation of a set of technology-intensive products, while firms in the South learn to imitate the North's innovations, and to produce them at low cost. They look at possible subsidies to either innovation or imitation, but find that such subsidies can either increase or decrease welfare. More generally, like Aghion and Howitt, they are unable to tell whether innovation is too fast or too slow. They do not consider possible improvements in intellectual property rights, so that innovators in the North earn profits from both quality improvements and low-cost production in the South.

Grossman and Helpman (1991b) study innovation and growth in the global economy. They emphasize *investing* in innovation, which creates both cost-reducing quality improvement and brand proliferation. They feel that the spillovers from imperfect property rights in knowledge help to drive growth, which would otherwise slow down due to the effects of fixed resources. They model innovation as creating monopoly profits for a time, but find certain cases where the equilibrium is efficient despite these profits. They recognize the negative externality when a new idea destroys the value of an old idea, and they say they are unable to tell, in general, whether the equilibrium in a competitive economy gives too much innovation or too little. I like their emphasis on investing in innovation, including the knowledge needed for further innovation, and on quality ladders and brand proliferation. However, I think we can model their basic process as containing rents but no monopoly profits, and I think we can model growth without invoking fixed factors. If we do that, spillovers will seem more harmful than beneficial, and strengthening property rights may improve welfare in cases where subsidies to innovation or imitation don't.

Grossman and Helpman (1994) argue that technology, rather than capital accumulation or external economies, drives growth. They think that most technical progress requires an intentional investment of resources by profit-seeking firms or entrepreneurs. They favor a model emphasizing successive improvements to a product, where each improvement creates temporary monopoly power. They treat knowledge "spillovers" as a problem, since spillovers cause growth to be slower than it should be. They even describe their approach as a general equilibrium one. Most of what they say does indeed seem consistent with the general equilibrium approach I favor. So I don't understand why they conclude with a statement that imperfect competition, incomplete appropriability, and increasing returns to scale are important in understanding growth. Indeed, the distinctions they make between their models and models emphasizing capital accumulation seem artificial. In effect, they are saying that technical growth is a form of capital accumulation. So why not use the capital accumulation models as a first approximation, and the "quality ladders" models with temporary monopoly power and local economies of scale as a second approximation? When we include various kinds of uncertainty in the simpler models emphasizing capital accumulation, they are sufficient to explain the broad facts, like continuing growth and differences across countries in realized growth. Why not just say we accumulate human and physical capital, much of which is technical?

Grossman and Shapiro (1982) look at the interaction between investment in general skills and availability of income insurance. In many of their models, but not all, insurance leads people to specialize more, and thus to invest less in general skills. Greater uncertainty reduces the amount of specialization in most cases. All of this is consistent with a general equilibrium approach, modified to allow for incomplete insurance markets. Their model shows how higher risk tolerance or more complete markets cause people to choose higher expected return and risk.

Hall (1978) says that consumer optimization implies that no variable other than current consumption should help significantly in predicting future consumption. That's his version of the "life cycle-permanent income hypothesis." He finds that past income doesn't help in predicting consumption, but that past stock market returns do. He modifies the hypothesis by saying that some part of consumption takes time to adjust to a change in permanent income, thus suggesting a preference for smooth consumption. I have no problem with the permanent income hypothesis as a rough measure of how people act, but with general utility functions, consumer optimization does not require it. Even if people use all available information in deciding on current consumption, they can have patterns in consumption that depend on the history of shocks to tastes and technology.

Hall (1988a) discusses the influence of career prospects on employment decisions. He notes that the value of employment fluctuates much more than the cash wage, partly because the probability of promotion varies (p. 273). He even mentions the effects of regional and sectoral shifts on unemployment (p. 275). His explanations rely on factors that go beyond normal forces of supply and demand in perfectly competitive markets, but much of what he says applies equally to a general equilibrium model.

Hall (1988b) develops a simple two-sector business cycle model with shocks to both preferences and technology. Preference shocks affect the relative demand for the two goods, rather than the relative demand for goods and leisure, as in a conventional real business cycle model. Thus this model moves in the direction of a full general equilibrium model. He is able to explain why relative prices need not move in any systematic way with business conditions. He has a version of the model where firms in one sector have market power, but I don't think he needs that to give the features he wants. I favor continuing to develop the competitive version of his model, by adding such features as commitment to technology and a multisector labor market. Having both taste and technology shocks will be sufficient, I think, to give noncyclical relative prices in a fuller model.

Hall (1988c) claims that price far exceeds marginal cost for most U.S. industries, because when output rises, firms sell the output for considerably more than they pay for the incremental inputs. He finds that variation in output is large compared with variation in labor input times labor's share of output. He figures a conventional Solow residual and relates it to those instrumental variables that he feels should be unrelated to variation in productivity: military spending, the world oil price, and the political party of the president. He interprets the strong relation he finds as evidence for imperfect competition. He considers, but rejects, overhead inputs and labor hoarding as alternate explanations. I consider many of his assumptions extreme and unrealistic, including (1) that the real wage doesn't vary, (2) that productivity growth is a constant plus an error term with special properties, and (3) that marginal cost is constant below 100% use of capacity and is otherwise high. More fundamentally, I object to his use of a conventional asymmetric, instantaneous production function with the capital input measured at book value and the labor input measured in hours. If we measure output and all inputs at market value, and include human capital along with physical capital, and allow for varying utilization of both physical and human capital through varying hours and varying effort per hour, his conclusions collapse. Labor's share of output is no longer a key element of the model, and the fractional change in output is essentially the sum of fractional changes in technology, composite capital, and utilization. Variation in utilization can easily explain all of the cyclical output variation, even without bringing in variation in technology and in composite capital.

Hall (1989) surveys the literature on consumption, emphasizing tests of the Euler equation, which he describes as "the rational expectations permanent income model with constant expected real interest rate" (p. 172). He notes that this model does not fit the data, since past values of real income and financial variables help in predicting consumption changes. He considers possible explanations of this poor fit, including durable goods and the durability of consumption, liquidity restraints, and intertemporal substitution. While I think all these "explanations" are important facts about the world, I don't think there is any puzzle to explain. The Euler equation is based on time-separable and state-independent utility with an unchanging local utility function. I can think of no economic reason to make these assumptions about utility.

Hall (1990) discusses the apparent failure of the invariance properties of the Solow residual. His possible explanations include

market power, increasing returns, external technical complementarities, chronic excess capacity, unmeasured fluctuations in work
effort and hours, errors in measuring capital, errors in measuring
output, and monopoly power in the labor market. He rejects such
explanations as overhead labor and labor hoarding, wage
smoothing, adjustment costs, and price rigidity. He favors
explanations involving market power and increasing returns. In a
general equilibrium world, I fail to understand this whole line of
inquiry. When we measure the human and physical capital inputs to
production in efficiency units, and when we think of both hours and
effort per hour as measuring utilization of human and physical
capital, the properties of the Solow residual change completely. For
reasons given in Alchian (1959), I think it's very hard to reject
constant returns to scale when an item's cost depends on such
factors as the total quantity produced, the time taken to produce it,
and the time to plan the production run. In sum, I don't see what we
learn from trying to measure Solow's productivity residual or its
invariance properties in a multidimensional general equilibrium
world.

Hall (1991) discusses business cycle models that fall mostly outside
the general equilibrium framework, because they have increasing
returns to scale, minor noise with big effects, and a price level that
matters. But many of his points sound remarkably similar to mine.
What he calls "temporal agglomeration," with externalities, I call
"team production," with constant returns to scale. What he calls the
"nonconvexity" that causes someone to work a full day or not at all,
I model as a big differential between the wages for full- and part-
time work. He has noise in the form of a few minor events that have
big effects on the timing of agglomeration, while my noise is a
collection of many mostly minor realizations of uncertainty about
tastes and technology. My noise has big effects too, but it's part of
general equilibrium. We differ most on monetary policy, which I
regard as largely passive, without a significant role in an economy
with good financial markets and tax collection.

Hall (1993) tries to understand the recession of 1990–1991 in the
context of a number of major schools of macroeconomic thought.
He lists eight possible causes, from a shift in monetary policy to a
spontaneous decline in consumption. He finds that none of the
major schools can explain the details of this recession: there was no
outside force acting at that time, nor was there a coincidence of

forces of the kind people usually talk about. He sees a "cascading of negative responses," as small events had large consequences, which we can only understand by moving away from established neoclassical models. He omits, however, a detailed sectoral analysis of the recession. He starts on one by discussing Iraq's invasion of Kuwait, which led to an oil price shock and a decline in willingness to buy cars. If he continues this analysis, adding more and more detail along many dimensions, I think he'll find that we can explain this recession, and others, within some versions of the traditional neoclassical framework.

Ham (1986) applies conventional econometric methods to PSID data for 1971 to 1979 in trying to "test" the hypothesis that unemployment is a form of nonmarket time chosen by individuals on the basis of current and expected future wage rates. He says his test rejects the simple model he tries. As he notes, independent residuals and especially separable utility are important assumptions for his test, but he gives no economic reasons for them. I find the model he tests, which implies that people act the same in years when they are unemployed as in years when they are employed, to be inherently unreasonable. But I find the view that people are "off their supply curves" equally unreasonable. Thus I favor moving to more complex models of intertemporal substitution, which Ham says will be very difficult to test. That means they will be difficult to reject, so it is good news for these models.

Hamilton (1988) has an equilibrium model of unemployment and business cycles. Workers are specialized. They are unemployed either because they are changing sectors or because they are waiting for better conditions. The marginal products of employed workers can exceed the reservation wages of those without jobs. He works out a specific example with two sectors, and emphasizes energy and other primary commodity shocks as having economywide effects. His model is an example like many of the examples I use, though I would put more emphasis on shocks to a broad range of tastes and technologies.

Hansen (1985) adds indivisible labor to a conventional real business cycle model as a way of explaining why employment fluctuates more than hours per worker, why total hours fluctuate a lot though the measured real wage doesn't seem to, and why part-time workers earn less per hour than full-time workers. In his equilibrium, workers are identical, and the ones who work in any period are chosen by lottery. With perfect unemployment insurance, the equilibrium is efficient. His model inherits all the problems of the conventional real business cycle model, especially the problems that come from assuming all workers are identical. Using a general equilibrium approach, we can explain all the facts without this device. We use durable goods, team production, unmeasured wages, and shocks to tastes and technology across many microsectors to explain unemployment variation. We find that the average real wage, properly measured, varies a lot, and we find that part-time workers earn less because obsolescence makes their human capital worth less.

Hansen (1993) constructs an "efficiency units" measure of labor input from 1955 to 1988 using U.S. data on hours and earnings in nonagricultural industries, classified by age and sex. He finds smaller fluctuations in the efficiency units series, as we expect if hours show greater cyclical fluctuations in low-wage categories. He also finds that productivity measured in efficiency units is more highly contemporaneously correlated with GNP than productivity measured in physical units. He finds that total hours increase over this period, while efficiency units do not. Though he doesn't say so, this discrepancy may reflect the arrival in this period of the "baby boom generation," plus the increasing proportion of women in the labor force. I agree that his measure of effort makes more sense than total hours worked, but effort is only one part of labor input. Human capital is the other part, and is especially important in explaining changes over long periods. I suspect that we can identify effort better by trying to isolate the temporary components of wage income.

Hansen and Prescott (1993) use a version of the conventional real business cycle model to explore the 1990–1991 recession. They use a model with three inputs (capital, hours, and land) and three outputs (consumer-nondurables, consumer-durables, and producer-durables); and they ask whether technology shocks caused the recession. They conclude that their model "predicts" the recession but not the slow recovery, so technology shocks caused the recession but not the slow recovery. I question both their model and their conclusions. Their model shares the problems of all similar models: for example, it has fixed factors (labor and land) but no human capital and no real estate improvements; it has a real interest rate but no price of risk; and it has temporary shocks to output but no permanent shocks. The model has special problems that show up because it has three sectors: the consumer and producer durables sectors have their own "technology shocks," which are also the inverses of the equilibrium relative prices of consumer durables and capital in terms of consumption. If technology shocks are "supply shifts," then Hansen and Prescott are using a price change to measure a supply shift without considering possible demand shifts; as I see it, price changes depend on both technology shifts and taste shifts. Three sectors are better than one and I think consumer durables played a special role in the Depression of the 1930s, but I think we need millions of sectors to understand the varying match between tastes and technology that causes business cycles. Calibration, like correlation, does not tell us about the structure of the economy, so I do not believe they have isolated the effects of technology shocks. They identify technology shocks with changes in knowledge, while I identify them with changing expectations about the uncertain payoff from sector-specific investments. They say that besides technology shocks, shifts in the legal, regulatory, and political environment affect business cycles; I think such shifts have a minor effect compared to taste shifts, though the *average* environment affects volatility, income, and growth. I am especially puzzled by their claim that lower saving or the deferral of business investment can slow a recovery; in their model, this means only a shift of resources to the consumption sector.

Hansen and Jagannathan (1991) show that when utility is time-separable and state-independent, and when we know the mean payoffs from risky assets (along with the payoff covariances), we can restrict the admissible region for means and standard deviations of consumers' intertemporal marginal rates of substitution (IMRSs). They discuss a relaxation of their separability assumption; but with fully general von Neumann–Morgenstern utility, their restrictions have no analogue. They claim that we can observe IMRSs in complete markets (p. 226), but I think that's true only when we know the joint payoff distribution.

Hansen, Sargent, and Tallarini (1993) explore a family of intertemporal stochastic economies that are easy to simulate and that have a rich pattern of transient dynamics. They generalize quadratic utility to allow for "precautionary savings," and they generalize Ryder–Heal utility to allow for "habit persistence." Utility depends on the deviation of a flow of services from a "bliss point" for each consumption good. The flow of services comes from durables or just from past consumption. Preferences of this kind fall outside the von Neumann–Morgenstern universe. Their form of habit persistence introduces an "appetite for growth" because past consumption creates a floor for current consumption in the utility function. I don't know how many of their results will carry over to a general equilibrium model with conventional nonseparable utility. I doubt we can even define "precautionary savings" in an interesting way with general von Neumann–Morgenstern utility, and I like to add "consumption smoothing" to utility instead of "habit persistence." I think higher consumption today, holding consumption at other times fixed, should always give higher utility. Since they choose a heavily restricted nonstandard model for easy simulation, I don't know what we can conclude from their graphs.

Hayashi (1982) derives a theoretical model of the relations among marginal q, average q, and investment, taking account of tax rules and installation costs. The theory makes some sense as applied to an individual firm, though I doubt we can measure the firm's opportunities well enough to see when it's investing at the wrong rate. But I don't see how we can apply the theory to the economy as a whole. In his empirical work, Hayashi uses replacement cost estimates from Christensen and Jorgenson (1973). We can see from Table 1 that estimated replacement cost doesn't fluctuate much (p. 222). This is because the figures are book values rather than market values. I don't know what to make of estimates of q based on replacement cost figures like this.

Heaton (1993) explores a utility function that allows both local substitution and habit formation. He says that he finds more evidence for local substitution than for habit formation. He considers the effects of time averaging in consumption noted by Christiano, Eichenbaum, and Marshall (1991), but finds that he must still allow for nonseparable utility, especially when looking at monthly seasonally adjusted data and quarterly seasonally unadjusted data. He uses a utility function that depends on deviations from a "bliss point" that grows at a sure exponential rate matched to the observed growth rate of consumption. Like the Ryder and Heal (1973), Sundaresan (1989), and Constantinides (1990) utility functions, his violates the von Neumann–Morgenstern axioms (with positive prices). Under certain conditions, higher local consumption can mean lower utility. Moreover, he must assume that the utility discount rate equals the growth rate of capital. Finally, he boldly applies a model with little uncertainty to actual U.S. data. I think a simpler way to show that Christiano, Eichenbaum, and Marshall (1991) do not rescue separable utility is to show that estimated instantaneous consumption with seasonal and cyclical factors removed is smoother than wealth.

Helpman (1992) discusses "endogenous macroeconomic growth theory" with either "quality ladders" or "expanding varieties." Both approaches seem relevant to the economics of knowledge, but he must make restrictive assumptions to make them relevant to growth: in particular, he assumes fixed factors like "labor" that drive down the return to capital as it accumulates, and he assumes no real uncertainty. Without fixed factors, these theories can explain income as much as they explain growth. With uncertainty, especially combined with differentiated primary, intermediate, and final goods and services, we have a major reason for differences in income and growth across countries, plus a way to explain business cycles and growth together. I especially favor recognizing variation in relative prices between differentiated goods and services, which this literature generally doesn't do. He emphasizes externalities, but when we add negative externalities to the positive ones, as Aghion and Howitt (1992) do, I think we can ignore all of them, at least as a first approximation.

Hercowitz and Sampson (1991) note that labor effort can fluctuate in equilibrium not only because of temporary changes in labor productivity, but also because of temporary differences between the productivity of market work and homework. In their model, permanent changes in labor productivity are associated with such differences, since the capital and knowledge that add to the productivity of homework take time to build up. I think these effects are part of a full general equilibrium model, but I'm not convinced they are central. Hercowitz and Sampson use the obvious cyclicality of total labor effort (which varies more in the U.S. through total employment than through the average workweek) to isolate cyclical elements in GNP for the period from 1954 to 1987. Like Arrow (1962) and Romer (Paul, 1986), they model endogenous growth by treating human capital as "knowledge" that accrues in proportion to physical capital in productivity units. Thus knowledge is external to both firms and workers. I don't feel we need to model human capital this way to give sustained growth or any other feature of the world. I prefer using absence of fixed factors to give sustained growth, and diminishing returns to human and physical capital separately to give balanced growth. Hercowitz and Sampson, like Lucas and Prescott (1971), use a capital evolution equation that shows decreasing returns, reflecting adjustment costs in increasing the capital stock or diminishing returns in research activities. I prefer to use Alchian's (1959) approach so we can stick to constant returns. They show some skepticism about their data (using wages to proxy for the spot return on labor effort) and identifying assumptions (assuming the two innovations are independent), but I think more skepticism is warranted.

Hicks (1965) makes a strong case for using a utility function with complementarity between successive consumptions. In other words, he favors putting a preference for smooth consumption into the utility function.

Hillinger (1987) believes that measures of business activity have a periodic element as well as a random element. His spectral analysis of German gross national product, fixed investment, and inventory investment seem to support this view strongly. In general, he attributes it to the (partly psychological) cost of shifting stocks and flows from one area to another, so he relates the periods to asset lives. With some moderate changes, I think we could make his story consistent with a general equilibrium approach, where sectors producing durables show strong periodic patterns. I wonder what a similar spectral analysis shows when applied to activity in other countries.

Hofstede and Bond (1988) discuss the role of Confucian values in the growth of Singapore, Taiwan, South Korea, Hong Kong, and Japan since 1955. The values they find most relevant are (1) ordering relationships by status and hierarchy, (2) avoiding shame, (3) saving, and (4) persevering. I suspect these factors are quite important, along with others like "intelligence" and "luck."

Hosios (1994) models unemployment and vacancies with sectoral shifts. He emphasizes temporary layoffs along with permanent separations. He finds that a change in the separation rate causes unemployment and vacancies to move together, while a change in the variance of relative output prices causes them to move in opposite directions, though some people say that movement in opposite directions is evidence of aggregate demand shocks. He also notes that sector definitions are arbitrary: he goes to the level of individual firms. The driving force in his model is an externality:

workers on temporary layoff may search for new jobs, but they demand higher wages than those on permanent separation because they have better alternatives. When the proportion of job candidates on temporary layoff increases, firms find it less attractive to hire right away so they create fewer vacancies. I don't believe he captures the impact of sectoral shifts on unemployment and vacancies; in particular, I don't think we need an externality to explain why unemployment and vacancies move in opposite directions. Even in a general equilibrium model, vacancies often represent temporary hires, which mirror temporary layoffs. They are also a symptom of job moves associated with career advancement; such job moves are procyclical. Thus I think we expect unemployment and vacancies to move in opposite directions even without any change in the variance of relative output prices. What causes them to move is a change in the match between tastes and technology; in other words, a drawing from a huge joint distribution, rather than a change in the shape of the distribution.

Howitt (1988) has a model where job changes are costly for both firms and workers. He uses a Lucas-type island model with limited communication and money supply shocks. He emphasizes two sorts of externality: greater recruiting effort by firms means people who are unemployed find jobs more quickly; and each firm fails to take account of the effect of its current recruiting activities in raising future hiring costs by depleting the stock of unemployed workers. Neither of these externalities strikes me as central to business fluctuations. If he assumes all job search costs are internal, and if he converts his islands to dimensions in a general equilibrium model (dropping the causal role of money), he will have a model like mine. Costly job search and recruiting are surely central to equilibrium labor market behavior.

Hulten (1992) develops a model that allows for both embodied and disembodied technical change. He uses conventional growth accounting to estimate that best-practice technology exceeds the average level by around 23%, and that about 20% of the residual growth of quality-adjusted output can be attributed to embodied technical change. He says that shortening the age structure of capital can improve its productivity, but that this would have little overall impact on output growth. I can see little value in this kind of growth accounting, and I don't believe his numbers have economic meaning. If we shift to a symmetric production function and recognize that the stock of human and physical capital (measured in efficiency units) changes more because relevance changes than because of depreciation and investment, this entire exercise collapses. I'm especially puzzled by Hulten's statement that upgrading old plant and equipment will make capital more efficient. This is always true, but if businesses are making optimal investment decisions, it does not pay to accelerate the upgrading of old capital.

Imrohoroğlu and Prescott (1991) explore a model where intermediated government liabilities are the only assets that people can use to smooth consumption. They find that high inflation has a substantial welfare cost, since it makes assets with fixed nominal returns costly to hold. People thus hold fewer assets, on average, and face more volatile consumption. They do not explain how monetary policy determines the inflation rate. I think it does not: the inflation rate is exogenous and monetary policy is passive. They note that they omit insurance markets, but I think their omission of markets for real assets is more serious. With such markets, people can smooth consumption easily at any level of inflation. Inability to borrow easily against human capital affects the path of consumption, but this happens at any rate of inflation. Thus I don't think their results generalize to a fuller model.

Jones (1992) simulates a trading strategy in U.S. bonds (over the period 1979–1990), based on Mankiw's (1986a) observation that steep yield curves predict declining long bond yields in the United States, Canada, the United Kingdom, and Germany. He finds that the strategy would have been successful, in several variations and in both halves of the period. He favors Froot's (1989) "explanation," which says (based on surveys of interest rate expectations) that market participants don't change their views on future long yields enough when short yields change. I interpret this, though, as evidence that central bank use of monetary policy creates profit opportunities in bond markets by artificially distorting prices and yields.

Jones and Manuelli (1990) show that we can have continuing growth with convex technology and "fixed factors" if we assume that the marginal products of the variable factors are bounded above zero. To me, this is like saying that the fixed factors are not really fixed. I don't understand why they want to preserve a model with fixed factors. They end, though, by calling for a model that combines growth and fluctuations, and for a model with multiple consumer goods and multiple capital goods.

Jones, Manuelli, and Rossi (1993) analyze optimal taxation in three endogenous growth models. The third model looks primarily at tax questions, but we can use the first two models to study growth, even though they assume a world of certainty. The models are all free of fixed factors, so we can take an economy's growth rate as depending on impatience and the return to capital rather than on the exogenous growth of technology. The models treat human capital seriously; in fact, the first model treats human and physical capital symmetrically. Both kinds of capital are used in producing output, which is then divided between consumption, new physical capital, and new human capital. The amounts of physical and human capital stay in balance as the economy grows. I find this the most natural model. The second model introduces endogenous leisure, but also suggests a special production process for human capital that is nothing like the process that gives consumption and physical capital. They treat output of human capital as a convex function of direct investment in human capital and effective labor devoted to production of human capital. Why a convex function of *investment* and effective labor rather than *capital* and effective labor? Among versions of their second model, I prefer one that treats output of human capital as simply the sum of direct investment and the wage value of time spent creating it.

Jorgenson and Fraumeni (1992) summarize their work on the relation between education and growth. They emphasize the role of human capital in production. Their estimates of the amount of U.S. human capital are more than ten times estimates by Kendrick (1976) and others, partly because they count the value of student time as one of the inputs to education. They emphasize the diversity of types of human and physical capital. They do not, however, seem to take account of capital revaluations due to shifts in tastes or technology among these types. In general, they have more faith in their econometric methods than I do. While they say it's less important than growth in inputs, they even think they can measure a Solow residual.

Jovanovic (1987) shows that in the presence of "strategic complementarities," independent micro shocks can produce any amount of aggregate risk in a unique equilibrium. In the general equilibrium approach, we have no strategic complementarities, and micro shocks along many dimensions are somewhat dependent across agents, since all rational agents make the same assumptions when they invest in human and physical capital. This approach can also explain any amount of aggregate risk in a unique equilibrium.

Jovanovic and Lach (1991) model growth in technology in the form of newly invented intermediate goods, as in Romer (Paul, 1990b). They observe that societies take a long time to adopt technology and technologies suit them differently, which can create a good deal of persisting inequality. They say that "invention" of new products and processes is the only kind of shock to technology. In their model, these shocks seem largely unrelated to conventional business cycles. I like their emphasis on diverse elements in technology, and I view their model as suggesting that random shifts can explain some of the persistence in inequality of GNP across countries; but I think they define their technology shock far too narrowly and ignore analogous taste shocks. If they make their production function strictly convex, generalize their technology shock, and add endowment differences and multidimensional taste shocks to a model with both human and physical capital, I think they will find that they can explain both conventional business cycles and inequality in GNP.

Jovanovic and Moffitt (1990) look at the mobility of workers who vary in age and experience, using the National Longitudinal Survey of Young Men, with observations every two years from 1966 to 1981. They find that mobility generally declined over this period (for workers of a given age). When they look at mobility among three sectors (manufacturing, services and trade, and other), they find that gross flows averaged about ten times net flows. The ratio of gross flows to net flows seems strongly procyclical, though they do not highlight this fact. Because gross flows are so much bigger than net flows (and for other reasons), they feel that "sectoral shifts" can explain only a small part of mobility. They explain the remaining part of mobility as due to "rematching" of workers with jobs, after discovering that the match is imperfect. This rematching process could also describe the situation where a match starts out well, but deteriorates because the worker outgrows his job. Normally such a worker is simply promoted to a better job, in the same firm or a different firm. They find that workers who shift sectors earn less than similar workers who stay put, which is consistent with the notion that starting on a new career path involves a loss of human capital. The worker who moves earns less at first, but expects to earn more than if he stays. Some of their findings are due to use of a crude sectoral analysis along a single dimension: if they treated each job as a separate sector and divided time finely, the ratio of gross to net mobility would fall sharply. I think a finer sectoral analysis would also change the proportion of mobility that they assign to sectoral moves rather than rematching. Finally, they estimate that the option to change firms increases GNP between 6% and 9%. If they could estimate the value of the option to change jobs rather than firms, this proportion would rise enormously.

Jovanovic and Rob (1990) analyze long waves and short waves in a Schumpeterian process of discovery and refinement. They give an axiomatic description of the space within which invention and development take place. (I find at least two of the four axioms restrictive rather than intuitive.) In their model, everything depends on a measure of growth opportunities and a measure of the relative cost of extensive and intensive search. (Extensive search is like basic research.) The model shows cycles when growth opportunities are in an intermediate range—not too low and not too high. They treat knowledge as freely available to all, so this is more a model of society's choices than a model of a firm's choices. As they note, it is not a model of macro fluctuations. Still, the idea that technology has many dimensions, where we can either develop an existing dimension or start a new one, is essential, I believe, in understanding both business cycles and variation in economic growth.

Kahn (1987) shows that we can easily explain the volatility of production relative to sales by creating an inventory model with stockout avoidance where sales rates show positive serial correlation and the firm can backlog orders. Thus he shows we do not need supply shocks to explain the volatility of production.

Kahn (1992) models the inventory behavior of the U.S. auto industry. He finds that demand uncertainty plays a bigger role than cost uncertainty, and that firms hold inventories more to avoid costly stockouts than to smooth production. He does not find "excess" production variability. He does all this with a model where sales shocks are independent and identically distributed. I think he'd strengthen his results if he used a model where some sales shocks are permanent. He comes close to that in his 1987 paper.

Kandel and Stambaugh (1991) use nonexpected-utility preferences (as in Epstein and Zin (1989)) to look at the means, volatilities, and predictability of asset returns. They separate the roles of risk aversion and intertemporal substitution; in particular, they find lower values of the elasticity of intertemporal substitution associated with higher equity return volatilities. They use the endowment framework of Lucas (1978), where consumption goods are exogenous and perishable, combined with a Markov regime-switching model for the mean and standard deviation of consumption growth. I think we can create as much flexibility as we need without going outside general von Neumann–Morgenstern preferences. Indeed, I think we can match any possible combination of means, volatilities, and predictability for asset returns with reasonable assumptions about risk aversion and willingness to substitute consumption through time.

Kelly (1992) uses a model in the spirit of Long and Plosser (1983), but with stochastic factor productivities, to show that output converges across economies in most cases with constant returns to scale and persistent growth. I think this is one among many multisector models showing convergence. In other models, we can easily create divergence too, without relying on increasing returns to scale.

Kemeny, Morgenstern, and Thompson (1956) generalize von Neumann's (1945) model of multisector economic growth to allow some production processes to use fewer than all the goods produced in the previous period, and to allow for consumption or outside demand. Then the growth rate can be less than the interest rate, which makes the model more plausible. It is still a kind of general equilibrium model with many sectors, but it lacks uncertainty, so we can't use it to model the causes of business cycles and growth variation.

Khan and Ohanian (1993) add heterogeneity in plants and managerial span of control to a conventional real business cycle model. Plants differ in productivity, which agents come to know only gradually. Production shows constant returns to managers, capital, and labor, but decreasing returns to capital and labor only. Closing a plant means a manager can open a new one that uses frontier technology. They try to explain things like the cyclical behavior of entry and exit for plants that differ in age and size. They even try to match certain quantitative features of the U.S. economy. Their model inherits the serious structural problems of the standard real business cycle model, including asymmetric production. I don't know why they focus on variation in productivity across plants. The effects of this kind of heterogeneity are swamped by the effects of heterogeneity in inputs and outputs. If we want to understand business cycles and growth, that's the kind of heterogeneity we need.

King (Ian, 1993) surveys the research on sectoral shifts in unemployment. He says the central message of this literature is that heterogeneity is important: among firms, workers, plants, and even jobs. He suggests creating models where workers differ in age and ability and can buy human capital, and where firms choose sector, technology, and plant size. His title comes from his feeling that we don't fully understand such facts as the large variation in job destruction over the business cycle, but I feel the kind of general equilibrium model he favors can easily explain all the facts he cites.

King (Robert, 1990) uses a conventional real business cycle model with separable utility, no human capital, and no uncertainty to analyze the impact on consumption, leisure, output, and investment of temporary and more permanent changes in government purchases (financed through lump-sum taxes). He follows Hicks in dividing the effects into wealth effects and substitution effects. He analyzes disturbances to a steady state. He can do this because labor acts as a fixed factor in the conventional model. If we take away the fixed factor by adding human capital on a par with physical capital, our conclusions change completely. Now there are only wealth effects, which depend on the present value of all future government purchases. The effects of temporary and permanent changes in government purchases differ only in magnitude. Hours do not fluctuate. In other words, with no fixed factors we cannot begin to think about shifts in government purchases as a significant force behind business fluctuations or cycles. King's goal is to give researchers a tool for analyzing existing business cycle theories, but his tool does not work on theories that lack fixed factors.

King, Plosser, and Rebelo (1988a, 1988b) describe the conventional real business cycle approach to growth and fluctuation. They emphasize the fact that in their models, fluctuation in effort is driven by changes in wealth and in the real interest rate, not by wage changes. They add human capital, but treat their revised production function as asymmetric in physical and human capital. They add "labor market heterogeneity," but only by assuming that agents differ in productivity; I think we must focus on heterogeneity in skills along many dimensions. They note that in a model with no fixed factors, there is no steady-state growth path, but that the ratio of human to physical capital can vary around a steady-state level. Since I think conventional real business cycle models have many structural defects,

I don't make much of the authors' attempts to "calibrate" the model to match the variances and covariances of various measures of economic activity. For example, they create a consumption series that is smoother than the output series without invoking a preference for smooth consumption. Even to use their models as examples, I think we need to change them. I would change their model with human capital by converting variation in the constant out front into variation in "effective" human and physical capital; by allowing utilization of physical capital to vary along with effort in both sectors; and by assuming that shocks to human capital, physical capital, effort, and utilization of physical capital are all highly correlated. I would interpret the shocks to all four variables as caused by underlying shifts in tastes and technology that we do not model explicitly in this simple reduced form.

King, Plosser, Stock, and Watson (1991) study output, consumption, and investment figures to find out what role permanent productivity shocks play. They say that when they add measures of money, the price level, and the nominal interest rate, permanent productivity shocks explain less than half of a measure of fluctuations. I am puzzled by their econometric methods: they adopt "identifying restrictions" that don't seem motivated by economics, and imply that they can then use correlations to infer causation. In particular, they assume that shocks to the common stochastic trend in output, consumption, and investment represent permanent productivity shocks. I can't think of any reliable way to identify productivity shocks using aggregate data, especially when most productivity shocks are sector-specific. Similarly, I can't think of a meaningful way to ask what proportion of the variability we see is explained by productivity shocks.

King and Rebelo (1988) extend Uzawa's (1965) analysis of endogenous growth. They allow investment in human capital, and they even look at a "one-sector model" where human and physical capital move together. This means they don't have a fixed factor, so surprises have permanent effects on the economy's path. Adding human capital and taking away the fixed factor are steps in the right direction, I think. We can reinterpret the technology shock in the one-sector version of their model as a shock to the price of capital. This makes growth entirely endogenous, and makes taste and technology shocks indistinguishable. They emphasize transformations that create stationary variables, but do not talk much about how those variables act. Thus they don't say much about cycles. A general equilibrium model could give the abstract macroeconomic behavior they describe, but I'd like to see more specific discussion of the sources of cyclical fluctuations involving stochastic shocks and mean reversion or cycles with specific periods, where temporary and permanent shocks are correlated. I'd like to see discussion involving consumption smoothing, durables, or even the match between tastes and technology. They also omit the trade-off between risk and growth through technology choice: people can choose large fluctuations with higher growth, or stability with lower growth.

King and Rebelo (1993) show a particular problem with the conventional neoclassical model of growth, where at least one factor of production is nonreproducible. Lengthy transitions to the steady state can occur only with very low intertemporal substitution, which implies very high initial marginal products. I suspect that their conclusion carries over somehow to a model with first order uncertainty and nonseparable utility, even though we must then distinguish between willingness to shift consumption through time and willingness to take risk. (With time-separable utility, these two aspects of preferences are inseparable.) They argue that these peculiar properties imply that we should move to a model with a broader definition of capital, and perhaps no fixed factors at all. I agree. I think this is one of many reasons to move to such a model.

Krane and Braun (1991) look at evidence of production smoothing for a number of commodities where they are able to find physical-product measures of production, inventories, and sales. In 25 out of 38 cases, the variance of detrended production is less than the variance of detrended shipments. Thus much of the evidence for the "production smoothing puzzle" may be just bad data. Their analysis also suggests that the standard optimization problem, with one-period trade-offs between production and inventory costs that are quadratic functions of production, inventories, sales, and seasonal factors, does not capture the decision-making environment of many industries. In other words, the model that suggests the puzzle is too restrictive. Rather than giving up our conventional general equilibrium assumptions, we can try another model.

Kremer (1993) describes a plausible production process in which a mistake at any point can greatly reduce the value of output. High-quality workers are those who make few mistakes. In his "O-ring" production function, named for the *Challenger* disaster, quantity cannot be substituted for quality. Workers are sorted into firms and countries by quality, and small differences in worker skill can give large differences in wages and output. He uses the theory to help explain the large income differences between countries, the predominance of small firms in poor countries, and the positive correlations among the wages of workers in different occupations within firms. When workers are perfectly matched, his analysis is consistent with general equilibrium, so it helps explain some facts that might otherwise seem puzzling. He suggests that when workers are imperfectly matched because their skill levels are uncertain, we may gain by subsidizing education; but he does not give a detailed model of how such subsidies might work. The same information problems that interfere with the match will interfere with an efficient system of subsidies. In fact, a subsidy system demands information about who gains the most skill from added training but is least able to finance his own training, and the political will to discriminate on this basis. On the surface, this seems even more difficult than matching, which requires only information about current skill levels.

Kremer and Thomson (1994) analyze convergence toward steady-state growth in several versions of the conventional neoclassical growth model supplemented with human capital and applied to a small open economy. They assume perfect capital markets (in a nonstochastic world). They write production as depending separately on the human capital of young and old workers, and they emphasize on-the-job training along with formal education. The features they add to the conventional model are reasonable and are similar in some ways to the models I use (especially my "migration" model above). They need these features to explain "slow convergence," because the conventional model predicts fast convergence. I prefer to eliminate the fixed factor in the conventional model, which eliminates the "instantaneous convergence puzzle" before we start.

Krieger (1989) looks at international data on output fluctuations by country and by industry. She claims to find evidence against a "strong" version of real business cycle theory in the fact that country shocks seem to "explain" more of the movements in output than industry shocks. She says she uses fewer identifying restrictions than Stockman (1988), but she gives no economic reasons for the ones she does use. I take her study to be an attempt to use correlation to infer causation. Nothing she finds seems inconsistent with a multidimensional general equilibrium model of output fluctuations.

Kydland (1984) looks at labor force heterogeneity in "equilibrium" business cycle models. He uses a standard growth model with a small number of free parameters. (I consider that a defect rather than a virtue.) His heterogeneity involves only two kinds of workers (skilled and unskilled), whereas I believe we must think of labor (and capital) as varying along many dimensions in order to understand business cycles.

Kydland (1995) adds a model of on-the-job learning to a conventional real business cycle model of aggregate labor market fluctuations. He assumes that in each period a certain fraction of workers at each skill level advances to the next level. Both the skill levels and the fraction advancing are constant in his model, while they are strongly procyclical in the world. Thus I don't think his results carry over to a more realistic model that corrects both the defects in conventional real business cycle models and the inflexibilities in his model of on-the-job learning.

Kydland and Prescott (1980) use an equilibrium model of fluctuations to ask whether stable tax policy pays. They find that stabilizing output is possible but undesirable. They use productivity shocks that vary across individual "islands" and monetary shocks. They use nonseparable utility with a form of work satiation: added hours of work increase the utility of leisure. They emphasize the time it takes to build a capital asset as providing persistence. They note that "the" real wage must be procyclical in their model, but that measurement error and long-term contracts make it look less procyclical. If I were to redesign their model, I would make the islands "jobs" that differ along many dimensions; I would make the shocks to tastes and technology mostly relative rather than aggregate; I would eliminate the monetary shocks; and I would not try to match the numerical values in the model with features of the economy. Since the shocks would not be comparable across islands, computing the "average" shock would not be meaningful, so we would not be able to set it to zero. People would change jobs (or move out of and into the same job) not because leisure substitutes easily between present and future, but because total compensation in a job changes sharply.

Kydland and Prescott (1982) create a model that combines growth and fluctuations, and matches both micro and macro stylized facts. They emphasize multiperiod construction of capital goods. They assume that leisure and unemployment are the same, and they make utility depend on an average of current and past leisure to induce large changes in hours worked over the business cycle. Instead of emphasizing a price per unit of capital that has random walk features, they have a technology shock with random walk features. Instead of treating "persistence" as a natural result of durable investments, they have persistent shocks and use multiperiod construction. They claim a model with "adjustment costs" fails to explain the facts, but I think a fuller cost model, as outlined by Alchian (1959), can easily explain the relevant facts. In general, they will have an easier time explaining things if they relax some of the constraints in their model. When they try fitting their model to data, they look at fluctuations around the model's steady state. A more general model with first order uncertainty and no fixed factors has no steady-state growth path, so their conclusions are unlikely to carry over to a model like that.

Kydland and Prescott (1990) report some business cycle facts, including the observation that the price level since World War II has moved countercyclically. They find that hours worked is strongly procyclical and varies almost as much as real GNP, while a conventional measure of the capital stock varies smoothly and lags the cycle by at least a year. The inventory stock lags the cycle by half a year and is nearly as volatile as quarterly real GNP. Employment accounts for about two-thirds of the standard deviation in total hours, while hours per worker accounts for about one-third. When they weight hours per worker by an estimate of average human capital in figuring the real wage, they find that the real wage is strongly procyclical. The bulk of the volatility in aggregate output is "due to" investment expenditures. Consumer nondurables and services are relatively smooth and government purchases are noncyclical. Imports are procyclical with no phase shift, while exports are procyclical with a lag of six months to a year. Capital income is more procyclical than conventionally measured labor income. Money is procyclical, but generally lags. If I were reporting similar facts, I would try harder to convert all quantities to efficiency units. This makes such quantities as capital, labor compensation, and the real wage much more procyclical.

Kydland and Prescott (1991a) describe a quantitative general equilibrium approach to business cycles, where we measure willingness and ability to substitute. They contrast their approach with the earlier "system-of-equations" approach, where we measure behavioral equations. They include both a household sector and a business sector. They use the conventional heavily restricted real business cycle model. They consider, but reject, a time-nonseparable utility function. Since they do not give economic reasons for restricting their model, I don't know what to make of the numbers they come up with. In particular, I think their estimate of the percentage contribution of technology shocks to business cycle fluctuations is highly model-dependent. Indeed, in a full general equilibrium model I'm not sure it makes sense to ask how shocks are divided between taste and technology shocks.

Kydland and Prescott (1991b) add simultaneous variation in both hours per worker and the number of workers to a conventional real business cycle model. They assume that workweeks of different lengths are different commodities, and that an agent is constrained to supply one unit of one and only one of this range of commodities. They assume that utilization of physical capital varies, and that resources are used when agents move between the household sector and the market sector. They estimate that the "Solow technology parameter" accounts for about 70% of the fluctuations of output around its steady-state path. All these assumptions take Kydland and Prescott in the right direction, but they are very far from overcoming the limitations of the conventional model. For example, adjustment costs for moves between labor and leisure (as with layoff and recall, if we count waiting for recall as leisure) are trivial compared with total adjustment costs in reallocating human and physical capital. Their definition of "technology shock" and mine have almost nothing in common, so I don't even know what they mean (in economic terms) when they say that technology shocks account for a certain percentage of output fluctuations. With my approach, if we assume that governments reflect the wishes of the governed, all shocks are either technology shocks or taste shocks, defined along many dimensions. If I had to guess, I'd say each accounts for about 50% of the shocks to output. But my 50% is not comparable to Kydland and Prescott's 70%.

Kydland and Prescott (1993) redefine the labor input to production. They weight hours for each person in a PSID sample by average compensation per hour over the entire period from 1969 to 1982. They take this weight to be roughly proportional to human capital. Their measure of the labor input fluctuates much less than unweighted hours, since people who earn more have more stable employment. Their measure of the "implicit real wage" is strongly procyclical and is strongly correlated with their labor input. Their measure of the Solow technology coefficient fluctuates nearly as much as their labor input. They are moving in the right direction, since adding hours of different workers surely does not make sense, but I don't think they put enough action into human capital. They treat human capital as fixed over the business cycle, but then analyze variations in the "productivity per unit labor input" over the cycle. Surely wage or productivity variation is associated with variation in human capital! Kydland and Prescott focus on units of capital rather than unit value, and define units as unchanging over their measurement period. This makes the return per unit vary a lot, and puts a lot of action into what they call the "Solow technology coefficient." They do not explain why that coefficient measures cyclical variation in technology rather than tastes. I like, though, their discussion of human capital as part of the labor input to production.

Leamer (1994) asks for a better balance among issues, theory, and data. He emphasizes trade, but his comments apply to almost all areas of economics. Once we have formulated a theory to fit the issues we care about, he suggests "estimating" rather than "testing." I'm more pessimistic: I think all we can do is "explore." When trying to use the Heckscher–Ohlin theory, he notes that the relative number of commodities and factors plays a key role, which is odd. He suggests exploring models with more commodities than factors, while I find models with more factors than commodities more reasonable. All of the examples in this book have more factors than commodities, and assuming as many commodities as factors gives peculiar results like the factor price equalization theorem. He finds openness in trade very hard to measure, and he thinks it better to relate change in openness to growth than to relate openness to growth. He struggles with attempts to estimate "total factor productivity," especially when technology is embodied in costly human capital. In the end, he finds that few studies cast light on the central issue of international economics: "How, if at all, should governments intervene in international commerce?"

Leonard (1987) looks at structural and frictional unemployment using a complete survey of Wisconsin establishments in the unemployment insurance program. In 1978, it covered 125,000 establishments averaging ten employees. He finds enormous changes in individual establishments not explained by industry or regional trends. This variance can explain much of the unemployment that Lilien's (1982) measures of cross-industry variance do not explain. He concludes that this part of unemployment arises "not from the instability of people nor the instability of aggregate demand, but rather fundamentally from the instability of jobs" (p. 161).

Lewis (1993) asks, in the context of the standard real business cycle model, why changes in consumption are not perfectly correlated across countries. She finds little evidence that nonseparability in utility between leisure and consumption explains it. Highlighting durable goods and nontraded goods explains more. Taxes and other restrictions on cross-border investment explain the most. She finds the loss of welfare associated with the imperfect correlation is modest for industrial countries, but could be equivalent to 2–3% of annual output in general. I find her conclusions plausible, but I question her methods. As is customary in the standard model, she makes extensive use of the simple Euler equation, even though we know that utility is time-nonseparable. She uses unemployment as a proxy for leisure, which fits the practice of treating leisure and unemployment as equivalent, but which I find very odd. Does that mean we can replace leisure with unemployment in the utility function? Holding consumption fixed, does unemployment make us happy? I think consumption growth is imperfectly correlated across countries because people in different countries consume different things; because people do not diversify their human capital holdings for incentive reasons; because of barriers to cross-border equity investments; because of the "home bias;" because of consumption smoothing; and because of measurement error. If our formal tests don't confirm this, we should throw out the tests.

Lilien (1982) tries to assess the contribution of sectoral shifts to unemployment. He measures dispersion across 21 two-digit manufacturing industries by the variance of their hire rates. He finds dispersion substantially related to unemployment in the 1970s, though not in the 1960s. He finds that unexpected monetary growth is related to unemployment too. When Davis and Haltiwanger (1990, 1992) look at individual plants, they find a more consistent correlation of the same kind. Dispersion in net hiring is countercyclical, while overall net hiring is procyclical, so "job destruction" varies much more than "job creation." We cannot say, though, that this means sectoral shifts cause unemployment or changes in unemployment. Shifts in tastes and technology along many dimensions cause most of it, but we can't classify such shifts as "aggregate" or "sectoral" in any meaningful way.

Long and Plosser (1983) show that comovement, persistence, and other business cycle features come out of a model without monetary disturbances, government activity, incomplete information, biased expectations, nonmaximizing behavior, adjustment costs, or any sort of market failure. They assume both tastes and technology are known, so they do not describe their multicommodity shocks to output as technology shocks. In a sense, they do have adjustment costs, since their production process involves perishable intermediate goods of many kinds. One of their basic ideas is that when wealth is high, people will add to spending on all goods, both current and future, even when the output shock involves only a single current good. Since they use separable and state-independent utility, and since they do not have human capital, their model of labor markets does not have much structure. In fact, in their specific example, neither the real wage nor unemployment fluctuates at all.

Long and Plosser (1987) study the covariance structure of innovations in output across 13 industries. They find that the first factor explains a median of 16% of the variance at monthly intervals and 41% at quarterly intervals. They interpret this increase with interval size as due to propagation of shocks across sectors. I interpret it as mostly due to natural and artificial smoothing of the reported output data. I would use stock returns for this kind of study. They view the common factor as evidence of aggregate shocks (perhaps from government policy), while I view it as evidence of the size of the first factor in the covariance structure of taste and technology surprises.

Loungani (1991) regresses British unemployment from 1920 to 1938 on (1) the crosssection standard deviation of industry stock returns, (2) monetary base growth, and (3) the unemployment-benefits-to-wages ratio. The stock return variable comes in most strongly, especially with a two-year lag. The others seem significant in some versions of the regression. Since it's just a regression, we can't really infer cause and effect directly. I especially doubt the relevance of monetary policy, though Loungani writes as if he assumes it matters. Similarly, I think unemployment benefits have to be important, even if they don't seem significant in the regression.

Loungani and Rogerson (1989) study data on sectoral reallocation from the Michigan Panel Study of Income Dynamics. They find that the flow of workers from durable goods sectors to services accelerates during recessions, while the flow from services to stable employment in durables accelerates during booms. The proportion of the unemployed who are changing sectors increases during recessions. They note that reallocation can occur either when its cost is low (as in a recession) or when gains are high (as when pay or growth differentials are high).

Loungani, Rush, and Tave (1990) find that a dispersion index that uses stock prices from different industries helps predict unemployment. They note that Lilien's (1982) relation between output dispersion and unemployment is close to coincident, but that dispersion measured from stock prices leads unemployment by as much as two or three years. Stock price dispersion reflects changes that investors expect to be permanent, while output dispersion may be temporary. They do not find that unemployment is related to their measure of aggregate demand once we allow for dispersion. I think the stock price measure that looks closest to what Abraham and Katz (1986) mean by "aggregate demand" is just the level of or return on the market as a whole. I think that measure does help explain unemployment, even after we account for dispersion, but I don't say it measures aggregate demand. Loungani, Rush, and Tave also find that the natural (or mean) rate of unemployment changed between 1968 and 1980.

Loungani, Rush, and Tave (1991) summarize their work on stock market dispersion and business cycles. They find that stock market dispersion predicts output growth two years later about as well as stock market return predicts output growth one year later. With both predictors together, only dispersion seems significant. (They even claim that dispersion predicts stock market return two years later.) Measures of fiscal and monetary policy don't help much. They note that stock market dispersion measures give an early signal of shocks that affect sectors differently, and put more weight on permanent shocks than on temporary shocks. Thus they doubt that "aggregate shocks" that affect different sectors differently are causing the relation that Lilien (1982) found. Their evidence seems consistent with a general equilibrium model of business cycles.

Lucas (1967) uses adjustment costs associated with gross or net investment (relative to capital) to analyze a firm's or an industry's supply response to a shock to price or some other input. He assumes that firms expect prices to remain constant, but concludes that "the long-run supply price for a competitive industry cannot be interpreted as an average cost curve derived from a 'long-run cost minimization problem'" (p. 332). I agree, though my alternative is to say that the firm tries to set short- and long-run *marginal* cost (along many margins) equal to price. For example, a retailer looks at the marginal cost of increasing sales by adding a store, the marginal cost of increasing sales by training salespeople better, and the marginal cost of increasing sales by more newspaper advertising; and sets the number of stores, the amount of training, and the frequency of advertising at levels where the marginal cost of each is equal to the marginal revenue from added sales. He rejects Alchian's (1959) approach because he says "the resulting theory cannot be applied to data at the balance sheet and income statement aggregation level or at higher levels of aggregation" (Lucas, p. 323, n. 7). I think the fact that Alchian's approach can't be applied means that these levels of aggregation are inappropriate. I am especially skeptical of the use of financial statement data to analyze investment for industries or for the economy. While Lucas suggests going on to a model with uncertainty, he does not say much about differentiating kinds of capital. I think we must use uncertainty and differentiated capital to understand investment. Moreover, when we do so, I think adjustment costs will have no special role to play at high levels of aggregation. At the micro level, an adjustment cost is just the cost of shifting capital from one use to another.

Lucas (1975) gives a theoretical example of a business cycle. In his "island" model, real output shows serially correlated movements about trend not explainable by movements in the availability of factors of production. The shocks are serially uncorrelated. Everyone is rational, but agents face "a succession of ambiguous, unanticipated opportunities which cannot be expected to stay fixed while more information is collected" (p. 1120, n. 8). Thus he emphasizes current uncertainty about the economy, whereas I emphasize future uncertainty. He has islands, while I have sectors, measured along many dimensions. We agree that a tax policy that reduces volatility also reduces desirable resource movements following relative demand shifts (pp. 1139–1140). We disagree most on the nature of the shocks: his are monetary/fiscal shocks that reflect "aggregate demand," while mine are simply multidimensional changes in current and expected future supply and demand.

Lucas (1987) says that (1) equilibrium models of business cycles based on rational expectations and details about such things as the employer-employee relation are the only kind worth exploring; (2) the variability in consumption growth that we have seen since World War II is too small to worry much about; and (3) we can and should use monetary policy to keep the average inflation rate below 10%. I agree with (1) but disagree with (2) and (3). In a world with well-developed financial markets (unlike the "cash-in-advance" world he describes), I think monetary policy must be essentially passive. (See Black (1987).) And the volatility of consumption, which reflects (at least in the long run) the volatility of wealth, is in my view inseparable from expected growth. We have a choice among production possibilities, some with low volatility and low growth, and others with high volatility and high growth. At the margin, when we make an optimal choice along this frontier, added expected growth and reduced volatility are equally important. (That's the nature of the optimum.) If we find a way to reduce the volatility of every choice, we will then move along the frontier to a point with higher expected growth. So an improvement in one is literally equivalent, in equilibrium, to an improvement in the other. (Again, see Black (1987).)

Lucas (1988) explores three growth models in the light of several stylized facts: that growth seems to continue without limit; that output levels vary widely across countries; that growth rates seem to vary across countries and through time; and that migration is mostly from poor countries to rich ones. He notes that in the conventional Solow model, output levels and growth rates should converge rapidly through physical capital movements, and that output and capital growth rates should satisfy a linear relation across countries even off their steady-state growth paths. He tries two ways of adding human capital (and removing the fixed factor) to solve these problems. With the first, average human capital affects production, so added human capital has external benefits. With the second, the economy produces two distinct goods using different technologies, as in the models of international trade that give factor price equalization without factor migration between countries. In this model, people accumulate human capital by working, but skill accumulation for each good depends on the average skill level in its industry.

Lucas feels that he needs the externalities to capture the notion that human capital involves groups and to explain migration from poor countries to rich countries: I model those things using the idea of "team production" involving people in the same city, the same country, or the same world. The team members have different skills, and in explaining migration, I specifically assume that some have more of a given skill than others. I like his move toward multiple goods, but I think we need to have multiple inputs as well as multiple outputs. In fact, I think we should always use more inputs than outputs, precisely to avoid the factor price equalization results, which strike me as peculiar. To explain differences in actual growth experiences across countries and through time he can add uncertainty to his model. Once he has human capital, team production, and multiple inputs and outputs in an uncertain world, he can explain all of his stylized facts without externalities, and without paying special attention to the continual introduction of new goods.

Lucas (1990) notes that conventional growth models predict that the marginal product of capital will be far higher in poor countries than in rich ones, until capital flows equalize it. He suggests two ways of adding human capital, both involving external effects. He uses a model with no uncertainty, and calibrates it with data from Krueger (1968) and Denison (1962). He rejects a model with constant returns to scale, saying it implies that Mexicans can earn the same wages in the United States and Mexico. He concludes that rather than giving aid in physical capital, we should encourage human capital growth in poor countries and should tie aid to openness to foreign investment on competitive terms (since corrupt rulers or foreign investors may have monopoly power). Krueger ties human capital to imperfect instruments like education and age, and Denison uses biased measures of both physical and human capital. Lucas, Krueger, and Denison all use certainty models, and make other arbitrary assumptions, so I don't know how we can take seriously the numbers in this exercise. Why do Mexicans earn more in the United States than in Mexico? Perhaps because property rights are more secure here, or because workers with few skills but the ability to learn can earn more working alongside skilled U.S. workers; I don't think it plausible that all conditions other than the aggregate level of capital are the same in the two countries. In a model with a single composite capital good and no fixed factors, aid in any form is helpful and puts the recipient onto a permanently higher income path. Aid tied to more secure property rights might even cause a long-lasting increase in the growth rate. I think we can easily explain everything in this paper using a simple general equilibrium model.

Lucas (1993) sets out to explain the growth differences between East Asian countries like South Korea and other countries like the Philippines. He includes human capital in his production function, especially human capital accumulated through on-the-job learning. In fact, he concludes that human capital matters more for growth than physical capital, partly because it has external benefits. He has trouble seeing growth as simply the accumulation of human and physical capital through saving and investment: for example, he wants to measure schooling capital by years in school (when it has no external benefits), without recognizing the steady increase in the value of a year in school. His model has no fixed factors, so we can easily explain large and continuing growth rate differences as saving and investment rate differences caused by differences in patience, without invoking things like quality ladders in any explicit way. As he recognizes, differences in risk tolerance, in willingness to work hard, in endowments of skills, or in luck play important roles; but all we need with his models are differences in saving and investment rates. We can easily choose the constants in his simplest models so that physical and human capital are accumulated at the same rate; the higher the rate, the faster the economy grows, and this growth never slows down. Lucas' claim that differences in saving rates are level effects only seems wrong for his models (p. 257), and the differences in saving and investment rates he cites do not include investment in human capital (p. 256). He claims that capital mobility blunts the effects of saving rate differences, but this is not true when human capital is immobile, as he assumes, and investment in human and physical capital is balanced. Let's put in human capital and include human capital accumulated on the job, but let's not go overboard: we can assume balanced accumulation of human and physical capital, and balanced accumulation of schooling and experience capital.

Lucas and Prescott (1974) have a general equilibrium model of search and unemployment with identical workers but differing labor markets. Shocks change demand curves in different markets, but do not affect the aggregate demand for labor. Since there are many small markets, unemployment is constant, but unemployment and the value of searching for a new job both rise with variability of demand. Higher persistence of demand shocks first increases, then reduces, equilibrium unemployment. Government policy that reduces unemployment also reduces welfare by reducing the equilibrium present value of wages.

Mankiw (1986b) shows that we can resolve the "equity premium puzzle" by assuming that shocks affect people differently in a world of incomplete markets. I think his analysis carries over to a world where markets are complete but where people vary along many dimensions. Of course, in a full general equilibrium model, the puzzle doesn't arise in the first place, since it depends on assuming time-separable, state-independent utility.

Mankiw (1989) compares "real business cycle" and "new Keynesian" theories of the business cycle. None of the real business cycle models he discusses is a multidimensional general equilibrium model with career paths. Most of them have a single kind of worker in a single kind of job and no human capital. He claims a real business cycle theory needs both substantial shocks to technology and leisure that is highly substitutable over time; but a full general equilibrium model need not have either of these features to explain business cycles.

Mankiw (1990) discusses the disarray in macroeconomics. In his treatment of one version of the "sectoral shifts" approach (which is part of a full general equilibrium approach) he says that it's not clear how to distinguish this approach empirically from Keynesian approaches to business cycles (p. 1654). Does that mean he thinks the data fit this story as well as they fit the Keynesian story? To me, any evidence in favor of the Keynesian model is evidence against the general equilibrium model. If Mankiw really feels he can't reject a version of the general equilibrium model, I rest my case.

Mankiw (1992) discusses the factors affecting growth and the rules for fast growth. He says that when we include human capital, total capital accounts for 80% of income and raw labor accounts for the remaining 20% (pp. 89–90). To get the 20%, he uses the minimum wage, which I think includes the return to lots of human capital; and he argues from estimates of the return to schooling, but does not include the return to work experience. Thus I find it easy to move his estimate from 80% to 100%; I think we can take all of income as a return to some form of capital. His four secrets to fast growth are: (1) start behind; (2) save and invest; (3) educate the young; and (4) keep population growth low. When we change his model so that all income comes from capital, secret (1) loses its force, and I think (3) is implied by (2), especially when education is financed privately. If people derive utility from children, (4) may not be relevant. Thus Mankiw's most important secret is (2) save and invest. But even this is beside the point if we prefer current consumption to growth.

Mankiw, Romer, and Weil (1992) claim that the Solow model, augmented to include human capital, is broadly consistent with the evidence on the relation between income growth and such inputs as saving and population growth. They look at convergence conditional on capital accumulation and population growth. They claim that rates of return on capital investments are higher in poor countries than in rich ones. And they find no evidence that capital accumulation has external effects. I don't understand why they defend an augmented Solow model rather than an augmented endogenous growth model with constant returns to scale. The endogenous growth model seems to explain more naturally why the world economy keeps growing, and it need not predict any special sort of convergence. "Conditional convergence" seems strange to me, since the capital accumulation it holds fixed is naturally correlated with growth. They make the usual assumption that schooling measures human capital, though I think far more human capital comes from on-the-job learning. Sometimes they assume that a country's "initial" endowment is independent of its saving rate, though the simplest endogenous growth model suggests these variables are highly correlated. In general, they infer causation from correlation. They assume a world of certainty where depreciation rates are known and constant and where real interest rates tell us about marginal products of capital. Thus they ignore the influence of "luck" in differences in realized growth. Finally, they claim to be puzzled by differences across countries in "exogenous" factors like tax policy and tastes for children. They seem to want to see a world where "all countries are created equal," but that is not the world we live in. At any given moment, different countries have made and inherited different investments in what the future will be like, along many dimensions. When the uncertain future becomes certain, some of these investments will pay off, and the countries that made or inherited them will show high growth, other things equal.

Mankiw, Rotemberg, and Summers (1985) find little evidence for models that include leisure but assume time-separable, state-independent utility. They test Euler equations for present and future consumption, for present and future leisure, and for present consumption and leisure. Their discussion of the pitfalls and arbitrary assumptions in this type of empirical work is so thorough that I wonder why they bother looking at the data. They suggest that the most obvious kind of nonseparability in utility (consumption smoothing) conflicts with what "intertemporal substitution theories" assume (p. 249). Perhaps, but I don't think it conflicts with theories that assume general von Neumann–Morgenstern utility. They argue persuasively that we can't test or estimate full intertemporal optimization models, and use that as a reason for working only with first order conditions. But this is too easy: it implies we can estimate utility without solving the identification problem. They say, "It is impossible to test the general proposition about continuous optimization discussed above" (p. 227). I take this to mean that the general equilibrium approach to business cycles may explain all we observe. If we can't reject it, we have to keep it!

Mankiw and Zeldes (1991) note that about three-fourths of U.S. families hold no common stock, based on the 1984 Panel Study of Income Dynamics. The consumption-based asset pricing model, as in Merton (1973) and Breeden (1979), depends on time-separable, state-independent utility, and on all consumers holding unconstrained positions in the assets we want to price. Mankiw and Zeldes say that nonstockholders explain some, but not all, of the "equity premium puzzle." In a full general equilibrium model, we don't limit the utility function, so there is no puzzle to explain.

Manuelli and Sargent (1988) raise many of the same questions about Lucas (1987) that I raise (and some that I don't). They accept the thrust of his claim that growth is more important than variability, while I believe that the two must be equally important along at least one margin. They note that Lucas asks for a model that integrates growth, business cycles, and such topics as unemployment; I claim that the general equilibrium model, including durables, career paths, and jobs that differ along many dimensions, does just that.

Mayshar and Solon (1993) use data from the Current Population Survey and the Area Wage Surveys between 1951 and 1990 to show that both second and third shift work in large manufacturing plants are highly procyclical. Late shifts operate without the day shift complement of overhead labor, so the elasticity of output with respect to the conventional measure of labor input is greater than one. This helps explain the procyclical behavior of conventional productivity measures. It also shows one way in which utilization of both human and physical capital can vary over the cycle.

McCallum (1989) surveys real business cycle models, emphasizing the Kydland and Prescott (1982) approach. He says that the economy may have a lot of inefficiencies even though unavoidable shocks (not generated by erratic monetary or fiscal policy) explain a substantial portion of output and employment variability. He questions the relevance of econometric studies, especially those aimed at "Granger causality." He also questions the value of thinking about growth and fluctuations at the same time. In general equilibrium, though, growth and fluctuations are intimately connected. Resolution of uncertainty causes both business cycles and variation in growth rates. Moreover, we can choose more or less specialization in tastes and technology, and more or less roundabout production. When we choose more of either, we have higher expected income or growth but larger fluctuations.

McCallum (1993) says that in properly done empirical work, the degree of differencing of the data matters little so long as we handle serial correlation of the residuals properly. Though he doesn't emphasize this, it does matter that we transform the variables so that the residuals are stationary. He says that in separating the "trend and cycle" components of a series (or the relation between temporary and permanent shocks), it's important to use theory along with statistical analysis of a single time series. I agree. We can also use related time series.

McLaughlin (1991) asks why, if labor turnover is efficient, people label some separations as "quits" and others as "layoffs." He answers that these terms are useful in summarizing the environment of the employment transition. Quits are procyclical, while layoffs are countercyclical. Quits signal a job change that is less likely to involve unemployment. In general, he views a quit as occurring when the worker finds out about a good job offer, and a layoff as occurring when the firm discovers a decline in the worker's productivity. I think his story would become even more plausible if he included temporary layoffs.

Mehra and Prescott (1985) claim that a full general equilibrium model cannot explain both the behavior of aggregate consumption and the apparent risk premium on stocks and other risky assets. In particular, they doubt that use of nonseparable or state-dependent utility resolves the puzzle, since they say this means making consumptions close together in time poorer substitutes than consumptions at widely separated dates (pp. 158–159). But Sundaresan (1989) and Constantinides (1990) have shown that just such utility functions suffice to resolve the puzzle. I think Greenig's (1986) utility function does even better. While Mehra and Prescott claim the essence of the puzzle involves the average growth rate of consumption (p. 146), I claim it involves the smoothness of consumption growth. Since Walras–Arrow–Debreu models with nonseparable preferences are so varied, I don't see why Mehra and Prescott claim that none of them fit what we observe. Once we use a model that separates risk aversion and the intertemporal elasticity of consumption, we can use risk aversion to explain the risk premium, and elasticity to explain consumption smoothing.

Miller (1985) notes that investment affects depreciation by making old capital obsolete. Most estimates of capital assume that depreciation depends only on age. If we use market values to measure capital, then Miller's effects are automatically covered.

Miller (1989) suggests aggregating diverse capital goods using their rental rates as weights (and aggregating workers using wage rates as weights). Even this, he claims, does not give a quasi-concave production function. I think his concavity point confuses a shifting equilibrium with a shifting supply curve. When we aggregate human or physical capital, I think we should simply add estimated market values.

Miller (1991) asks again Joan Robinson's question, In what units is capital measured? Her preferred answer relies on a labor theory of capital value (according to Miller), while he claims that no consistent definition exists. I believe that we can measure capital consistently at market value, and can even decompose the time series of market values into changes in the number of units and changes in unit value. However, I am reluctant to use either capital units or total capital value as an input to a conventional neoclassical production function (except one that simply gives the distribution of returns on total capital). For production, the composition of capital matters. Miller also claims that the quantity of capital in an old machine can't be related consistently to the quantity of capital in a new machine by the ratio of their rents. I think this is true only in the sense that the quantity of capital relates to both current and future rents. I think he confuses an equilibrium relation with a supply schedule (p. 42).

Mortensen and Pissarides (1993) use a model with vacancies, unemployment, and costly matching of workers with jobs to explain some of the features of job creation and destruction as described by Davis and Haltiwanger (1990, 1992) and others. Jobs vary only in productivity. A filled job has an option value, because its productivity may improve. I don't feel this kind of model captures the essence of matching. I think about the match between wants and skills along many dimensions rather than the match between workers and jobs where jobs vary only in productivity. I think about investing in skills more than investing in finding a new starting point when the earlier investments don't work out. When the match between wants and skills is good, income and employment are high and dispersion across plants is low. That generates all the stylized facts about job creation and destruction.

Mulligan and Sala-i-Martin (1993a) explore the "transitional dynamics" of models with two inputs and two outputs but no fixed factors. They concentrate on the case where physical capital is low relative to human capital. They give three forces that influence the transition: a Solow effect, because the marginal product of physical capital is high; a consumption smoothing effect, because consumption is forward looking; and a relative wage effect, because wages can vary between sectors and through time. They use time-separable utility and very special production functions that allow them to avoid writing prices for human and physical capital. Indeed, I think they need separate prices for the human and physical capital used in each sector, plus a process that better captures the adjustment costs in moving capital between sectors. With consumption smoothing and true adjustment costs in production, their first order conditions and many of the "interesting facts" will collapse. They can continue to use state variables and control variables, but the prices or relative prices of different kinds of capital will become important. In general, I think the specific allocations of human and physical capital are more important for understanding business cycles and growth than the relative amounts of capital in these two broad classes. I'd especially like to see some uncertainty in their models. Thus I doubt that this analysis of transitional dynamics will help them much in creating integrated theories of business cycles and growth.

Mulligan and Sala-i-Martin (1993b) discuss the relation between income and various schooling-based measures of human capital, looking across U.S. states at ten-year intervals from 1940 to 1980, and across 97 countries at five-year intervals from 1960 to 1985. One version of their model has no fixed factors, which implies that human capital and output should move together, at least roughly. Across states, they weight years of schooling by estimated wage-income ratios for schooling categories. Their "efficiency unit" measure of human capital is thus similar to total wage income, except for variation in "participation rates" and in the human capital of high school graduates, which they use as numeraire. Across countries, they use years of schooling only, though they do allow for added schooling beyond a certain point to have a negative effect on human capital. They summarize their findings by saying that across U.S. states, incomes have become more similar but human capital stocks have not; while across countries, incomes have become less similar while human capital stocks have become more similar. I think wage income is a far better measure of human capital than anything based on schooling, partly because experience capital is a major part of human capital along with schooling capital. I suspect the differences in their various dispersion measures reflect mostly measurement errors and luck, so we can't conclude anything from them. I think the best use of their data is in relating schooling to wage income or total income, rather than in relating income and human capital; but even that would be hard to interpret, because it's only a correlation.

Mulligan and Sala-i-Martin (1994) explore various measures of human capital, especially one based on the ratio of the average wage to the estimated wage of a person with no schooling. The zero-schooling wage is the intercept from a regression, across states within the U.S. and over years, of average weekly earnings on schooling and other characteristics. Because of variation in the relevance of schooling, human capital using their measure grew very rapidly in the 1980s. The connection between schooling and their measure of human capital is far from perfect; in fact, they find only minor differences in human capital in 1990 across four broad areas of the country. I don't think their statistic measures human capital at all, because I don't accept their assumption that a zero-schooling worker is the same always and everywhere. In fact, I think a zero-schooling worker's human capital is roughly proportional to average human capital and both are roughly proportional to physical capital per person. Thus I use unnormalized wage income or even a measure based on the changing market value of physical capital, and I find consistent strong growth in human capital between 1940 and 1990. I interpret their measure of "human capital" as simply a measure of the ratio of average human capital to zero-schooling human capital. The sharp rise in this ratio during the 1980s is simply the often noted increase in wage differentials for different schooling levels over that period.

Murphy (1985) looks at correlations between state unemployment rates and factors such as the teenage and nonwhite population plus personal income as a measure of product market demand. He recognizes that all these factors affect both labor demand and labor supply. He finds that the structural factors have bigger correlations with unemployment rates than the product-market demand factors. I think he can "explain" a great deal more if he expands the product-market demand factors to include measures of the demand for specific products and services provided in each area. Surely, in general equilibrium, demographic structure interacts with the match between skills and labor demand along many dimensions to create geographic differences in unemployment rates.

Murphy and Topel (1987) use data from the Current Population Survey covering years from 1968 through 1985 to analyze the evolution of unemployment through time and across business cycles for men with strong labor force attachments. They break their sample down by one- and two-digit industry, age, schooling level, and region. They find a steady increase in unemployment over the period for the entire sample and all subgroups, with local peaks at business cycle troughs. They find that overall mobility across two-sector industries, both with and without intervening unemployment, is strongly procyclical. Mobility across one-sector industries fell while unemployment increased. Unemployment due to industry changers is steady after 1970 and has no prominent cyclical pattern. They say that this evidence is inconsistent with a large role for "sectoral demand shifts" in explaining unemployment. They interpret some regressions across industries and states as providing evidence on "spillovers" across industries. I accept most of their observations, and I agree that "sectoral demand shifts" do not play a big role in explaining unemployment, especially when we define sectors as one- and two-digit industries. At the finest level of detail, unemployment is almost always a sector change or a layoff followed by a return to the same job. Along some dimensions, two different jobs are always in different sectors even if they are in a single firm. I claim that shocks to tastes and technology cause most unemployment and whatever pattern of sectoral demand shifts or sectoral supply shifts we see. I don't think that regressions involving states and industries can tell us much about the causes of unemployment. Murphy and Topel like theories that make "strong" predictions that we can "test" by looking at these kinds of data. I agree only when we have good economic reasons for the restrictions that make a theory "strong" in their sense. I can't think of any good economic reasons for the sectoral shifts hypothesis they test. In the end, they suggest that specialized human capital can help explain many of their results. They even point out that "aggregate shocks" generating unemployment reduce the average amount of specific capital in the economy, which helps explain the persistence of unemployment. Exactly! Indeed, one explanation for the upward trend in unemployment over this period is simply the increasing specialization of workers. A more specialized worker is more likely to face a shock that forces a job change, but is no more likely to face a shock that forces a change across broad sectoral boundaries.

Neumann and Topel (1991) study the effects of industry diversification of employment within states. Thus they look at two important dimensions (industry and geographic area) at once. They find cross-industry mobility to be greater than cross-state mobility. Their formal model (pp. 1346–1350) is similar in spirit to the one I outline above, except that they have only demand shocks, while I have shocks to both tastes and technology. To identify their empirical model, they assume only demand shocks, and they make other assumptions that I consider unjustified such as: "aggregate fluctuations are nonneutral across spatially distinct markets only through their nonneutral effects on industries" (p. 1354). They talk about covariances among demand shocks as important in explaining unemployment: this is like the covariances among and between taste and technology shocks in my model. Their covariances are entirely exogenous, while mine are partly endogenous since people can choose technologies that have both high means and high covariances.

Pack and Page (1994) use both regressions and case studies to analyze the growth of "high performing Asian economies." They use conventional regressions, relating real per capita income or output growth to growth in conventionally measured capital and labor or to the share of investment in income, educational attainment, population growth, and initial income relative to the U.S. They do not say much about the problems with "perpetual inventory" estimates of the capital stock or the use of numbers of workers or hours to measure labor input. They do not say much about reverse or common causation, such as the fact that people seem to consume more education when their incomes rise. They touch only briefly on the large number of omitted variables, such as willingness to work hard and save, or tolerance for the risk involved in manufacturing jobs. They say very little about data mining, though they select high performing countries in general and two of the highest performers in particular for close study. Given these problems in interpreting their observations, and especially the difficulty in inferring causation from correlation, I don't know what to make of their conclusions. They see countries moving toward "international best practice," while I see countries accumulating different kinds of capital, including technical capital. They see countries "learning by exporting," and especially "learning by exporting manufactured goods," while others see firms "learning by investing" or "learning by investing in equipment," and I see individuals "learning by working." They see growth in "total factor productivity," while I see growth in properly measured human and physical capital. They favor promoting exports and restricting imports at certain stages of development, but give few reasons why this dominates a policy of immediate and unilateral free trade and investment.

Parente and Prescott (1993) study changes in the distribution of wealth across nations as defined by GDP per capita. They find great disparity in wealth, with the distribution shifting up over time. They find no convergence from 1960 to 1985, and no convergence among Western nations from 1870 to 1979. They find divergence among Southeastern Asian nations from 1900 to 1985. They also find great mobility in relative wealth. I wish they could do this study using estimates of total wealth at market value, but I imagine it would show the same thing.

Parente and Prescott (1994) believe that "barriers to technology adoption" can explain all the differences in income between countries and growth spurts such as Japan's. They assume that freely available technology, growing at a fixed rate, acts as a fixed factor in production, so differences in patience or tax rates among countries affect their relative income levels but not their long-run growth rates. They justify their use of a fixed factor by saying that development miracles like Japan's are just not possible with the reproducible capital income share near one. I like their emphasis on barriers to technology adoption. I think these barriers can have big effects on growth rates, just as taxes on capital can. The barriers they list include regulatory and legal constraints, required bribes, violence or threats of violence, sabotage, and worker strikes. I presume they have in mind hostility to changes in production methods that lower cost or create new services but require a lot of reallocation of human and physical capital. But I don't see why they insist that we use these barriers alone to explain income or growth rate differences, when differences in talent, patience, willingness to work hard, and luck, among other things, also seem important. Since I think their model has structural problems as a complete explanation for growth, I don't take seriously their attempt to calibrate it to fit the growth experiences of selected countries. I don't think barriers to technology are special. Violence and threats of violence, for example, matter when they are aimed at transfers of political power as well as when they are aimed at preventing technology adoption. Taxes affect growth in a similar way when we have no fixed factors. Most generally, anything that takes away or threatens to take away a share of assets, or that weakens property rights, affects growth in a similar way. In my view, all these factors work together.

Phelps (1990) discusses "neo-neoclassical real business cycle theory" as one of seven schools of macroeconomic thought (pp. 82–93). He seems to favor a blend of the seven schools and does not think anyone believes in a wholly nonmonetary theory of economic fluctuations. He is wrong about that: I believe in such a theory, at least for economies with developed capital markets and more or less balanced budgets. To Phelps, a neo-neoclassical theory is one that escapes the imperfect information of an island economy, partly by using a single representative agent. The theories he describes depend on temporary or permanent productivity shocks (though he finds odd the concept of "negative technical progress") and on a major role for shifts in the real interest rate. I share his skepticism about a theory with these three features. The driving forces in a general equilibrium model depend on diversity in wants and resources, and a representative agent model hides this diversity. With many dimensions, shocks to tastes and technology can have big effects, and a negative shock is one that worsens the match. And in a general equilibrium model, the real rate plays only a minor role.

Pissarides (1992) notes that people lose some of their skills when unemployed. He constructs a matching model with a "thin market externality" that reduces the supply of jobs when the duration of unemployment increases. He finds that multiple equilibria are possible. I don't understand how we can have a matching model when workers differ only in whether or not they are employed. In my models, we can think of "the match" between desired and available worker skills in great detail along many dimensions. Job search is costly, partly because skills become obsolete while someone is searching. Any factors like government subsidies to unemployment that lengthen job search also cause skills to become obsolete more quickly: that's one of the costs of such policies. When the match is very poor, unemployment is bound to be high for a long time even when the government doesn't subsidize it. Thus I don't see why we need to invoke thin market externalities or multiple equilibria to explain the persistence of unemployment.

Plosser (1989) argues that the standard neoclassical growth model with uncertainty, converted into the conventional real business cycle model, helps us understand both growth and business cycles. He does not seem to worry about the structural problems in the conventional model or its use of concepts that many people find hard to swallow: that unemployment is "leisure," that "the" real interest rate governs decisions about allocating work effort over time, and that changes in a single measure of "technology" drive the economy. He discusses adding realistic features such as human capital and multiple sectors, but is reluctant to go all the way to a full general equilibrium model. I suspect he doesn't want to give up the kind of simple algebra he uses in his appendix.

Plosser (1992) contrasts recent work on endogenous growth with earlier work based on the Solow model. He feels that human and physical capital accumulate as if we faced no fixed factors, and that government taxation of capital or income can have big effects on growth. He does not think the steady states in Solow's model are reasonable. He says clearly that cross-sectional correlations over many countries using poor quality data do not tell us much about growth, but then tries to interpret the correlations. He seems to feel that growth is a good, rather than simply something that we can trade off against current consumption. I think he takes too seriously the idea that human capital or knowledge gives net positive externalities. In general, though, his approach is consistent with general equilibrium.

Poterba and Summers (1986) discuss the effects of reporting errors on estimated transition frequencies between labor market states. They find that conventional measures may understate the duration of unemployment by as much as 80% and overstate the frequency of labor force entry and exit by even more. I think this illustrates a major problem with economic data generally. We have trouble defining many quantities (like the capital and labor inputs to production), and we have trouble measuring those we can define. This is another reason not to take the results of econometric studies too seriously.

Prescott (1986) says that real business cycle theory based on a stochastic growth model, as in Kydland and Prescott (1982), can explain most of the behavior of the U.S. economy. What it doesn't explain, he says, may be due as much to measurement problems as to problems with the theory. This is the sense in which theory is ahead of business cycle measurement. He concludes that costly efforts at stabilization are likely to be counterproductive, since fluctuations are optimal responses to uncertainty in the rate of technical change, but that policy may well affect the average rate of technical change. I think we can improve the theory even without better data: one way is to stop relying on variation in the aggregate rate of technical change.

Prescott (1991) says that conventional real business cycle theory is both "strong" and "real." It is strong in that it allows quantitative predictions that are sometimes wrong, and it is real in that it explains much of what we see. He says, citing Sonnenschein (1973), Mantel (1974), and Debreu (1974), that competitive equilibrium theory is "virtually vacuous." He means that we can explain almost any series of observations of prices and quantities; but as he himself emphasizes, we have all kinds of data other than prices and quantities. (For example, we have marketing studies of tastes and engineering studies of technology.) He likes "calibration," but I think calibration tells us almost nothing when we apply a badly structured model to data that is often mismeasured. He says that persistent technology "shocks" are important. I agree, in the sense that we can model permanent improvements in technology as additions to capital. But the surprises that change the match between wants and resources can affect both tastes and technology, and we reduce any mismatch we see through our future investments. Prescott says that, "surprisingly," business cycles are induced by highly persistent changes in growth factors; I think that temporary and permanent shocks have partly common causes and are highly correlated. He says that labor indivisibilities are important, but I think we can use depreciation in human capital to explain why part-time work is rare. He says that "labor hoarding" doesn't work as an explanation of procyclical measurement errors in labor input. I don't like the phrase, but I do think people work more intensively in good times. When both are properly measured, effort per hour is procyclical partly *because* the real wage is procyclical. He says that neither efficiency wages nor increasing returns are key to understanding business fluctuations. I agree. He says that incomplete markets (when agents differ) are not important. I agree, but I think "agent heterogeneity" even when markets are complete is very important for the role of both tastes and technology. He says that the dimensions of technical change don't matter. I think they matter a lot, since they affect the match between wants and resources. He says that inventories behave just as they should, and I agree. He says that nominal wage contracting doesn't explain much, and I agree. He is even skeptical, as I am, about the role of money in business cycles. In general, he likes "quantitative" models more than I do, because he has more faith in the available measures of economic activity, and because microeconomic phenomena play a bigger role in my explanations for business cycles than in his.

Prescott and Mehra (1980) model "recursive general equilibrium" using a structure that is the basis for the one used in conventional real business cycle models. They look only at cases where capital, output, and consumption are bounded. They allow utility to depend on the state of the world, so we can use their approach to model a type of consumption smoothing (and other state dependencies).

Przeworski and Limongi (1993) argue that secure property rights foster growth, but that we can't tell whether democracies or dictatorships better secure these rights. They note that democracy sometimes gives political stability, but can hurt growth by encouraging current consumption or by promoting distorting transfers. They note the difficulty in settling the issue through regression, partly because regime changes sometimes depend on economic performance.

Quah (1992) shows that the underlying permanent component in every integrated series can be taken to be arbitrarily smooth, so the transitory component dominates at all finite horizons. Without explicitly identifying the underlying economic structure, we cannot quantify the relative importance of permanent and transitory components. I like using composite capital at estimated market value to identify the permanent component in many economic series, though changes in market value may be smoothed in a series like output or consumption; and I like using unemployment or durables output to identify the transitory component.

Ramey and Ramey (1994) explore the relation between unpredictable economic fluctuations and growth, both across a sample of 24 OECD countries and through time (from 1875 to 1992) in the United States. They note that uncertainty raises expected production cost because firms must commit to technologies that usually turn out to be higher in cost than other available choices. They assume that volatility in government spending causes the volatility in output. In their regressions, both across countries and through time, they find that greater uncertainty is associated with slower growth. They hold a number of things fixed in their regressions, so they find only a *conditional* relation between volatility and growth. They interpret their conditional correlations as indicating causation, but I do not. They note that a relation between political instability and growth may help explain their results: I like that idea better than the notion that uncontrolled shifts in government spending affect growth. Though they do a simple test for this, I think reverse causation explains a lot of what they find: an economy with very low growth is apt to experience high volatility for several reasons. For example, low growth can *cause* political instability. I like the idea that uncertainty is costly because firms must commit to technologies in advance, but I think uncertainty about the composition of output is far more important than uncertainty about its scale. I think uncertainty is important for tastes and technology generally, rather than for government spending in particular.

Ramey (1991) claims to find evidence of declining marginal cost in the production functions of firms in the food, tobacco, apparel, chemicals, petroleum, and rubber industries. She says this helps explain the volatility of production relative to sales and procyclical labor productivity. I don't think we need to abandon the conventional notion of convex technology just yet. If we distinguish short- and long-run marginal cost, and if we use all the richness in Alchian's (1959) analysis of costs and outputs, we can explain the data easily. I don't think her econometric results shed much light on technology, because the identification problems are extremely hard to solve. In a full general equilibrium model, production is volatile partly because inventories are durable, so small changes in desired inventories mean large changes in production for inventory. Properly measured labor productivity is procyclical because human capital and physical capital are specialized in the same ways.

Rebelo (1991) explores a class of endogenous growth models with constant-returns-to-scale technologies. He generalizes the simple linear model by assuming that fixed factors enter the production of consumption goods but not the production of capital goods. Fixed factors can also be used in producing some capital goods, so long as they are not used in producing a "core" of capital goods. The fixed factors cause physical output of consumption goods to grow more slowly than physical output of capital goods, but relative prices evolve in such a way that the relative value of each part of output is constant. In this model and most of its variants, higher taxes on physical capital and weaker property rights cause growth to fall. He adds human capital and shows that workers will migrate from countries with high tax rates and low growth rates to countries with low tax rates and high growth rates, because wages are higher there. Thus he does not need the externalities that Lucas (1988) relies on. I like these results, but I think fixed factors are so unimportant that the simpler course is to ignore them. I think his reason for migration is important, but I believe we can explain much of it without relying on either externalities or government behavior like taxes or enforcement of property rights. He claims that the wide cross-country disparity in rates of economic growth is the most puzzling feature of the development process, but he assumes a world of certainty, so he doesn't analyze two of the major reasons for this disparity: variation in risk tolerance and the influence of chance. Indeed, he assumes that countries hardly differ at all, so it's natural that he needs differences in taxes to explain different growth experiences.

Rebelo (1992) surveys growth models without fixed factors. He notes that when the world has no uncertainty and when people in different countries all have the same preferences, such models imply common growth rates, even when returns vary across countries, so long as physical capital is free to move to the country where it earns the highest return. He also notes that such models fail to explain why the saving rate is higher in poor countries than in rich countries. He introduces uncertainty briefly, and notes that risk and expected growth need not be correlated across countries. He suggests a utility function with a subsistence level of consumption that can help explain differences in growth rates and systematic variation in saving rates even without preference differences across countries. His modified utility function obeys the von Neumann–Morgenstern axioms, but he can explain the facts more easily, I think, by relaxing his two main assumptions. First, even when variation in expected return doesn't explain variation in expected growth, variation in realized return can certainly explain variation in realized growth. Second, variation in patience, which I think we can measure directly in various ways, can explain variation in saving rates and thus in growth rates. While people in poor countries may save less, it's more true, I think, that people who save less are relatively poor. Thus luck and thrift, in a world with immobile human capital but mobile physical capital, can explain large differences in realized growth rates even without any fixed factors of production.

Ríos-Rull (1994) finds that restricting trades that transfer the risk of particular realizations of the productivity shock does not change the qualitative — or quantitative — properties of a conventional real business cycle model. In other words, market completeness does not matter much. I believe the same is true of most general equilibrium models. Because he adopts most of the conventions of the conventional real business cycle literature, I don't know what to make of his specific conclusions, like the variation in consumption and leisure volatility across age groups. In particular, I give no weight at all to his claim that the risk premium is near zero, or to his belief that allowing trading in a riskless asset should lower a model's risk premium. That result will vanish when he abandons time-separable utility.

Rissman (1993) looks at the Phillips curve relating unemployment and inflation in the light of the impact of sectoral shifts on unemployment. She says that unemployment due to sectoral shifts should not affect inflation. When she takes out estimates of unemployment due to sectoral shifts, she finds no decrease in the strength of the inflation-unemployment trade-off during the 1970s. I would like to see her extend her analysis to sectors defined in great detail along many dimensions and emphasize the difficulty of inferring causation from correlation. If she does this, I think she will find it very difficult to attribute any shifts in unemployment unambiguously to monetary and fiscal policy.

Rogerson (1987) discusses a simple two-period, two-sector world with permanent sectoral shocks. A worker who changes sectors loses income and utility and faces a chance of being unemployed for more than one period. He can reduce the chance of being unemployed by spending time and money on job search. A shock to technology (it could as easily be to tastes) produces a response that looks like a cyclical fluctuation. Employment and output fall sharply while the reallocation is going on, then rise again. Since he treats his model as just an example, we can take it as suggesting some of the elements of a full general equilibrium model. I like the fact that he doesn't try to "test" or "estimate" his model.

Rogerson (1988) shows that an economy of people who work full time or not at all can behave smoothly in the aggregate. When everyone is identical, the equilibrium involves lotteries to allocate jobs to people, and an insurance market that transfers money from the employed to the unemployed. This equilibrium is efficient. Moreover, a shock can cause a large change in hours without a large change in the real wage. I think we can understand labor supply without invoking lotteries. When we include the unmeasured part of the wage (the part that adds human capital) and average marginal pay over everyone, whether or not he is working, we will find that the real wage is highly cyclical, just as hours are. Part-time work is rare, but I think we can understand that in a convex environment by noting that human capital increases with average hours worked per week.

Rogerson (1990) uses theory and simulation to study a world where workers gain specialized human capital by following specific careers. Total compensation includes both current wages and expected higher future wages that come with greater experience. Shocks change the slope of the age-experience curve, the wages (and employment) of the young, and the employment (and wages) of experienced workers. Inexperienced workers are first to be displaced, but they find new jobs more quickly. Output declines tend to occur suddenly, followed by gradual recoveries. Thus he has many of the key features of a general equilibrium model with specialized human capital and careers. Because careers are so important in his model, a shock that reduces output can sometimes *raise* the spot wage for inexperienced workers.

Rogerson (1991) finds that in thirteen countries, the flow from manufacturing to services speeds up in bad times, while the flow from agriculture to services speeds up in good times. This fits the fact that of these three, manufacturing is most cyclical and agriculture is least cyclical. He notes that a common shock to technology across all sectors might give this pattern, but feels it's unlikely that specific sectoral shocks will do so. I disagree. I can't think of many aggregate shocks to technology, and I can think of ways that shocks to tastes and technology across many dimensions give effects that look like they are caused by aggregate shocks. If he looks at more dimensions I think he'll find aggregate shocks less persuasive. The pattern he finds is consistent with an overall flow from manufacturing and agriculture to services, combined with cyclical fluctuations that are bigger in manufacturing than in services, but smaller in agriculture than in services.

Rogerson and Rupert (1991) estimate the intertemporal elasticity of substitution of leisure. They note that prime-aged married males are apt to be working the maximum practical number of weeks, so have limited ability to substitute work and leisure through time. For others, and for those working less than the maximum number of weeks, the elasticity of substitution is much greater. Their theory makes sense, but their empirical work relies on the usual attempts to find "instrumental variables" to relate correlation and causation. I don't find the empirical work very informative for this reason. I also wonder why people think intertemporal substitution has to be high to explain unemployment. The values of different career paths can differ greatly, especially in bad times. Once we separate individuals along many dimensions, many people can face sharp changes in total compensation through time without sharp changes in "the" measured wage. I don't feel comfortable treating job search as leisure, either. I think we can understand the principal forces behind business cycles without thinking about intertemporal substitution at all.

Romer (Christina, 1990) notes that the Great Depression started with a stock market decline that led to great uncertainty for both forecasters and investors. The volatility of stock prices was much greater after the crash of 1929 than after the crash of 1987, and only the earlier one led to a depression. She says that uncertainty can lead people to postpone durables purchases because they don't know how high to go on the quality scale. Since they spend less on durables, they may even spend more on perishables. When she does a regression, she finds that uncertainty over the last year "explains" more of the change in spending on durables than the stock market change over the year (lagged one quarter). She seems inclined toward Keynesian interpretations of her facts, but I find a general equilibrium interpretation more plausible. I think one of the causes of the Great Depression was a sharp change in tastes from durables to perishables. (That would explain Romer's finding of a small increase in consumption of perishables at first.) For this and other reasons, the mismatch between wants and resources became unusually great, causing a large decline in the values of human and physical capital. That decline increased stock price volatility because it added to both financial and operating leverage in firms. The decline also caused a further decrease in purchases of durables, because a given decline in demand for the services of durables means a much larger decline in output of durables. I think that if Romer did her regression using five- or ten-year intervals rather than one-year intervals, she would find the wealth variable much stronger and the volatility variable weaker. As it is, I think volatility is largely a proxy for earlier decline in value. (We know that stock price declines are generally followed by increases in volatility.)

Romer (Christina, 1991) adds to her work on aggregate data (1986, 1989) by looking at consistent annual data on 38 individual commodity series giving outputs (or inputs) in agriculture, minerals, and manufacturing for the period 1889 to 1984. She finds little change in the short-run behavior of individual series between the prewar and postwar periods, though they show generally greater volatility interwar. She finds a mix of permanent and temporary shocks in all periods. Most of the variation in production of minor goods is "due to" industry-specific shocks (I would say "associated with"), while much of the variation in major goods is "due to" a common factor. She does not look for common factors other than an overall aggregate factor. She speaks of "demand shocks" and "supply shocks," with a presumption that demand shocks are apt to be more temporary than supply shocks. I'm not sure how she would classify a shift in the match between tastes and technology (along many dimensions) of the kind that I think is important. She fails to find evidence that government attempts to stabilize have succeeded. I think we can find such evidence if we look elsewhere: for example, government subsidies for declining industries and professions and for unemployed people may have slowed the shift to growing industries; I think such actions stabilize output and reduce welfare for most people. In general, I like her use of data on individual industries, and I consider her results consistent with a general equilibrium approach to business cycles. Shifts in tastes and technology continue to act as they always have, even as the industrial structure of the economy changes.

Romer (Paul, 1987b) applies conventional econometric methods to a conventional Solow model using conventional measures of capital and labor to explain an apparent slowdown in growth of "labor productivity" and an apparently high "capital elasticity of output." He feels that he needs to assume that investment has external benefits or that noncompetitive elements play a large role in product differentiation to explain the "facts." I think he has both the facts and the explanations wrong. Growth in output per worker varies for many reasons, including variation in the strength of property rights and the resolution of uncertainty about the allocation of investments to specific sectors defined in great detail. The slowdown in growth of labor productivity can be for a combination of reasons like these. Over long periods, effective human capital and effective physical capital grow about as much as output, and we can't use conventional econometric methods to find out how output would change if we increased one without increasing the other. This is partly because the econometric pitfalls Romer lists are worse than he says, and partly because current output depends on both current and past inputs. In general, we can easily explain the facts using versions of the competitive general equilibrium model, so we need not reach for "crazy" explanations.

Romer (Paul, 1989) describes the facts and theories of growth. We can explain Kaldor's (1961) six stylized facts in a simple general equilibrium model with specialization by countries and no fixed factors, though Romer doesn't emphasize this. He favors a multicommodity model with monopolistic competition that comes from fixed costs causing a single firm to produce each good, as in Romer (Paul, 1987a). He seems to assume these fixed costs just to make his model work, since otherwise, "Holding the amount of initial resources Z constant, output could be increased indefinitely by increasing the range M of different specialized inputs that are used" (1989, p. 109). He thinks that the rate of growth of factor inputs is not large enough to explain the rate of growth of output (p. 55), but I think that's only because factor inputs are mismeasured. He says the reason to go from the Uzawa (1965) model to the Lucas (1988) model is to explain the growth in the wage of a new high school graduate (p. 102); I think the graduate has more valuable human capital each year, so we don't need the increasing returns of the Lucas model. He claims that it may be acceptable to create a growth model that doesn't also have business cycles (p. 105), but I think we can't understand why people choose a certain expected rate of growth without including the costs of high growth embodied in business cycles, and I think realized growth reflects the accumulation of shocks that also drive business cycles. In general, I think we can use the differentiation and specialization that Romer likes without assuming that a single firm produces each output.

Romer (Paul, 1990a) argues persuasively that examples of "nonrival inputs to production," like engineering drawings, abound. More generally, we have nonconvexities with products like movies, where the production cost can be high whenever the likely market is large. Indeed, I think human capital generally has some of this quality, since a person can pass on his skills by teaching or managing. Romer assumes, though, that innovations and the things they replace are neither substitutes nor complements. I feel they are more often substitutes: the word "new" implies that. When they are, external losses from "market stealing" ("creative destruction") can offset the external gains from nonrival inputs.

Romer (Paul, 1990b) explores the implications of viewing technology as a nonrival, partially excludable good. In his model, people invest too little in human capital, so we can improve welfare by reducing the distortions that cause this or by subsidizing investment in human capital. He talks about factors that affect growth, but I think all that he says about growth can be rephrased as applying to income. I think his paper tells us about technology and innovation, but has little relevance for growth per se. He assumes that human capital depends on years of schooling and experience, and thus does not grow from one generation to the next, but I think this ignores increases in the cost and value of human capital. He is comparing years of schooling or experience at two different times without counting changes in the implicit and explicit prices of these forms of human capital. I assume that human capital grows about as fast as physical capital: the fact that humans have finite lives is not special, since machines and other forms of physical capital have finite lives too. Because of obsolescence, even knowledge and ideas and designs have limited lives. Thus he assumes that growth is limited by both labor and human capital (in the absence of innovation) while I assume no limiting factors. Because he assumes limits to growth, he needs to assume knowledge "spillovers" to explain persistent growth. He also assumes that firms or individuals continually create new goods in which they have monopoly power. Though he assumes a world of certainty, he could use this differentiation as the basis for a close-to-general-equilibrium model that explains business cycles and growth-rate differences as uncertainty is resolved along many dimensions. Finally, he shows that a market with more human capital (other things equal) has higher growth. The corresponding result in a general equilibrium model is that a market whose residents have more total capital (human and physical) has higher income or growth. High income becomes high growth whenever people choose to consume substantially less than all their income. In the light of Aghion and Howitt (1992), I see no reason (as a first approximation) to treat knowledge as differing from other forms of capital.

Romer (Paul, 1993) says that Mauritius has grown rapidly by using ideas about sewing garments brought in by Hong Kong Chinese; and that Taiwan has grown even more rapidly by creating ideas in areas that include textiles, chemicals, and electronics. He says that ideas are always nonrival, but may or may not be excludable. He does not mention the fact that new ideas can destroy the value of old ideas, or the role of factors other than government policy in growth. He discusses free trade and cross-border investment as ways of improving access to ideas, but does not mention reducing capital taxes as a way of promoting ideas (if we want to promote them). He mentions Taiwan's "industrial policy," but does not explain how that might have helped. He feels that on balance, there is a strong case for government subsidies in certain areas like education and research; but in other areas, he sees only a role for removal of barriers and protection of property rights.

Romer and Romer (1994) find that the U.S. Federal Reserve has influenced bank lending directly (in the postwar period), rather than indirectly through open market operations and other instruments of monetary policy. This is consistent with my view that bank loans and deposits are unrelated. They also find that the Federal Reserve maintains its ability to control overnight rates. I agree, but I think that this implies an opposite movement in longer-term rates. As a result, open market operations have little impact on the level of prices or economic activity.

Rotemberg and Summers (1990) use a model with fixed prices and "labor hoarding" to explain the procyclical behavior of measured total factor productivity. They believe their explanation works better than Hall's (which relies on market power and a difference between price and marginal cost). They note that productivity seems more procyclical in Japan, with its tradition of employment security. They regress a measure of the apparent difference between price and marginal cost for eighteen manufacturing industries on measures of market power and labor hoarding. Since both of these observations tell us only about "correlation," I don't see how we can use them to infer causation. Rotemberg and Summers also use a model from Prescott (1975) which seems to show that with competition and flexible prices, both Solow residuals and a naive measure of labor productivity are acyclical, even though firms hoard labor. I don't understand this alleged "puzzle." When firms and workers have investments in specific human and physical capital, an improvement in the match between wants and resources causes an increase in the return to extra hours of work (so hours go up), an increase in measured output and productivity, and a permanent increase in wealth. Since the match fluctuates at business cycle frequencies, we don't have to raise "the possibility that technology fluctuates at business cycle frequencies" (p. 871), as they say Kydland and Prescott (1982) suggest.

Rotemberg and Woodford (1994) compute the "forecastable changes" in output, consumption, and hours. They use forecastable changes, which are stationary, to identify the cycle. They show that standard real business cycle models cannot explain the behavior of forecastable changes. They conclude that real business cycle theorists have failed to show that technical progress, as reflected in stochastic growth, drives business cycles. I find their discussion of forecastable changes interesting, especially when they use only a simple statistical model to produce their forecasts. I don't know why they spend so much effort on the real business cycle model, which has so many structural problems. And I don't know why the whole economics profession spends so much effort analyzing aggregates, when the keys to the causal structure of the economy are in the details.

Rouwenhorst (1991) shows that Kydland and Prescott's (1982) "time-to-build" feature does not add much to their model's ability to explain persistent responses to temporary shocks. The other features of their model (nonseparable utility and inventories as a factor of production) don't seem to add much either. The shocks themselves must have the persistence pattern that we want output to have. Rouwenhorst points out that use of a single source of uncertainty limits the kinds of behavior we can model. I think that conventional real business cycle models like Kydland and Prescott's have many other problems as well. I think their time-to-build feature is special, though, because it hints at the efficiency and uncertainty inherent in roundabout production.

Saint-Paul (1993) asks whether recessions are good for long-term growth, because firms spend more time on productivity-improving activities then. He refers to this as the "opportunity cost" theory of productivity growth. In other words, when production is less profitable, a firm can redirect resources into preparing for future production. He uses a "semi-structural vector autoregression approach" to explore these ideas, using annual data for twenty-two OECD countries from 1950 to 1988. He concludes, tentatively, that there is some support for the opportunity cost approach; that transitory demand fluctuations affect productivity more than permanent ones; that this might explain 10–20% of productivity fluctuations; that he finds no evidence that higher volatility causes faster growth; and that high frequency components of fluctuations hurt long-term growth, while low frequency components help it. I find the whole idea that recessions are good for growth strange. I endorse the objections he lists to the idea: that productivity-enhancing activities are similar to other forms of investment and that the few forms of investment that are countercyclical are swamped by the many that are procyclical. I think his econometric methods rely on arbitrary identifying assumptions, and I doubt that the Solow residual he uses measures productivity improvements, so I don't accept his conclusions. The idea is that this unmeasured form of investment might be countercyclical; I think unmeasured investment in human capital through on-the-job learning, which is strongly procyclical, makes this negligible.

Sala-i-Martin (1990) surveys some basic models of endogenous growth. He notes that even models with externalities have versions without externalities that can give indefinite steady growth. Since he considers only certainty models, he does not discuss the connection between growth and variability. He discusses government spending, which can displace private activity; learning by doing, which can simply add to human capital without externalities; human capital accumulation through studying; and capital heterogeneity, which (though he doesn't note this) can also operate without externalities. For an example, look at the simple fixed proportions "business cycle model" above.

Samson (1991) relates employment growth across eight countries and nine sectors for the period 1968 to 1985. She finds that national shocks and sectoral shocks seem about equally important. She tentatively interprets national shocks as aggregate demand shocks. I question that interpretation. In fact, I think she will find that she can make national shocks quite unimportant by adding detail to her sectoral analysis along many dimensions. I think that regional and political shocks *are* sectoral shocks.

Sargent (1980) constructs a simple model where aggregate investment is irreversible, so the market price of capital can differ from its replacement cost and Tobin's q can differ from one. His model has aggregate shocks to both tastes and technology. Even in this simple model, there is no way to recover firms' aggregate demand for investment by analyzing behavior of output, investment, and q. Even in principle, instrumental variables and lagged values of q don't help. He concludes that the same "frictions" or "adjustment costs" that allow q to differ from one also establish a presumption that agents' investment decisions are not expressible in any simple way as depending on q.

Schmitz (1993) says that neither traditional neoclassical growth theories nor modern theories that stress differences in human capital can explain the observed inequality in the world. He likes theories like Parente and Prescott's (1994) that stress differences across countries in the incentives provided to entrepreneurs to adopt new technology and create businesses. He notes that groups in society with a vested interest in the status quo create barriers to the adoption of new technology and the creation of new businesses. He says that a model with human capital and no fixed factors doesn't work because it implies that countries will diverge over time, and because it implies that the overall rental rate on capital equals the output-capital ratio (p. 30, n. 28). To explain why countries don't diverge, all we need are a few factors that aren't fully reproducible (going back a little toward the traditional neoclassical model), or team production, using inputs from different countries. And I think the overall rental rate on capital *is* equal to the output-capital ratio; it only seems different because output, capital, and rental rates are hard to measure. Thus I think the intangible physical capital that Schmitz emphasizes is an important input to production, but is combined in a symmetric way with tangible physical capital and human capital. It is not special.

Schultz (1961) pleads for more attention to human capital. He thinks that growth in human capital explains most of the growth in output not explained by growth in physical capital. Moreover, he notes that our national accounts omit much or most of our investments in human capital, including investments through on-the-job training. He says that human capital, like other forms of reproducible capital, becomes obsolete and deteriorates when it is idle. Indeed, he says that the most distinctive feature of our economic system is the growth in human capital.

Shapiro (1993) asks why, if the capital input to production is quasi-fixed, output expands more than worker hours in booms. He suggests it may be from increases in utilization of physical capital, as when plants are operated for extra shifts. In fact, using data from the Census Bureau's Survey of Plant Capacity, he finds that utilization of plants is highly procyclical, and explains the relation between output and hours without invoking increasing returns. In my symmetric production functions, we include both human and physical capital, together with utilization of both human and physical capital. With fixed capital, variation in the utilization of physical control that just matches variation in the utilization of human capital gives comparable variation in output. So we need to add in the permanent shocks to effective capital to explain the behavior of output. Since temporary and permanent shocks are correlated and since labor utilization rarely has permanent shocks, output varies more than either labor or capital utilization.

Shiller (1987) observes that we should probably include a great many different kinds of shocks in explaining aggregate variability. I agree, though he includes some (like unexpected changes in the money stock) that I would not include. In discussing weather as a source of variability, he illustrates the kinds of detailed analysis we need to show the relevant structure of just one part of the economy. He even suggests that a properly specified large-scale econometric model may have a role in understanding fluctuations. I agree again, though I'm not sure we need to understand them fully, if the government is largely powerless to improve on the competitive equilibrium. He notes that we should interpret models with just a few shocks as exploratory exercises.

Shoven and Whalley (1992) survey the literature on "applied general equilibrium models." I like these models because they rely on general equilibrium, because they emphasize estimation rather than testing, and because they are heavy on economic content. But they handle uncertainty by including expected values inside utility functions (often using myopic expectations), and the results of policy experiments are often highly sensitive to elasticities that we know little about. Thus I am very cautious about using the specific numbers that come out of these exercises. I think we can look to these models mainly for insights into the unintended consequences of changes in government policy.

Singleton (1988) shows several pitfalls in "estimating" real business cycle models. He discusses biases that prefiltering or seasonal adjustment can introduce, especially when the same underlying causes lie behind both secular and cyclical fluctuations. He shows that "calibration," as Kydland and Prescott (1982) recommend, can be inappropriate if the micro and aggregate models are incompatible or just different. He shows that additive decomposition of economic series into trend, cyclical, and seasonal components doesn't make sense in some models. Yet he fails to mention some problems that to me seem much bigger. How do we use apparent "Granger causality" to draw inferences about true cause and effect? How do we justify (except by citing researcher convenience) the restrictions we need to derive or test an Euler equation? What do our conventional econometric methods tell us in an unrestricted general equilibrium model?

Solow (1956) creates a model of long-run growth that contrasts with the Harrod–Domar model with fixed proportions of capital and labor. He likes the idea of balanced growth, where the capital-labor ratio approaches a stable steady state. I don't know why he likes that, since we see no tendency in real economies for the rate of growth to slow down as they become wealthier. I view it as a version of Malthus' fallacy of the fixed factor. In Solow's case, the fixed factor is labor. One way to correct this problem is to let the two factors of production be human and physical capital. Then it's the ratio of human to physical capital, where both are measured in efficiency units, that approaches a steady state.

Solow (1957) initiates or endorses many of the features of the conventional production function as a way of accounting for growth. His function is asymmetric, since he includes physical capital but not human capital. He refers to the growth in output not explained by his asymmetric inputs as "technical change," though in general equilibrium this residual can reflect all sorts of shocks to tastes and technology. He even tries crude measures of the inputs and the resulting residual, but I don't know what to make of the result. With a more refined model, including better defined and better measured inputs, his results will change completely. In particular, growth will show up more in the inputs than in the residual.

Solow (1988), in his Nobel lecture, defends the models of growth and technical change that he developed (Solow (1956, 1957)). He raises again the Harrod–Domar question: "When is an economy capable of steady growth at a constant rate?" He notes that Harrod and Domar assume that the saving rate, the labor force growth rate, and the capital-output ratio are given constants. He says this implies that government policies that increase saving also increase growth, which seems odd to him. He allows the capital-output ratio to vary, but keeps the other two assumptions. He is alarmed at the use of his work in real business cycle models, which he says treat business cycles as "optimal blips in optimal paths in response to random fluctuations in productivity and the desire for leisure." Still, he says that Prescott's model is hard to refute with time-series data. Thus he admits the difficulty in interpreting econometric studies; but he does not yet admit equal difficulty in interpreting his measures of technical change, partly because we have no good way to aggregate the inputs to production. And he still doesn't allow uncertainty to play a significant role.

Solow (1991) suggests adding insights from analysis of industrial structure to macroeconomics, in a way that makes precise Schumpeter's ideas about innovation. He prefers Krugman's (1990) analysis to Romer's (Paul, 1986) and Lucas' (1988) more conventional analyses. In Krugman's kind of model, the social return to innovation exceeds the rate of interest, so the equilibrium entails underinvestment in innovation. Solow seems to feel that a model that captures innovation must involve such a difference between the rate of return and the rate of interest. I don't agree. For example, if we assume that innovators capture *all* the rents they create (because we enforce their property rights), or if we recognize the negative externalities from innovation along with the positive externalities, then I think we can create a model where the equilibrium is efficient. It's an ex ante competitive equilibrium, though it involves rents. Thus I don't think the existence of Schumpeterian innovation necessarily implies gains from government intervention.

Solow (1994) surveys the varieties of growth theory, from Harrod and Domar through Solow to Aghion and Howitt, with many variations. He thinks some technical progress is endogenous, but he doesn't think we have quite the right model for this yet. He is highly skeptical of empirical work that takes the form of cross-sectional regressions on the Summers and Heston data. He does not care for models with "intertemporally optimizing representative agents," because heterogeneity may be crucial to macroeconomic outcomes, and because infinite-time optimization may gloss over some crucial features of equilibrium. He feels that a model where greater saving and investment can lead to permanently higher growth rates makes growth seem too easy! He notes that a model with constant returns to capital must have increasing returns to scale, or else non-capital factors will have negative marginal products. I assume constant returns to scale rather than constant returns to capital; and I assume that non-capital factors are negligible for the foreseeable future. He wants to add to Aghion and Howitt's (1992) model the chance that innovations are complementary with predecessors and add to their rents. I feel that some innovations are like that, but that the vast majority reduce the rents that might otherwise have accrued to previous innovations. I think most innovations don't add much in a technical sense: they are mainly intended to take market share away from previous innovations.

Stadler (1990) points out that both real business cycle models and models with monetary or other "aggregate shocks" can generate a nonstationary random-walk-like pattern for output. When technology is endogenous, either directly or through growth in human or physical capital, good times (regardless of source) can lead to a permanent addition to output and capital. Thus the existence of "unit roots," as in Nelson and Plosser (1987), does not let us distinguish among business cycle theories. I agree with this point, but in a general equilibrium model I don't see a place for aggregate shocks. I don't even see how to define them.

Starr–McCluer (1993) uses a sophisticated statistical technique to refine estimates of the extent to which unemployed workers switch sectors in expansions and contractions. Loungani and Rogerson (1989) say sector switches are much more common in recessions, while Murphy and Topel (1987) say they're more common in expansions. By correcting the biases in their studies, Starr–McCluer finds that sector switches are more common in recessions, but not by as big a margin as Loungani and Rogerson claim. This seems to support a sectoral explanation of unemployment. I believe we can find stronger support when we use a finer sectoral breakdown along many intersecting dimensions. Indeed, the general equilibrium approach does not necessarily predict that sector switches will be more common in recessions. Changing sectors is risky, and in some ways is easier to do when times are good. We can regard it as a form of investment, since a worker sacrifices short-term pay to do it. Like other forms of investment, it may be higher in good times than in bad times. Moreover, in good times many firms are more willing to hire trial workers with little industry experience. We may find that sector switches with intervening unemployment are more common in recessions, while sector switches without intervening unemployment are more common in expansions. Thus I do not regard these as crucial tests of the general equilibrium approach.

Startz (1994) models an economy where a single factor can produce either of two goods using linear technology and can shift freely between the two sectors. The rate of external technical growth in each sector depends on the amount of capital in that sector. This externality means that the economy can have multiple stable "growth states," and small shifts can have large effects if they move the economy to a new region. Thus he can explain business-cycle-like fluctuations with a model like the one Lucas (1988) uses to explain variation in long-run growth rates. Uncertainty has no special role in his analysis. I just don't see why he feels compelled to go outside the universe of general equilibrium models. In general equilibrium, the "state of the world" involves tastes, technology, and allocations of human and physical capital along many dimensions. There are many "stable" states, and a shift or shock in tastes or technology moves us from one to another. An "improvement" in technology that affects one sector more than another can make existing capital obsolete, so it can look like "technical regress." We can use the same underlying mechanism to explain business fluctuations and growth variation. So why look elsewhere?

Stockman and Tesar (1995) add taste shocks to a version of the conventional real business cycle model with a traded good and a nontraded good in each of two countries. They compare certain features of their models with summaries of annual and quarterly data from the early 1970s to the late 1980s, detrended using the Hodrick-Prescott filter or by taking first differences of logs. They feel they need taste shocks to explain the high standard deviation of consumption, the low correlation between consumptions across countries, and the fact that the correlation between relative price and relative consumption across the two sectors is so far from −1.0. I agree that we must include taste shocks in a model that explains business cycles in detail, but I don't think we need them to explain these particular facts. A more general version of the basic model can explain these facts. For example, if we create a model with "first order uncertainty" in the capital stock, we can make consumption as volatile as we like. Also, a varying match between tastes and technology can give a positive correlation between relative price and relative consumption across broadly defined sectors, even when the variation comes from shocks to technology. They take Solow residuals seriously as measures of productivity shocks, but I interpret their Solow residuals as combinations of additions to human capital and noise, confounded by the use of an accounting measure of the capital input to production. I agree with their approach to data. They say, "We do not formally estimate or test hypotheses about the model because the model is clearly false..." They even show how modest changes in data or procedures can raise the estimated correlation between the average product of labor and output from .33 (in Prescott's work) to .87 (in their work). Actually, I'd like to apply that same skepticism to the calibration they do for their model and to their method for analyzing its dynamics. They linearize the first order conditions around the nonstochastic steady state; so their results will change sharply if they use time-nonseparable utility, adjustment costs in production, and a model that has no steady state because it has no fixed factors.

Stokey (1991) creates a growth model where individuals have finite lives and where human capital is the only factor of production. Investments in human capital have external effects because they increase the efficiency of schooling for later cohorts. She finds that a small country that opens trade may sometimes reduce its own human capital investment and growth. She does not explain why investment and growth are desirable, and she does not consider the negative externalities of schooling in destroying the value of old ideas. Most important, she does not balance the human capital added by working against the amount added by further schooling. She allows human capital and schooling to vary in both quantity and quality, but not by sector. She concludes that subsidies to education, child labor laws, and practices that encourage investment will raise welfare; but I feel these conclusions are specific to her restricted model. As she notes, even her conclusions about the effects of trade may be specific to her model.

Summers (1986) says that conventional real business cycle models have nothing to do with actual real business cycle phenomena in capitalist economies. He notes that a theory's ability to mimic quantitative stylized facts does not mean it is even close to right. He complains that conventional real business cycle models use poorly estimated parameters and rely on implausible shocks to technology. He feels that most of what theorists call "technology shocks" come from labor hoarding and other behavior that they do not model. He wonders how a model that largely omits prices can be accurate. He suggests a model where "breakdowns in the exchange mechanism" prevent willing buyers and sellers from meeting. In sum, he feels that "a lengthy professional detour into the analysis of stochastic Robinson Crusoes" can't be productive. I agree with his conclusion and with most of his arguments, though not with his alternative model. I think a Robinson Crusoe model is bound to fail because it ignores crucial differences among workers and consumers and among products and services.

Summers (1991) argues persuasively that formal econometric work almost always fails. He says the search for "deep structural parameters" and the less formal analysis of time-series data using "VAR" methods both fail to distinguish cause and effect. He likes empirical work that gives us simple stylized facts to think about. He says attempts to falsify theories based on overidentifying restrictions are unenlightening, since the auxiliary assumptions matter so much. He suggests that researchers choose tractable assumptions for their own convenience, and that they use difficult statistical methods to demonstrate their prowess. My only reservation about his message is that I feel he understates the difficulty of informal empirical work. I am not persuaded by Friedman and Schwartz's (1963) use of natural experiments, and I don't believe that Mehra and Prescott's (1985) observation survives the relaxation of time-separability. In general, though, I agree with Summers' conclusion that "progress is unlikely as long as macroeconomists require the armor of a stochastic pseudo-world before doing battle with evidence from the real one" (p. 146).

Sundaresan (1989) explains consumption smoothing using nonseparable utility that depends on both current consumption and a weighted average of past consumption. While this kind of utility can give either smoothing or its opposite (satiation), he makes assumptions ensuring that people smooth their consumption. In his most specific example, the weighted average of past consumption serves as a floor level for consumption, as in Ryder and Heal (1973). I'd be happier with utility that depends more directly on the smoothness of the consumption path, as in Greenig (1986), or with fully state-dependent utility. Sundaresan's utility function has the feature that higher consumption today, holding fixed past and future consumption, can mean lower utility.

Tamura (1991) uses an endogenous growth model that gives convergence in *per capita* income and output growth rates because production of human capital uses a person's own human capital plus the average amount of human capital in society. He notes that it's easier to learn an old idea than to create a new one, but he does not consider the fact that creating new ideas destroys some of the value of old ones. Moreover, we can create convergence easily in a model without externalities by making production depend on both domestic and foreign human capital: in a sense, that's a competitive version of what Tamura is doing.

Uzawa (1965) analyzes a certainty model with linear separable utility of consumption, separable production with constant returns to scale, and an "education" sector that uses only labor inputs. Thus labor-augmenting technical growth in knowledge is one of the economy's outputs. Along his optimal equilibrium growth path, the ratio of capital to augmented labor remains fixed. In a multidimensional version of this with uncertainty, the economy will move toward balance among many produced inputs to production, while shocks will keep throwing the balance off. Human capital will be one of those produced inputs.

Von Furstenburg (1977) finds that the use of Tobin's q in explaining real orders or investment as a percentage of the real gross capital stock of nonfinancial corporations, using data from 1952 to 1976, is optional. Using q alone, the residuals have lots of serial correlation. With other variables like measures of capacity utilization and tax credits for investment in plant and equipment, q doesn't add much. He creates quarterly estimates of replacement cost by interpolating annual figures from the flow-of-funds accounts. He notes that estimates of replacement cost by the Bureau of Economic Analysis are average rather than marginal, and exclude intangible assets. In discussing the fact that measured q usually comes out less than one, he says that the BEA replacement cost estimates "do not reflect the current cost of putting a given number of efficiency units in place but instead measure the current cost of the same amount of resources as was previously used to produce capital goods; thus 'costless' technical progress is ignored" (p. 358). I claim that if we think carefully about how to measure "efficiency units" and how to aggregate measures of replacement cost for different assets, we are led inexorably to a theoretical value of q that is always one, except for possible tax effects using one definition of q. Still, q as von Furstenberg measures it indicates movements in market value in past quarters and years, so it is naturally correlated with investment. Measured q, capacity utilization, and investment are all roughly procyclical, though with different phases, so it's natural that he finds them correlated.

Von Neumann (1945) creates an elegant model of general equilibrium where goods are transformed from one time and state into the next through *production*. He has a certainty model with many goods and no fixed factors. The many actual and potential production processes show constant returns to scale; and they may be "circular," in that good A may be used, directly or indirectly, in producing good B, while good B is used in producing good A. Consumption is implicit in the production process; it is not chosen to maximize utility. An equilibrium exists where all quantities expand at a constant rate equal to the rate of interest, so the interest rate is net of consumption. Up to an important transformation, the equilibrium is unique. This is a special case, since the world is certain and prices don't change, but it has multiple goods and multiple production processes, which are both important in a realistic general equilibrium model of growth, labor, and business cycles.

Weil (1989) finds both an "equity premium puzzle" and a "risk-free rate puzzle," using either time-separable, state-independent von Neumann–Morgenstern utility or a class of Kreps–Porteus nonexpected utility preferences with constant intertemporal elasticity of substitution and constant but unrelated relative risk aversion. The first puzzle says we don't see enough risk to explain the equity risk premium. The second says we don't see enough intertemporal substitution to explain the short-term real interest rate. Since nonexpected utility doesn't help, I don't know why he explores it. Instead, he could move to nonseparable or state-dependent utility and show that both puzzles vanish.

Weiss (1984) assumes that firms find it less costly to fire workers than to hire them. He considers both relative sectoral shocks and overall shocks that affect all sectors the same way. He finds that either sort of shock can explain Lilien's (1982) findings. He suggests that skewness patterns favor an explanation involving overall shocks over one involving relative shocks. I think that's reading too much into the data, especially since I have trouble imagining any overall shocks.

West (1990) uses a simple inventory model to show how cost and demand shocks interact to cause fluctuations in aggregate inventories and GNP. He refers to the fact that production is more variable than demand as "excess volatility," but his model shows that both cost and demand shocks can easily have this effect, because inventories are durable. When firms keep inventory-sales ratios close to constant, changes in expected sales (possibly due to changes in expected cost) cause larger percentage changes in output temporarily. He uses a bivariate VAR model to try to separate the movements in inventories and output due to cost and demand shocks. To do this, he must use "identifying restrictions." He gives few economic reasons for the ones he adopts. I am tempted to say, "No identification without justification." He says that he can imagine more complex models that are unrejected (pp. 963–964). I think a fuller general equilibrium model would be an example.

Williamson (1990) notes that sectoral shifts can disrupt production partly by reducing the value of prior sorting in the labor markets. People seek out the kinds of jobs where they are most productive, and shifts in the pattern of jobs can reduce the value of what they know about matching their skills with jobs. This carries over to the general equilibrium approach. The same argument gives one reason why an unexpected shift in tastes or technology can hurt (or help) the match between wants and resources.

Yang and Ng (1993) model growth as a process of increasing specialization through learning about efficient ways to organize production and about specific production processes. Specialization and roundabout production add to production efficiency but increase transportation and bargaining costs. Comparative advantage is acquired, and it works between countries and within countries in the same ways. Firms increase efficiency by reducing transaction costs. Contracting costs imply an optimal degree of vagueness in property rights; even many "externalities" are endogenous and optimal. Money and credit are essential after specialization reaches a certain point, but do not affect the evolution of the real economy. Even business cycles and unemployment are endogenous and optimal. In fact, they show that their equilibrium is efficient even though they include transportation costs, transaction costs, bargaining costs, and costs of enforcing contracts. They note that their models are hard to "test," and present them mostly as a series of examples. All this is consistent with a general equilibrium approach to growth and business cycles, but I would add several features to their models. The most important is uncertainty. Specialization and roundabout production increase expected costs as much because of uncertainty about future tastes and technology (plus costs of reallocating resources) as because of transportation and coordination costs. This would also let them model business cycles and unemployment without relying on "indivisibilities." If they distinguish between a person in his role as consumer and the same person in his role as producer, they will not need to contrast their approach with work that treats consumers and producers as distinct. In their models, consumers prefer "diversity," which makes different consumption goods "complements" in utility. I think it is far more important to model tastes as "specialized" so that consumers gain extra utility from goods that have precisely the desired features. This makes specialization in tastes parallel to specialization in technology.

Finally, as they note, they can fill in their models by adding human and physical capital more explicitly and by allowing people to differ in their endowments of tastes, skills, and resources.

Young (1992) presents a fascinating comparison of the 30-year growth experiences of laissez-faire Hong Kong and government-controlled Singapore. He finds that measured technical progress was very rapid in Hong Kong, but virtually zero in Singapore. He thinks Singapore caused this by pushing the economy constantly into new sectors where it had to start over (up the experience curve) repeatedly. He uses conventional measures of capital (from investment history with geometric depreciation) and labor (number of workers). This causes a particular problem in his study, since Singapore seems to have encouraged the growth of physical capital but not human capital. Since he doesn't measure human capital (except through the change in formal education in part of his study), he finds that the inputs to production grew faster (relative to output) in Singapore than in Hong Kong. Thus what he labels "slower technical progress" in Singapore may be slower growth in human capital due to the government's distortion. Indeed, I suspect that we can interpret his measures of technical growth as entirely growth in human capital in both countries. (This makes his Solow residuals identically zero.) Moreover, it's possible that some of the "shortfall" he finds for Singapore is due to a lag between added capital and the resulting increase in output. Similarly, I can interpret some of his other models in a conventional way. Rather than saying the marginal product of each accumulable factor is bounded above zero, I simply say that all factors are accumulable. So-called unskilled labor may learn from experience just as much (in percentage terms) as skilled labor. What he calls "invention" I consider creation of a type of intangible physical capital. When he says that learning by doing on the factory floor has diminishing returns until the next invention, I say that human capital (especially experience capital rather than schooling capital) has diminishing returns when we hold physical capital fixed.

Young (1993) explores the interplay of creation and destruction arising from substitution and complementarity among technologies in an endogenous growth model built around external effects. New final goods substitute for old final goods but create new markets for old intermediate goods. Costly invention creates valuable patents, but some activities create knowledge as an "unappropriated by-product." Since new knowledge has both positive and negative external effects, we don't know whether to subsidize it or tax it. He uses a certainty model but finds multiple equilibria, some of which are unstable. He mentions "linear models of factor accumulation" with no fixed factors and no externalities (p. 805), but does not explain why he rejects such models. I think he should reconsider.

Zarnowitz (1985) surveys the then-recent work on business cycles. He concludes that the evidence is, on balance, unfavorable to equilibrium theories (p. 555). He also says, in relation to my earlier work, that changes in tastes and technology can "penalize some sectors and benefit others, causing numerous shifts in relative prices and outputs; they may occasionally have significant net favorable or adverse effects on growth but can hardly be responsible for *recurrent sequences* of expansions and contractions in aggregate economic activity" (p. 567). I hope this book shows how such changes can indeed explain such "recurrent sequences" as we observe.

Zarnowitz (1992) surveys both pure and applied research on business cycles, especially work sponsored by the National Bureau of Economic Research. He repeats his comments in Zarnowitz (1985) on the causal role of changes in tastes and technology (p. 71). In general, he says that "new classical" equilibrium models "have no multiplier mechanisms, and compensatory combinations of large shocks to technology and a strong instantaneous accelerator lack credibility. The models also fail to produce the sizable positive autocorrelation of investment that is observed" (p. 9). He even claims to see no important connections between growth and cycles (pp. 203–231). I hope this book shows how we can deal with all of these issues. In particular, we have autocorrelated investment whenever we have shocks that are permanent or that take time and effort to unwind.

Summary

I believe that versions of the full general equilibrium model, with complete markets, unrestricted utility, and convex production, can explain most of what we see in business cycles, labor economics, and growth. A number of empirical "puzzles" dissolve when we use the full model, even when we assume constant returns to scale and secure private ownership of all technology.

For example, when we use general von Neumann–Morgenstern utility, the "equity premium puzzle" is no longer a puzzle, and apparent violations of Euler equation restrictions vanish. The simplest way to generalize time-separable, state-independent utility is to add a preference for smooth consumption by replacing each period's consumption with a weighted geometric average of current and past consumption. To model local substitution, we can then replace each period's consumption with a weighted arithmetic average of current and past consumption.

Similarly, a full model of convex production takes a huge array of inputs at times ranging from the present to the distant past. We can't rearrange past inputs, though we almost always want to. If we insist on summarizing production as depending only on current inputs, we should look for symmetry: if output depends on physical capital, it should also depend on human capital; and if we let effort or hours vary to capture changes in utilization of human capital, we should also include changes in utilization of physical capital. The conventional neoclassical production function, with inputs of physical capital and labor, is hopelessly asymmetric.

To understand business cycles, we need to see the world in great detail along many dimensions. I believe that the driving force is investments in human and physical capital that commit us to our expectations about future tastes and technology along all these dimensions at many future times. More roundabout production and more specialized investments mean higher expected income and growth, but only at the cost of higher output volatility and higher expected unemployment.

We cannot aggregate shocks, because the details matter. Changes in aggregate prices and quantities depend on a whole array of shocks to tastes and technology. Thus we cannot infer, from macroeconomic data, anything we might call an "aggregate demand shock" or an "aggregate supply shock." This means we cannot isolate shocks to technology.

At the finest level of detail, we can always see many expanding sectors and many contracting sectors. But when our expectations turn out to be right, we have a good match between wants and resources, and we will see many more expanding sectors than contracting ones. Moreover, when many sectors work together to produce things, more effective capital in one sector increases output in other sectors. When times are good, almost all broadly defined sectors expand; and when times are bad, almost all broadly defined sectors contract.

Making property rights more secure or increasing political stability, up to a point, can increase the expected payoffs from investments and reduce risk. Thus "environmental risk" is associated with low output. But by choosing the level of specialization in our investments and the degree to which we use roundabout production methods, we trade off volatility and expected output, or volatility and expected growth. Along these margins, added consumption volatility and added consumption growth are equally important. Overall, though, we need not have a positive correlation across countries between average volatility and average growth.

Similarly, we can choose the amounts of specialization in production and consumption separately. If we have little specialization along either dimension, the payoff from added specialization is high. We keep increasing it until expected utility stops rising. Added specialization in production makes technology shocks more important, while added specialization in consumption makes taste shocks more important. At the margin, shocks to tastes and technology are equally important.

The factors that cause business cycles also cause growth rates to vary, across countries and through time. We can have continuing growth in output and in composite capital because we consume less than we produce, and because we have not yet encountered any fixed factors of production.

The market value of capital depends in part on its current and expected future relevance, and on its current and expected future utilization. Relevance and utilization tend to move together. Changes in output are highly correlated, over longer intervals, with market value changes. In the short run, we can distinguish between changes in the number of units of capital and changes in unit value, but in the long run, only total market value counts. We can even assume that human capital has a market value that closely tracks the market value of physical capital.

Lots of specialization means lots of unemployment, since it increases unemployment as a process of redirecting careers and since it makes temporary layoffs more common. Durables have a special role in temporary layoffs, since durables output is much more volatile than output of nondurables or services. These temporary changes in output and unemployment define business cycles, but they are highly correlated with permanent fluctuations in the market values of human and physical capital.

Inventories are durable. Thus we see temporary, cyclical changes in inventories along with other cyclical changes. Production is naturally more volatile than sales, even though inventories are sometimes used to smooth production.

Both long-run growth and short-run cycles are largely driven by *luck*: by whether the assumptions and expectations behind our investments turn out to be correct. We don't need to assume that volatilities or interest rates or expected returns or inflation rates or tastes for leisure change over time. All we need is the resolution of uncertainty.

Temporary changes in output, whether or not associated with production of durables, can help explain vacancies as well as temporary layoffs. Some vacancies represent temporary hires to meet temporarily high demand. Other vacancies represent openings created when careers are advancing rapidly. The two kinds of vacancies rise in good times, just as the two kinds of unemployment rise in bad times.

Sometimes it helps to think of production as done by teams that combine different sorts of human and physical capital in fixed proportions. We choose the proportions before we know how much of each input we have. Variation in the availability of the few constraining resources can drive common variations in output and labor demand throughout the economy.

More generally, it helps to think of production as combining inputs from different age groups, different sectors, and different countries. This helps us understand rapid increases in wages with age, migration from poor to rich countries, comovement among sectors, and convergence of income levels across countries. An increase in one input increases the marginal products of all the other inputs.

We add human capital through schooling and through experience. Experience is a form of compensation, so jobs with lots of growth potential pay lower current wages than those that make maximum use of existing skills, other things equal. On-the-job gains in human capital represent an unmeasured but strongly procyclical part of output, investment, and labor compensation.

Some human capital becomes obsolete rapidly, so full-time workers maintain higher levels of human capital than part-time workers. This makes hourly pay higher for full-time workers than for part-time workers, and it causes firms to lay off employees instead of just cutting back their hours when times are bad.

Conventional measures of Tobin's q reflect the relation between current and past levels of capital at market value. We can interpret Tobin's q as a ratio of market value to replacement cost only by arbitrarily excluding a portion of replacement cost. When we use the full cost of replacement, Tobin's q is identically one.

Conventional measures of the Solow residual use a physical capital input measured at book value, and omit the human capital input entirely. When we use symmetric inputs, the numbers change completely. No matter what inputs we use, the Solow residual reflects both tastes and technology. If we bring in variation in the relevance and utilization of composite capital, both now and in the expected future, the Solow residual can vanish entirely.

Knowledge and ideas sometimes travel from person to person, from firm to firm, or from country to country without compensation. They can be used over and over without any physical deterioration. But ideas do become obsolete, especially when new but related ideas arrive. New ideas are more apt to steal markets from old ideas than to increase the values of old ideas. Thus, as a first approximation, we can assume that ideas are like any other kind of capital. They are costly to create, valuable to use, and perishable.

We use new public and private technology by investing in specialized human and physical capital. Adoption of new technology takes time. All sectors are like this: as a first approximation, innovation affects sectors like human capital or equipment in the same way it affects other sectors.

The distribution of relative output levels across countries hasn't changed much for decades or centuries, but countries at the extremes of the distribution show mean reversion. Permanent shocks to output can cause divergence, but joint production involving teams from countries with close economic ties tends to reduce the dispersion in output levels, so it causes convergence.

I believe the real equilibrium, in a world with fully developed and freely operating financial markets, is almost entirely independent of price levels. In fact, I don't even think we can use monetary policy to control the inflation rate. Active monetary and exchange rate policies create opportunities for speculators, but have no significant macroeconomic effects. Passive policies break down only when governments run large deficits, which causes hyperinflation, and when nominal interest rates approach zero.

In principle, we can test the general equilibrium approach by looking at marketing and engineering data in great detail. We can identify our models by going beyond price and quantity data. We can observe preferences and production possibilities. In practice, testing the general equilibrium approach would be enormously costly. Instead of restricting our models in arbitrary ways so they are easy to reject, I suggest that we create many examples of the general equilibrium approach that we can use to explore the various aspects of the economy.

Part IV

Neutral Technical Change

Introduction

Were the 1980s characterized by "skill-biased technical change?" Did research and development, especially in computers and other equipment, lead to innovations that made education and experience more valuable? Did these innovations actually reduce wages for those without relevant skills? What role did freer trade play in the evolution of the wage structure?

I claim that we can understand many of the stylized facts as arising from rapid but neutral technical change. We can model neutral technical change in a world with no fixed factors as the balanced accumulation of human and physical capital. This works even if technical change starts with ideas that we must embody through investment in new capital. It means that we can capture all gains in "total factor productivity" (TFP) as gains in capital (measured in efficiency units).

Neutral technical change varies in speed, and is sometimes negative, as when unexpected obsolescence outweighs the normal accumulation of capital. In every decade, we also see very sector-specific shifts in tastes and technology that we do not expect to persist. In fact, these shifts also cause the unexpected portion of neutral technical change.

I claim that both human and physical capital, measured in efficiency units, grew rapidly in the 1980s. The most direct evidence for this was the increase in the market value of physical capital, as measured by stock, bond, and real estate prices. The increase in efficiency units of human capital is suggested by both the rise in the mean real wage and the dispersion of real wages. If we use an inflation measure that takes full account of quality changes, the real wage rose a lot during the 1980s. Human capital probably rose even faster, because a rapid rise in human capital is not reflected in wages right away. The increase in human capital through on-the-job learning is itself part of labor compensation.

Because we use human and physical capital together in production, neutral technical change can look like skill-biased technical change. An increase in physical capital, measured in efficiency units, increases the marginal product of investments in human capital and reduces the marginal product of investments in physical capital. Thus we will slant future investments toward human capital. If human capital measures "skill," we will see the original increase in physical capital create an increase in the returns to skill and the accumulation of human capital. An improvement in physical capital will look like "skill-biased" technical change.

To have a balanced increase in human and physical capital, we must increase human capital. A single business can do that by replacing a worker with one who has more skill. The economy can do it by replacing retiring workers with others on a faster track of human capital accumulation, and by encouraging all workers to obtain more education (before or after starting work) and more experience (in efficiency units). When capital accumulation is rapid, we expect to see wide education and experience differentials (especially when we use good measures of education and experience).

Periods of rapid accumulation of human capital will appear to be periods when the "demand for skill" is unusually high. The price of skill will be high, and its quantity will be increasing rapidly. Thus the "supply of skill" will be increasing along with demand. Skill differs from other goods because the amount of it can increase without limit (measured in efficiency units). It is a capital good rather than a consumer good.

In general, more skill should mean a higher wage, but rapid growth in skill should mean a lower wage, as compensation is diverted from direct pay to added human capital. When neutral technical change is rapid, most labor compensation can take the form of accumulating human capital, while direct wage compensation grows slowly for a while. Direct pay will reach its peak only as growth slows down. Also, human capital in efficiency units can change abruptly (up or down) as shifts in tastes and technology make it more or less relevant to current conditions. It follows more of a geometric random walk than a smooth growth path.

Part of capital accumulation involves added specialization, both across industries and within industries. In an open economy, added specialization usually means increasing trade and investment, and wholesale shifts of certain kinds of jobs among countries. We upgrade human capital partly by "exporting" industries that make heavy use of workers with little human capital, and partly by exporting low-skill jobs within each industry. Thus all technical change can appear to be "skill-biased," and the extra trade that comes with added specialization can appear to cause the export of low-skill jobs.

Neutral technical change, then, means the accumulation of capital, including technical capital like ideas and knowledge generally. In open economies, it usually involves added trade and investment. It shows up especially in certain industries and in certain kinds of activity within each industry. It often involves added specialization. At the most general level, though, we can model it as simply the balanced accumulation of human and physical capital.

Modeling Neutral Technical Change

Technical change seems to involve "ideas," with properties that ordinary capital doesn't have. We can transfer ideas to new people more easily than we can create new ideas. New ideas have positive externalities, but they also may steal the market from old ideas. When a new way of making polyethylene makes the old way obsolete, much of what we invested in the old way turns to waste. Thus we can start by ignoring both positive and negative externalities, and treat investment in ideas the same as investment in any other kind of capital.

Roughly, then, technical change can take any of three equivalent forms. It can make old capital more effective, which is like multiplying the amount of capital. It can create freely available opportunities to invest in new kinds of human and physical capital. This new capital then embodies the new technology. Or it can take the form of intentional investment in research and development, the results of which are owned by the investor. As a first approximation, we can model any of these forms as the balanced accumulation of human and physical capital through saving and investment. It's that simple.

We can interpret neutral technical change as coming out of nowhere (or abroad) to change the effectiveness of human and physical capital, as creating opportunities to invest in new human and physical capital, as the human and physical capital we create through research and development, or (most simply) as all the human and physical capital created in any way at all. In a world with no externalities and no fixed factors of production, all of these are equivalent.

Write y_t for output, h_t for human capital, and k_t for physical capital. Human capital is in efficiency units, so it grows faster than average years of schooling or experience. Physical capital is in efficiency units, and is both tangible and intangible. Both kinds of capital change with investment, obsolescence, and shifts in the relevance of existing capital to current conditions. We are abstracting from variation in hours worked or effort, so we omit any labor input other than human capital. The simplest production function goes a long way:

$$y_t = A_t k_t^a h k_t^{1-a},$$ (1)

In principle, A, k, and h can all change through time, but we lose no generality by incorporating changes in A into k and h. In other words, we can assume that A is constant, and that technical change takes the form of accumulation (not always positive) of human and physical capital.

Solow (1957) defines "neutral technical change" as a shift in the conventional two-factor production function that leaves marginal rates of substitution unchanged. He simply multiplies the production function by a factor that depends only on time. Because he doesn't allow for variation in the efficiency units embodied in a piece of physical capital, and because he doesn't recognize human capital explicitly, he concludes that the increase in gross output per man over the period 1909–1949 was 87.5 percent technical change and 12.5 percent increased use of capital. Since we can model all technical change as accumulation of human and physical capital in efficiency units, I don't understand this distinction.

In a world of uncertainty, human and physical capital can be out of balance, but then we shift our investments toward the kind of capital in short supply, which tends to restore the balance. This random progress of the two kinds of capital, with uneven growth and varying degrees of balance, can make neutral technical change look like technical change that is biased toward skill or high-tech physical capital.

We can choose to take output in the form of consumption goods and services, new human capital, or new physical capital. At this level of abstraction, we do not distinguish among the processes that give these various forms of output. When we add more detail, though, we might model production of human capital, for example, as making more use of human capital inputs, and production of physical capital as making more use of physical capital inputs.

Accumulation of physical and human capital

Since the production function has no fixed factors, we can model endless growth without assuming that abstract growth in technology drives everything. Technology can be just one form of capital, and growth can be balanced accumulation of all kinds of capital.

How can we think of technical progress as the accumulation of human and physical capital? Don't finite lifetimes limit the amount of education and experience that workers can accumulate? Doesn't accumulation of physical capital eventually lead to diminishing returns?

Diminishing returns require fixed factors of production, and we have not encountered any fixed factors over recorded history. People have pointed to many potential fixed factors, ranging from food to clean air to oil, but none have turned out to be truly limiting. We have always found ways to increase supply or to substitute away from potential fixed factors. Thus the returns to accumulation of capital have not diminished.

Someday we will encounter a fixed factor. Human life will end, either on the earth or on distant planets. But this will not likely happen for many millennia.

We can measure physical capital at cost when we first invest to create it. It includes tangible assets like plant and equipment and inventories, consumer durables, and intangibles like reputation and brand awareness. Over time, physical capital tends to deteriorate. Obsolescence, though, is more important than deterioration. Obsolescence is very erratic, and depends partly on shifts in tastes and technology that change the relevance of existing physical capital. We create much of the obsolescence in existing physical capital by investing in new physical capital. Research and development can also make existing physical capital less relevant.

We accumulate physical capital by investing enough to offset the obsolescence and deterioration in existing physical capital. Some years, obsolescence is negative because of shifts in tastes and technology that increase the relevance of existing capital. Other years, obsolescence is so severe that we can't invest enough to offset it. On average, though, we invest more than enough to offset the obsolescence and other sorts of depreciation in existing physical capital, including obsolescence caused by our investments in new kinds of capital.

Human capital accumulates in much the same way. We create new human capital through formal education and training, but mostly through living and working. We create a big part of it before starting school. Human capital becomes obsolete just as physical capital does, at a highly variable rate that is sometimes negative. Finite lifetimes don't really change the picture much, because we lose most of our human capital through obsolescence rather than death.

Note in particular that we are assuming endless growth in human capital. Sometimes this takes the form of added years of schooling and experience, but that kind of growth has clear limits. The most general form of growth in human capital is an increase in the value of a year of schooling or a year of experience. We can see this increase in rising wage levels and in the rising cost of providing schooling and experience. Thus the limits to human life do not imply limits to the human capital a person can acquire in his lifetime.

People accumulate units of capital through education and experience. Each unit has a cost or price and a rental rate. Wages can rise steadily over time because units of human capital are accumulating, even though unit prices and rental rates are generally stable.

On-the-job experience is a major source of human capital. We pay for it mostly by taking lower direct wages than we see in jobs that don't provide useful experience. The cost of this kind of human capital rises and falls as labor compensation rises and falls.

Similarly, the cost of a unit of formal training rises and falls, but mostly rises over time. We certainly do not measure the human capital provided by schooling in years of schooling. Initially, we measure it at cost. A thousand dollars worth of schooling this year, though, is not equivalent to a thousand dollars worth of schooling last year. This year's schooling is more relevant (on average), and we retain more of it.

Because gross investment in human capital is so rapid (though much of it is unrecorded in the national product accounts), and because its cost and value continue to rise indefinitely (on average) we can accumulate human capital indefinitely. Human and physical capital can remain in balance, and the shares of GDP going to "labor" and "capital" can remain roughly constant.

In a world of accumulating and sector-specific human and physical capital, supply and demand shifts can operate in counterintuitive ways. As people become more skilled, wages generally rise. An increase in the quantity of people with more than a given level of skill is associated with an increase in their wages, even though we see no special increase in demand for people with those skill levels.

It looks like a simultaneous increase in price and quantity, which suggests an upward shift in demand. In fact, though, it is an increase in supply as much as an increase in demand. It may reflect a simple desire to accumulate human and physical capital so future consumption can be high. In other words, it may reflect the desire to save. We don't need to assume a shift in any supply or demand curve to explain it.

In a sense, this is a case where supply creates its own demand. No matter how much human and physical capital we have, we can always use more. When production is governed by (1), or by a variant of (1) that includes many varieties of human and physical capital, adding more capital does not reduce wages or rental rates on physical capital.

Since units of human and physical capital are very sector-specific, where we define sectors very narrowly, shifts in tastes and technology along many dimensions can cause major changes in relative wages among different kinds of workers. This happens both within and across conventionally defined industries. In fact, human and physical capital usually respond in similar ways to these shifts. Because these shifts have such big effects, we cannot simply apply a constant depreciation rate to the cost of new investments in human and physical capital. Measured in efficiency units, human and physical capital vary much as stock and bond prices vary.

In effect, shifts in tastes and technology across microsectors cause changes in supply and demand for different workers. Because some kinds of human capital become obsolete quite slowly, these changes have long-lasting effects. Swings in the fortunes of different sorts of workers that last a decade or more are superimposed on the upward drift of human and physical capital. I see no reason to believe that taste shifts are usually more important than technology shifts, or that technology shifts are usually more important than taste shifts. Similarly, I don't know how to rank the relative importance of supply and demand shifts for units of different kinds of human capital. In fact, if demand shifts are more important, people will change the nature of their production processes to increase the importance of supply shifts. I can see no reason to assume that supply is fixed, either within or across industries, when analyzing data.

In equilibrium, supply and demand schedules interact to fix price and quantity. Excess supply and excess demand are both zero. It doesn't make sense to say that supply and demand are out of balance or mismatched, because price and quantity can adjust so that a mismatch never occurs. Except when governments (or unions supported by governments) intervene, the same is true in labor markets. Wages and supplies of different kinds of workers adjust to balance supply and demand.

Once we move to a dynamic model with uncertainty and lots of sectoral detail, though, the picture changes a bit. Supply and demand are still balanced at every moment, but we must make detailed decisions about investments in human and physical capital based on incomplete information about the future. When the future arrives, we may be happy or unhappy about the specific investments we made.

If we made our investments in the right areas, we will see a good match between wants and resources, and the market value of human and physical capital will be high. Otherwise, it will be low. We can think of shifts in tastes and technology as affecting the quantity of human and physical capital measured in efficiency units, as reflected in market values.

Can we see a mismatch between the amount of human and physical capital the economy wants and the amount available? No: the economy can use any amount of human and physical capital. With no fixed factors, adding human and physical capital doesn't even drive down wages, or rental rates on physical capital. In this sense, we can't see a mismatch between the skill requirements of available jobs and the skills available (together with a mismatch between required and actual sophistication levels for physical capital).

We can, however, have an imbalance between human and physical capital. An unexpected shift in tastes or technology can affect human and physical capital differently, causing one to be more relevant to current conditions than the other. Over time, we can correct the imbalance by investing more in the kind of capital that has become less relevant. While we are investing, assuming that we are investing more than normal in human capital, we can say that the jobs available require more skill (on average) than the workers have. In effect, the skill level of available jobs is set by the sophistication level of our physical capital.

The balance between human and physical capital is a relatively minor aspect, though, of the match between wants and resources. We can have "too much" or "too little" capital in all sorts of sectors, as defined in great detail along many dimensions. Having too little capital in a microsector means directing an unusually large fraction of new investment in human and physical capital to that microsector.

In general, I don't think Say's Law makes much sense. Supply creates its own demand only by causing price changes that bring us back to equilibrium. As applied to accumulation of human and physical capital, though, it does make sense. With no fixed factors, we can save and invest as much as we want without affecting prices in any predictable direction. Supply of skill, as embodied in human capital, when accompanied by supply of sufficiently sophisticated physical capital, does indeed create its own demand.

Interpreting the 1980s

I think we can explain the 1980s partly with unusually rapid neutral technical change, but mostly with unique shifts in tastes and technology. These shifts increased the values of some kinds of human and physical capital and reduced the values of other kinds. To describe these shifts, we need models with sector-specific human and physical capital, where we define the sectors in great detail along many dimensions.

In the 1980s, barriers to international trade and investment fell, and gross volumes of trade and investment rose. This facilitated the added specialization and other forms of upgrading of human and physical capital. It allowed us to export more of our low-skill jobs. People speak of the effects of trade on jobs, but trade itself is hardly a causal factor. Reduced barriers to trade and investment come closer to the causal factors, but these changes had more fundamental causes in turn.

Immigration also changed its character somewhat in the 1980s. Immigrants had lower skills, on average, than prior immigrants. This too was related to the change in the wage structure, and tied in with the increased wage dispersion. Women also entered the labor force on balance consistently over the decade, partly because the divorce rate was high. This reduced the mean growth in real wages. The decline in union membership over the decade had a similar effect. All of these factors suggest that the mean growth in human capital was probably greater than the mean growth in real wages.

Lots of differentials changed in the 1980s. For example, the differential between the mean wage of college graduates and the mean wage of nongraduates increased. We sometimes describe this as an increase in the "education premium." We even say that it reflects greater demand for college graduates. Note, though, that this is exactly what we expect when the mean education level rises. In a sense, it is a statistical artifact. The mean education level of college nongraduates did not change much, but the mean education level of college graduates continued to rise, even when measured very crudely, as by years in school. Thus the increase in this differential may be simply one aspect of the neutral technical change (or balanced growth in human and physical capital) that highlights this period.

The same is true of other differentials, like the blue-collar/white-collar differential and the production worker/nonproduction worker differential in manufacturing. By themselves, the increases in these differentials don't tell us much. They go along with rapid but neutral growth in composite capital.

The general lesson here is that we must be very careful about reading things into the statistics we get by classifying data. Just as correlation does not imply causation, classification does not imply structure. We should be especially wary when we set out to "decompose" some preliminary results. Decomposition is as likely to deceive us as to tell us what we really want to know.

People writing about wage structure often speak of trade and technology as if they were alternative causes of the changes we have seen, especially in the 1980s. They create models where expanded trade or a trade deficit or advancement of high technology or advancement of computers in particular hurts workers, especially workers with few skills.

Curiously, both of these proposed "explanations" of wage structure changes sound very familiar. Businesspeople have for centuries called for protection against competing imports. Economists have generally rejected such mercantile arguments, saying that the benefits of free trade generally outweigh the costs to businesses and workers most affected by imports.

Similarly, unions and workers have for centuries called for restraints on automation, saying that new machines and more efficient production methods cost workers their jobs. Such arguments are named for the Luddites, who used violent methods to slow the introduction of new technology. Again, economists have generally rejected these arguments, saying that the benefits of adopting new technology are high.

Economists' arguments are somewhat subtle, since the benefits of trade and technology are widespread while the costs are sometimes concentrated. That's why the media tend to emphasize the costs, while economists emphasize the benefits. In most cases, even people with very low wages gain from free trade and added technology.

The literature on wage structure, though, is an exception. At least for the 1980s, economists identify trade and technology as the main causes of slow growth in median wages and increased wage dispersion. The main debate concerns the relative weights to assign to trade and technology.

I am mystified by this approach. I find it hard to believe that either trade or technology had a generally negative effect in the 1980s. If either or both did, then that decade was very unusual. I doubt that it holds lessons for the future.

Moreover, reduced barriers to trade and investment can contribute to technical progress and capital accumulation. You can have technical progress without added trade, or increased trade without technical progress, but normally they go together. When trying to explain something like a change in the structure of wages, I see no reason to assume that trade (which means reduced barriers to trade and investment) and technical change (which goes hand in hand with capital accumulation) are mutually exclusive.

Both freer trade and advancing technology work their wonders partly by reducing consumer prices and partly by adding to the available array of consumer goods and services. To measure their benefits, we must have good price indexes that capture transactions prices on an expanding list of items. Existing indexes fall short on both counts. With better price indexes, I think we'll find that average real incomes and even median real incomes (including benefits) rose in the 1980s.

Normal sources of growth affected the 1980s as they do most decades. Some things, though, were specific to the 1980s. Relative prices and relative wages changed in ways that we have not generally seen and do not expect to generally see in the future. The dispersion of real wages rose, but it is unlikely to continue growing indefinitely.

Increased wage dispersion doubtless had many causes, some related to the specific sectors that did relatively well or badly in the 1980s. It may have reflected a better alignment of pay with marginal product, as artificial barriers (like those created by unions) fell. If technical change was unusually rapid in the 1980s, ability to adapt to rapid change may have been especially well rewarded. More able people are typically more able to adapt to rapid change, as discussed by Welch (1970). In this sense, rapid technical change may almost always be skill-biased. Beyond that, the particular sectors and subsectors favored by the changes in tastes and technology that we saw in the 1980s may have been sectors where workers tend to have lots of human capital. Both technical change and taste change can be skill-biased in this sense (in particular periods).

Technical growth and capital accumulation are always concentrated in certain sectors. In the 1980s, much of the growth involved computers. Firms added physical capital in the form of computer hardware and software. To balance that, they added programmers, systems engineers, and the knowledge needed to interpret computer output.

In this sense, the technical change was skill-biased. Computers require computer skills. Computer skills require computers. This is a kind of complementarity. But we can model it, at either the industry level or the aggregate level, using ordinary Cobb-Douglas production functions. The causation does not run from technical change in physical capital to skills. The technical change affects human and physical capital at roughly the same time; at least, neither consistently leads the other. If this is bias, then all technical change is skill-biased.

One way for an open economy to add human capital is to export the less skilled parts of its production process. This can happen both across industries and within industries. An industry that takes less skill can move to join similar industries abroad. Or the parts of an industry that take less skill can move abroad. I can see no way to attach meaning to the percentage of exports of less skilled jobs that occur within industries.

Note that exporting low-skill jobs need not mean reducing the skill levels in the target economies. The exported jobs can have lower-than-average skills for us, but higher-than-average skills for them.

Another way for an open economy to add human capital is to increase its degree of specialization. When specialization becomes more extensive, all economies involved can gain human capital together. Again, this can occur both across industries, as when some industries effectively disappear from some economies, and within industries, as when some kinds of jobs effectively disappear from all industries in a given economy. While some industries or jobs disappear, entirely new ones may appear.

Like capital accumulation generally, added specialization involves a simultaneous increase in demand and supply. More specialized capital is like more capital, when measured in efficiency units. And more specialization requires more investment and more human and physical capital.

Readings

Here's a sampling of the papers on the changes in the wage structure in the 1980s, with comments on problems I see in them. Perhaps the most common problem is discussing skill-biased technical change without considering neutral technical change as an alternative. Maybe the decade of the 1980s was simply a period of unusually rapid neutral technical change.

Berman, Bound, and Griliches (1994) review new and old evidence on the shift in demand away from unskilled and toward skilled labor in U.S. manufacturing in the 1980s. They find that production labor-saving technological change is the chief explanation. They do not consider the simplest explanation: that the 1980s saw rapid accumulation of human and physical capital. They claim to see meaning in the fact that the shift is due mostly to increased use of skilled workers within the 450 industries rather than a reallocation of employment across industries. I think that reduced barriers to trade and investment are as likely to stimulate intra-industry trade as inter-industry trade, and that we can as easily export low-skill jobs within industries as across industries. They note that sectors showing increased use of nonproduction workers are also apt to be sectors showing investment in computers and R&D, but something like that will be true under any story, including my simple story of capital accumulation. Similarly, they treat trade and technical change as alternate explanations for skill upgrading, but these explanations can easily be two parts of a single story of human and physical capital accumulation.

Blanchard (1995) looks for macroeconomic implications of shifts in the relative demand for skills. He notes both relative demand and relative supply of skills have increased; this is similar to the notion that both supply of and demand for human and physical capital have increased. He says that much of what we see can be explained by an adverse neutral shift in aggregate demand for labor. This is similar to my notion that much of what we see is a neutral gain in skills and technology; an increase in average capital can eliminate domestic jobs for people with human capital levels that are well below fixed thresholds. It also reduces the supply of such people. He says that the forces causing a shift in wage structure may well reverse in the future, which is consistent with a large role for unexpected shifts in tastes and technology across many sectors and subsectors. Even though he includes some empirical work that effectively uses correlation to infer causation, he says it is hard to draw definite conclusions from the empirical literature. He is quite tentative, as I would be, about drawing policy conclusions from this literature.

Borjas and Ramey (1994) find that a high correlation between wage inequality and durable goods trade is a persistent feature of the U.S. economy for the period 1963–1990. They take this correlation to indicate causation. I feel that's a leap of faith, and is unjustified. Wage inequality and durable goods trade do, I believe, have some common causes. Variation in the pace of neutral technical change is one common cause of variation in wage inequality and trade, especially when we measure wage inequality using truncated educational categories. Finally, they look for technological progress in the residuals of their regressions. This is another unsound way to use correlation to indicate causation. It is no more justified here than it is in the use of conventional measures of TFP.

Bound and Johnson (1992) use data from the Current Population Survey to analyze the 1980s increase in the relative wages of highly educated workers. They use an interesting theoretical structure that allows each group of workers to have a higher marginal product in one sector than in any others: in effect, they assume sector-specific human capital. They also allow for changes in "unmeasured labor quality," which might mean human capital beyond what's associated with things like years of education and experience. But they make other assumptions that are so restrictive that I don't know what to make of their results: for example, they assume that the aggregate supply in each group of workers does not depend on its relative average wage (p. 376). They conclude that "the" major cause of the wage changes of the 1980s was a shift in the skill structure of labor demand brought about by biased technological change. But they refer to the cause in their empirical work as "general" or sector-specific technical change, which suggests that we can easily reinterpret it as neutral rather than biased technical change. In general, their empirical work involves attempts to read causation into decompositions and other forms of correlation.

Davis et al. (1991) analyze the Longitudinal Research Datafile, which has observations on more than 300,000 manufacturing plants, with more frequent observations on fewer plants since 1972. They also use wage data from the Current Population Survey. They decompose the total variance of wages in various ways. I feel that decomposition is like correlation, and can't tell us what we want to know. They find (as others have) that workers at large plants earn more, and that this size differential increased from 1967 to 1986. They find an upgrading of skills in manufacturing, especially at large plants. All this is consistent with a rapid increase in both human and physical capital. They claim that the facts support their view that skill-biased technical change has been the major driving force behind rising wage inequality in the United States, but almost all their facts seem equally consistent with rapid but neutral technical change as the driving force. They talk about product demand shifts as an alternate explanation, but not supply shifts. Even neutral technical change will always be concentrated in certain sectors. Thus sectoral shifts in both demand and supply can help explain facts like the shift in the distribution of hours worked toward small plants from 1967 to 1972. (As they note, much of this was related to massive shrinkage of a few large plants in aerospace and defense.)

Johnson and Stafford (1993) show that improvements abroad can hurt real wages at home. I agree that this can happen, and may have figured into the 1980s changes in wage structure. They use a Heckscher-Ohlin model where labor moves freely between sectors in each country, so I don't put much weight on the details of their analysis. But similar things happen in more realistic models with sector-specific human and physical capital. In particular, innovation in one country can cause obsolescence in another country's human and physical capital, even when all sectors in all countries are perfectly competitive. In open economies without government intervention, these gains and losses are likely to be largely random, so we do not expect future gains and losses to be similar to those of the 1980s.

Juhn, Murphy, and Pierce (1993) show large increases in U.S. wage inequality over the 1970s and 1980s. These increases occur both within and across conventional education and experience groups, and both within and across cohorts of workers who entered the market at the same time. The increases occur at varying times for different groups. Since the proportion of skilled workers (using fixed categories or the right tail of the wage distribution) rose along with inequality, they say it was an increase in "demand for skill." They claim it was not an increase in dispersion in unobserved ability, because we see it within cohorts (423). Everything changes, though, when we think of skill as human capital. Human capital (measured in efficiency units) can change greatly, within cohorts as people invest in it at varying rates, and as its relevance changes with changed circumstances. An increase in wages together with an increase in supply of skilled workers can simply reflect added human capital, which is added supply as much as it is added demand for units of human capital. They try to read causation into decomposition and the timing of variance changes, but I am not persuaded. The human capital point of view undercuts their conclusion that demand for skill rose in the United States over this period. My conclusion from their data is that both demand for and supply of units of human capital rose over this period, and shifts in tastes and technology defined in great sectoral detail caused a change in wage dispersion both within and across conventional categories.

Katz and Murphy (1992) analyze the wages and numbers of workers in various groups from 1963 to 1987. Their "simple supply and demand framework" (35) suggests a role for the supply of college graduates and for both within-sector and across-sector shifts in labor demand in the changing structure of wages. They make so many simplifying assumptions, though, that I don't know what to make of their conclusions. Much of the time, they treat labor supply as exogenous, so they don't allow for supply curve shifts. They feel that within-industry demand shifts and across-industry demand shifts have different causes, perhaps because they have a Heckscher-Ohlin model in mind. In their formal model, they assume that labor inputs are not sector-specific. They say that they hold sector-specific unit cost functions fixed (59). They consider the possibility of "factor-neutral technological change" and "neutral demand shifts" (48), but do not go on to analyze their effects on the wage structure as we normally show it. Supply and demand surely explain wage structure along with most other things, but not in the particular way that Katz and Murphy suggest. The first step toward a more realistic model is to think about the supply of and demand for human capital (of various kinds) rather than labor.

Krugman, Cooper, and Srinivasan (1995) use a conventional general equilibrium trade model to analyze the causes and consequences of growing world trade. He notes that trade has only recently returned to its nineteenth-century levels, but that it has new features, including (1) growth in trade in similar goods among similar countries; (2) use of many-step production processes, with each step in a different country; (3) the emergence of countries like Singapore that specialize in trade; and (4) rapid growth in exports of manufactured goods from low wage countries. He notes that the causes of recent trade growth include technology (as in shipping costs) and politics (as in tariffs). He feels that these factors cannot explain much of the increase in unemployment in Europe, or the increase in wage inequality in America. Much of his discussion is consistent with worldwide neutral technical change, including added specialization made possible by increased trade and investment. The general equilibrium model he uses, though, has the fatal flaws of the Heckscher-Ohlin approach. He assumes that both skilled and unskilled labor can shift freely among sectors and subsectors.

Lawrence et al. (1993) look at proposed explanations for slow growth in average wages during the 1980s, and for greater wage inequality. They conclude that "trade" was not a major causal factor, but that technological change biased toward nonproduction labor was. I consider their methods unsound, since they rely on Stolper-Samuelson analysis and an industry-by-industry study of TFP growth. They also note that wages deflated by a basket of goods produced in the United States grew faster than wages deflated by a basket of goods consumed in the United States. They think this bears on causation, but I think it simply reflects relative price changes associated with shifts in tastes and technology across many sectors. They note in particular the increase in housing costs associated with increasing real estate values, but do not mention the corresponding increases in wealth and income for those who owned real estate.

Levy and Murnane (1992) survey the literature on earnings levels and earnings inequality. They accept the notions that within-group inequality differs somehow from between-group inequality (where we define groups by age, education, and gender), that higher numbers and higher wages imply greater demand for that kind of labor, and that classification or correlation can tell us about causation. They omit any discussion of human capital, which makes their "Economics 1 test" for shifts in demand misleading or wrong. When human capital per person is increasing within a group, its numbers and wages can both increase through a joint supply/demand effect, as discussed earlier. Their implicit models, like those in the literature, are static rather than dynamic, so they fail to see the truth in the "mismatch hypothesis." They think a mismatch between desired and available skills can be eliminated by wage changes; but, in fact, if workers acquire skills over many years that turn out to differ in sectoral detail from those the economy wants, equilibrium wages will be low. Even though supply and demand are always in equilibrium, we may spend years or decades eliminating the mismatch by shifting human capital investments to more suitable minisectors and microsectors.

Sachs et al. (1994) say that increased trade with developing countries follows Heckscher-Ohlin-Samuelson patterns, and has contributed to a decline in low-skill employment and a rise in high-skill employment, both within and across sectors. They say increased trade contributed also to growing wage inequality over the last fifteen years. In reaching their conclusions, they repeatedly use forms of correlation, including decomposition and regression, to indicate causation. They use the fatally flawed Heckscher-Ohlin—Samuelson theory and the equally flawed conventional estimates of TFP. They claim that falling low-skill employment together with falling low-skill wages indicate biased technical change, but neutral technical change can give the same patterns, when we define skill in absolute rather than relative terms. Neutral technical change, operating partly through increased trade, can explain everything they observe except the increased wage dispersion of the 1980s.

References

Berman, Eli, John Bound, and Zvi Griliches. "Changes in the Demand for Skilled Labor within U.S. Manufacturing: Evidence from the Annual Survey of Manufacturers." *Quarterly Journal of Economics* 109 (May 1994): 367–397.

Blanchard, Olivier. "Macroeconomic Implications of Shifts in the Relative Demand for Skills." *FRBNY Economic Policy Review* 1 (January 1995): 48–53.

Borjas, George J., and Valerie A. Ramey. "Rising Wage Inequality in the United States: Causes and Consequences." *American Economic Review* 84 (2): 17–22.

Bound, John, and George Johnson. "Changes in the Structure of Wages in the 1980's: An Evaluation of Alternative Explanations." *American Economic Review* 82 (June 1992): 371–392.

Davis, Steve J., John Haltiwanger, Lawrence F. Katz, and Robert Topel. "Wage Dispersion between and within U.S. Manufacturing Plants, 1963–86." *Brookings Papers on Economic Activity, Microeconomics* 1991 (1991): 115–200.

Johnson, George E., and Frank P. Stafford. "International Competition and Real Wages." *The American Economic Review* 83 (2) (May 1993), Papers and Proceedings of the Hundred and Fifth Annual Meeting of the *American Economic Association Papers and Proceedings*: 27–130.

Juhn, Chinhui, Kevin M. Murphy, and Brooks Pierce. "Wage Inequality and the Rise in Returns to Skill." *Journal of Political Economy* 101 (June 1993): 410–442.

Katz, Lawrence F., and Kevin M. Murphy. "Changes in Relative Wages, 1963–1987: Supply and Demand Factors." *Quarterly Journal of Economics* 107 (February 1992): 35–78.

Krugman, Paul, Richard N. Cooper, and T. N. Srinivasan. "Growing World Trade: Causes and Consequences." *Brookings Papers on Economic Activity* 1995 (1995): 327–377.

Lawrence, Robert Z., Matthew J. Slaughter, Robert E. Hall, Steven J. Davis, and Robert H. Topel. "International Trade and American Wages in the 1980s: Giant Sucking Sound or Small Hiccup?" *Brookings Papers on Economic Activity, Microeconomics* 1993 (1993): 161–226

Levy, Frank. and Richard J. Murnane. "U.S. Earnings Levels and Earnings Inequality: A Review of Recent Trends and Proposed Explanations." *Journal of Economic Literature* 30 (September 1992): 1333–1381.

Sachs, Jeffrey D., Howard J. Shatz, Alan Deardorff, and Robert E. Hall. "Trade and Jobs in U.S. Manufacturing." *Brookings Papers on Economic Activity, Microeconomics* 1994 (1994): 1–84.

Solow, Robert M. "Technical Change and the Aggregate Production Function." *Review of Economis and Statistics* 39 (August 1957): 312–320.

Welch, Finis. "Education in Production." *Journal of Political Economy* 78 (January/February 1970): 35–59.

References

Abel, Andrew B. "Asset Prices under Habit Formation and Catching Up with the Joneses." *AEA Papers and Proceedings* 80 (May 1990): 38–42.

Abel, Andrew B. "The Equity Premium Puzzle." *Federal Reserve Bank of Philadelphia Business Review* (September/October 1991): 3–14.

Abel, Andrew B., and Janice C. Eberly. "A Unified Model of Investment Under Uncertainty." *American Economic Review* 84 (December 1994): 1369–1384.

Abraham, Katharine. "Help-Wanted Advertising, Job Vacancies, and Unemployment." *Brookings Papers on Economic Activity* No. 1 (1987): 207–248.

Abraham, Katharine. "Comment" (on Davis and Haltiwanger (1990)). In Olivier J. Blanchard and Stanley Fischer, eds. *NBER Macroeconomics Annual* 5 (Cambridge, MA: MIT Press, 1990): 169–177.

Abraham, Katharine, and Lawrence Katz. "Cyclical Unemployment: Sectoral Shifts or Aggregate Disturbances?" *Journal of Political Economy* 94 (June 1986): 507–522.

Abramovitz, Moses. *Thinking About Growth* (Cambridge, MA: Cambridge University Press, 1989).

Aghion, Philippe, and Peter Howitt. "A Model of Growth through Creative Destruction." *Econometrica* 60 (March 1992): 323–351.

Aghion, Philippe, and Peter Howitt. "Growth and Unemployment." *Review of Economic Studies* 61 (July 1994): 477–494.

Aghion, Philippe, and Gilles Saint-Paul. "Uncovering Some Causal Relationships between Productivity Growth and the Structure of Economic Fluctuations." NBER Working Paper No. 4603 (December 1993).

Aiyagari, S. Rao. "On the Contribution of Technology Shocks to Business Cycles." *Federal Reserve Bank of Minneapolis Quarterly Review* 18 (Winter 1994): 22–34.

Alchian, Armen. "Costs and Outputs." In Moses Abramovitz, *et al. The Allocation of Economic Resources* (Stanford: Stanford University Press, 1959): 273–299.

Alesina, Alberto, Sule Özler, Nouriel Roubini, and Phillip Swagel. "Political Instability and Economic Growth." Harvard University Working Paper (November 1993).

Ambler, Steve, and Alain Paquet. "Stochastic Depreciation and the Business Cycle." *International Economic Review* 35 (February 1994): 101–116.

Ando, Albert. "Equilibrium Business-Cycle Models: An Appraisal." In F. Gerard Adams and Bert G. Hickman, eds. *Global Econometrics: Essays in Honor of Lawrence R. Klein* (Cambridge, MA: MIT Press, 1983): 39–67.

Andolfatto, David, and Glenn M. MacDonald. "Endogenous Technological Change, Growth, and Aggregate Fluctuations." University of Waterloo Working Paper (August 1993).

Arrow, Kenneth J. "Le rôle des valeurs boursières pour la répartition la meilleure des risques." *Econométrie, Colloques Internationaux du Centre National de la Recherche Scientifique* 11 (1953): 41–47.

Arrow, Kenneth J. "The Economic Implications of Learning by Doing." *Review of Economic Studies* 29 (June 1962): 155–172.

Arrow, Kenneth J. "The Role of Securities in the Optimal Allocation of Risk Bearing." *Review of Economic Studies* 31 (1964): 91–96.

Ashenfelter, Orley. "Macroeconomic Analyses and Microeconomic Analyses of Labor Supply." *Carnegie-Rochester Conference Series on Public Policy* 21 (1984): 117–156.

Atkeson, Andrew, and Patrick J. Kehoe. "Industry Evolution and Transition: The Role of Information Capital." Federal Reserve Bank of Minneapolis Working Paper (August 1993).

Backus, David K., Patrick J. Kehoe, and Finn E. Kydland. "International Real Business Cycles." *Journal of Political Economy* 100 (August 1992): 745–775.

Backus, David K., Patrick J. Kehoe, and Finn E. Kydland. "Dynamics of the Trade Balance and the Terms of Trade: The J-Curve?" *American Economic Review* 84 (March 1994): 84–103.

Backus, David K., Patrick J. Kehoe, and Finn E. Kydland. "International Business Cycles: Theory and Evidence." In Thomas F. Cooley, ed. *Frontiers of Business Cycle Research* (Princeton: Princeton University Press, forthcoming 1995).

Baily, Martin Neil. "Productivity and the Services of Capital and Labor." *Brookings Papers on Economic Activity* No. 1 (1981): 1–65.

Bak, Per, Kan Chen, José Scheinkman, and Michael Woodford. "Aggregate Fluctuations from Independent Sectoral Shocks: Self-Organized Criticality in a Model of Production and Inventory Dynamics." *Ricerche Economiche* 47 (1993): 3–30.

Barro, Robert J. "Output Effects of Government Purchases." *Journal of Political Economy* 89 (December 1981): 1086–1121.

Barro, Robert J. "Introduction." In Robert J. Barro, ed. *Modern Business Cycle Theory* (Cambridge, MA: Harvard University Press, 1989): 1–15.

Barro, Robert J. "Government Spending in a Simple Model of Endogenous Growth." *Journal of Political Economy* 98 (October 1990a): S103–S125.

Barro, Robert J. "The Stock Market and Investment." *Review of Financial Studies* 3 (1990b): 115–131.

Barro, Robert J. "Economic Growth in a Cross Section of Countries." *Quarterly Journal of Economics* 106 (May 1991): 407–443.

Barro, Robert J., and Robert G. King. "Time-Separable Preferences and Intertemporal-Substitution Models of Business Cycles." *Quarterly Journal of Economics* 99 (November 1984): 817–839.

Barro, Robert J., and Jong-Wha Lee. "Losers and Winners in Economic Growth." Proceedings of the World Bank Conference on Development Economics 1993 (1994): 267–297.

Barro, Robert J., N. Gregory Mankiw, and Xavier Sala-i-Martin. "Capital Mobility in Neoclassical Models of Growth." NBER Working Paper No. 4206 (November 1992).

Barro, Robert J., and Xavier Sala-i-Martin. "World Real Interest Rates." In Olivier J. Blanchard and Stanley Fischer, eds. *NBER Macroeconomics Annual* 5 (Cambridge, MA: MIT Press, 1990): 15–74.

Basu, Susanto. "Procyclical Productivity: Overhead Inputs or Cyclical Utilization?" University of Michigan Working Paper (December 1993).

Baxter, Marianne, and Mario J. Crucini. "Explaining Saving-Investment Correlations." *American Economic Review* 83 (June 1993a): 416–436.

Baxter, Marianne, and Mario J. Crucini. "Business Cycles and the Asset Structure of Foreign Trade." University of Rochester Working Paper (June 1993b).

Baxter, Marianne, and Urban J. Jermann. "The International Diversification Puzzle Is Worse than You Think." University of Rochester Working Paper (May 1993).

Becker, Gary S., Elisabeth M. Landes, and Robert T. Michael. "An Economic Analysis of Marital Instability." *Journal of Political Economy* 85 (December 1977): 1153–1189.

Becker, Gary S., and Kevin M. Murphy. "The Division of Labor, Coordination Costs, and Knowledge." *Quarterly Journal of Economics* 107 (November 1992): 1137–1160.

Bencivenga, Valerie R., Bruce D. Smith, and Ross M. Starr. "Liquidity of Secondary Capital Markets, Capital Accumulation, and the Term Structure of Asset Yields." Cornell University Working Paper (February 1994).

Benhabib, Jess, and Boyan Jovanovic. "Externalities and Growth Accounting." *American Economic Review* 81 (March 1991): 82–113.

Benhabib, Jess, Richard Rogerson, and Randall Wright. "Homework in Macroeconomics: Household Production and Aggregate Fluctuations." *Journal of Political Economy* 99 (December 1991): 1166–1187.

Bental, Benjamin, and Benjamin Eden. "Inventories in a Competitive Environment." *Journal of Political Economy* 101 (October 1993): 863–886.

Bergman, Yaacov Z. "Time Preference and Capital Asset Pricing Models." *Journal of Financial Economics* 14 (March 1985): 145–159.

Bernanke, Ben S. "Irreversibility, Uncertainty, and Cyclical Investment." *Quarterly Journal of Economics* 98 (February 1983): 85–106.

Bernanke, Ben S. "The World on a Cross of Gold." *Journal of Monetary Economics* 31 (April 1993): 251–267.

Bernanke, Ben S., and Mark Gertler. "Agency Costs, Net Worth, and Business Fluctuations." *American Economic Review* 79 (March 1989): 14–31.

Bernanke, Ben S., and Martin L. Parkinson. "Procyclical Labor Productivity and Competing Theories of the Business Cycle: Some Evidence from Interwar U.S. Manufacturing Industries." *Journal of Political Economy* 99 (June 1991): 439–459.

Bertola, Giuseppe, and Ricardo J. Caballero. "Irreversibility and Aggregate Investment." *Review of Economic Studies* 61 (April 1994): 223–246.

Beveridge, Stephen, and Charles R. Nelson. "A New Approach to Decomposition of Economic Time Series into Permanent and Transitory Components with Particular Attention to Measurement of the 'Business Cycle'." *Journal of Monetary Economics* 7 (March 1981): 151–174.

Bils, Mark. "The Cyclical Behavior of Marginal Cost and Price." *American Economic Review* 77 (December 1987): 838–855.

Black, Fischer. "Equilibrium in the Creation of Investment Goods under Uncertainty." In Michael C. Jensen, ed. *Studies in the Theory of Capital Markets* (New York: Praeger, 1972): 249–265.

Black, Fischer. *Business Cycles and Equilibrium* (Cambridge, MA: Basil Blackwell, 1987).

Blanchard, Olivier J. "Consumption and the Recession of 1990–1991." *AEA Papers and Proceedings* 83 (May 1993): 270–274.

Blanchard, Olivier J., and Peter Diamond. "The Beveridge Curve." *Brookings Papers on Economic Activity* No. 1 (1989): 1–76.

Blanchard, Olivier J., and Charles Wyplosz. "An Empirical Structural Model of Aggregate Demand." *Journal of Monetary Economics* 7 (January 1981): 1–28.

Blinder, Alan S. "Can the Production Smoothing Model of Inventory Behavior Be Saved?" *Quarterly Journal of Economics* 101 (August 1986): 431–453.

Blinder, Alan S., and Louis J. Maccini. "Taking Stock: A Critical Assessment of Recent Research on Inventories." *Journal of Economic Perspectives* 5 (Winter 1991): 73–96.

Blomström, Magnus, Robert E. Lipsey, and Mario Zejan. "Is Fixed Investment the Key to Economic Growth?" NBER Working Paper No. 4436 (August 1993).

Boeri, Tito. "Why Are Establishments So Heterogeneous?" OECD Working Paper (January 1994).

Boldrin, Michele. "Perfectly Competitive Models of Endogenous Business Fluctuations." *European Economic Review* 35 (April 1991): 300–305.

Bosworth, Barry. "The Stock Market and the Economy." *Brookings Papers on Economic Activity* No. 2 (1975): 257–290.

Boyd, John H., and Bruce D. Smith. "Capital Market Imperfections, International Credit Markets, and Nonconvergence." Federal Reserve Bank of Minneapolis Working Paper (May 1994).

Brainard, S. Lael, and David M. Cutler. "Sectoral Shifts and Cyclical Unemployment Reconsidered." *Quarterly Journal of Economics* 108 (February 1993): 219–243.

Brainard, William C., Matthew D. Shapiro, and John B. Shoven. "Fundamental Value and Market Value." In William C. Brainard, William D. Nordhaus, and Harold W. Watts, eds. *Macroeconomics, Finance, and Economic Policy: Essays in Honor of James Tobin* (Cambridge, MA: MIT Press, 1991): 277–307.

Breeden, Douglas T. "An Intertemporal Asset Pricing Model with Stochastic Consumption and Investment Opportunities." *Journal of Financial Economics* 7 (September 1979): 265–296.

Bresnahan, Timothy F., and Valerie A. Ramey. "Segment Shifts and Capacity Utilization in the U.S. Automobile Industry." *AEA Papers and Proceedings* 83 (May 1993): 213–218.

Brock, William A. "Asset Prices in a Production Economy." In John J. McCall, ed. *The Economics of Information and Uncertainty* (Chicago: University of Chicago Press, 1982): 1–46.

Brock, William A., and Leonard J. Mirman. "Optimal Economic Growth and Uncertainty: The Discounted Case." *Journal of Economic Theory* 4 (June 1972): 479–513.

Brock, William A., and Leonard J. Mirman. "Optimal Economic Growth and Uncertainty: The No-Discounting Case." *International Economic Review* 14 (1973): 560–573.

Burnside, Craig, Martin S. Eichenbaum, and Sérgio T. Rebelo. "Labor Hoarding and the Business Cycle." *Journal of Political Economy* 101 (April 1993): 245–273.

Caballé, Jordi, and Manuel S. Santos. "On Endogenous Growth with Physical and Human Capital." *Journal of Political Economy* 101 (December 1993): 1042–1067.

Caballero, Ricardo J. "Durable Goods: An Explanation for Their Slow Adjustment." *Journal of Political Economy* 101 (April 1993): 351–384.

Caballero, Ricardo J., and Eduardo M.R.A. Engel. "Dynamic *(S,s)* Economies." *Econometrica* 59 (November 1991): 1659–1686.

Caballero, Ricardo J., Eduardo M.R.A. Engel, and John Haltiwanger. "Aggregate Employment Dynamics: Building from Microeconomic Evidence." Massachusetts Institute of Technology Working Paper (November 1994).

Caballero, Ricardo J., and Mohamad L. Hammour. "The Cleansing Effect of Recessions." *American Economic Review* 84 (December 1994): 1350–1368.

Campbell, Jeffrey R. "Technical Change, Diffusion, and Productivity." Northwestern University Working Paper (February 1994).

Campbell, John Y. "Inspecting the Mechanism: An Analytical Approach to the Stochastic Growth Model." *Journal of Monetary Economics* 33 (June 1994): 463–506.

Campbell, John Y., and N. Gregory Mankiw. "Are Output Fluctuations Transitory?" *Quarterly Journal of Economics* 102 (May 1987a): 857–880.

Campbell, John Y., and N. Gregory Mankiw. "Permanent and Transitory Components in Macroeconomic Fluctuations." *AEA Papers and Proceedings* 77 (May 1987b): 111–117.

Campbell, John Y., and N. Gregory Mankiw. "Consumption, Income, and Interest Rates: Reinterpreting the Time Series Evidence." In Stanley Fischer, ed. *NBER Macroeconomics Annual* 4 (Cambridge, MA: MIT Press, 1989): 185–216.

Cardia, Emanuela. "The Dynamics of a Small Open Economy in Response to Monetary, Fiscal, and Productivity Shocks." *Journal of Monetary Economics* 28 (December 1991): 411–434.

Carroll, Christopher D., and David N. Weil. "Saving and Growth: A Reinterpretation." *Carnegie Rochester Conference Series on Public Policy* 40 (June 1994): 133–192.

Cheng, Leonard K., and Elias Dinopoulos. "A Schumpeterian Model of Economic Growth and Fluctuations." University of Florida Working Paper (July 1991).

Cheng, Leonard K., and Elias Dinopoulos. "Schumpeterian Growth and International Business Cycles." *AEA Papers and Proceedings* 82 (May 1992): 409–414.

Chirinko, Robert S. "Business Fixed Investment Spending: A Critical Survey of Modeling Strategies, Empirical Results, and Policy Implications." *Journal of Economic Literature* 31 (December 1993): 1875–1911.

Christensen, Laurits R., and Dale W. Jorgenson. "Measuring Economic Performance in the Private Sector." In Milton Moss, ed. *Measurement of Economic and Social Performance* (New York: Columbia University Press, 1973): 233–338.

Christiano, Lawrence J. "Is Consumption Insufficiently Sensitive to Innovations in Income?" *AEA Papers and Proceedings* 77 (May 1987): 337–341.

Christiano, Lawrence J., and Martin S. Eichenbaum. "Current Real Business Cycle Theories and Aggregate Labor-Market Fluctuations." *American Economic Review* 82 (June 1992): 430–450.

Christiano, Lawrence J., Martin S. Eichenbaum, and David Marshall. "The Permanent Income Hypothesis Revisited." *Econometrica* 59 (March 1991): 371–396.

Clark, Peter K. "The Cyclical Component of U.S. Economic Activity." *Quarterly Journal of Economics* 102 (November 1987): 797–814.

Cochrane, John H. "Production-Based Asset Pricing and the Link between Stock Returns and Economic Fluctuations." *Journal of Finance* 46 (March 1991): 209–237.

Cochrane, John H. "Permanent and Transitory Components of GNP and Stock Prices." *Quarterly Journal of Economics* 109 (February 1994): 241–266.

Cochrane, John H. "Shocks." *Carnegie–Rochester Conference Series on Public Policy* (forthcoming 1995).

Constantinides, George M. "Habit Formation: A Resolution of the Equity Premium Puzzle." *Journal of Political Economy* 98 (June 1990): 519–543.

Cook, Timothy, and Thomas Hahn. "Interest Rate Expectations and the Slope of the Money Market Yield Curve." *Economic Review* 76 (September/October 1990): 3–26.

Cooley, Thomas F., Jeremy Greenwood, and Mehmet Yorukoglu. "The Replacement Problem." University of Rochester Working Paper (October 1993).

Cooley, Thomas F., and Edward C. Prescott. "Economic Growth and Business Cycles." In Thomas F. Cooley, ed. *Frontiers of Business Cycle Research* (Princeton: Princeton University Press, forthcoming 1995): 1–51.

Cooper, Russell, and John Haltiwanger. "Inventories and the Propagation of Sectoral Shocks." *American Economic Review* 80 (March 1990): 170–190.

Cooper, Russell, and John Haltiwanger. "Evidence on Macroeconomic Complementarities." NBER Working Paper No. 4577 (December 1993a).

Cooper, Russell, and John Haltiwanger. "The Aggregate Implications of Machine Replacement: Theory and Evidence." *American Economic Review* 83 (June 1993b): 360–382.

Cowen, Tyler, and Randall Kroszner. "German-Language Precursors of the New Monetary Economics." *Journal of Institutional and Theoretical Economics* 148 (September 1992): 387–410.

Cromwell, Brian. "The Regional Concentration of Recessions." *Federal Reserve Bank of San Francisco Weekly Letter* 91-40 (November 1991): 1–2.

Cummins, Jason G., Kevin A. Hassett, and R. Glenn Hubbard. "A Reconsideration of Investment Behavior Using Tax Reforms as Natural Experiments." *Brookings Papers on Economic Activity* No. 2 (forthcoming 1994).

Danthine, Jean Pierre, and John B. Donaldson. "Methodological and Empirical Issues in Real Business Cycle Theory." *European Economic Review* 37 (January 1993): 1–36.

Davis, Steve J. "Allocative Disturbances and Specific Capital in Real Business Cycle Theories." *AEA Papers and Proceedings* 77 (May 1987a): 326–332.

Davis, Steve J. "Fluctuations in the Pace of Labor Reallocation." *Carnegie-Rochester Conference Series on Public Policy* 27 (1987b): 335–402.

Davis, Steve J., and John Haltiwanger. "Gross Job Creation and Destruction: Microeconomic Evidence and Macroeconomic Implications." In Olivier J. Blanchard and Stanley Fischer, eds. *NBER Macroeconomics Annual* 5 (Cambridge, MA: MIT Press, 1990): 123–168.

Davis, Steve J., and John Haltiwanger. "Gross Job Creation, Gross Job Destruction, and Employment Reallocation." *Quarterly Journal of Economics* 107 (August 1992): 819–863.

Davis, Steve J., and John Haltiwanger. "Driving Forces and Employment Fluctuations: New Evidence and Alternative Interpretations." University of Chicago Working Paper (January 1994).

Debreu, Gerard. *Theory of Value: An Axiomatic Analysis of Economic Equilibrium* (New York: Wiley, 1959).

Debreu, Gerard. "Excess Demand Functions." *Journal of Mathematical Economics* 1 (1974): 15–23.

De Long, J. Bradford. "Facets of Interwar Unemployment: A Review Essay." *Journal of Monetary Economics* 25 (March 1990): 305–312.

De Long, J. Bradford. "Depressions." In Eric Foner and John A. Garraty, eds. *Readers' Guide to American History* (Boston, MA: Houghton–Mifflin Company, 1991).

De Long, J. Bradford, and Lawrence Summers. "Equipment Investment and Economic Growth." *Quarterly Journal of Economics* 106 (May 1991): 445–502.

De Long, J. Bradford, and Lawrence Summers. "Equipment Investment and Economic Growth: How Strong Is the Nexus?" *Brookings Papers on Economic Activity* No. 2 (1992): 157–212.

Denison, Edward F. *The Sources of Economic Growth in the United States* (New York: Committee for Economic Development, 1962).

Denison, Edward F. *Trends in American Economic Growth, 1929–1982* (Washington, DC: Brookings Institution, 1985).

Detemple, Jerome B., and Larry Selden. "Risk and Time Preferences Implicit in Kreps–Porteus Temporal Von Neumann–Morgenstern Preferences." Columbia University Working Paper (March 1992).

Detemple, Jerome B., and Fernando Zapatero. "Asset Prices in an Exchange Economy with Habit Formation." *Econometrica* 59 (November 1991): 1633–1657.

Devereux, Michael, Allan Gregory, and Gregor Smith. "Realistic Cross-Country Consumption Correlations in a Two-Country, Equilibrium, Business-Cycle Model." *Journal of International Money and Finance* 11 (January 1992): 3–16.

Díaz-Giménez, Javier, Edward C. Prescott, Terry Fitzgerald, and Fernando Alvarez. "Banking in Computable General Equilibrium Economies." *Journal of Economic Dynamics and Control* 16 (1992): 533–559.

Dixit, Avinash K., and Robert S. Pindyck. *Investment under Uncertainty* (Princeton: Princeton University Press, 1994).

Donaldson, John B., and Rajnish Mehra. "Stochastic Growth with Correlated Production Shocks." *Journal of Economic Theory* 29 (April 1983): 282–312.

Donaldson, John B., and Rajnish Mehra. "Comparative Dynamics of an Equilibrium Intertemporal Asset Pricing Model." *Review of Economic Studies* 51 (July 1984): 491–508.

Donaldson, John B., and Larry Selden. "A Note on the Recoverability and Uniqueness of Changing Tastes." *Economics Letters* 7 (April 1981): 105–112.

Dotsey, Michael, and Robert G. King. "Rational Expectations Business Cycle Models: A Survey." In John Eatwell, Murray Milgate, and Peter Newman, eds. *The New Palgrave: A Dictionary of Economics* (New York: Stockton Press, 1987). Reprinted in *Federal Reserve Bank of Richmond Economic Review* (March/April 1988): 3–15.

Dynarski, Mark, and Steven M. Sheffrin. "New Evidence on the Cyclical Behavior of Unemployment Durations." In Kevin Lang and Jonathan S. Leonard, eds. *Unemployment and the Structure of Labor Markets* (New York: Basil Blackwell, 1987): 164–185.

Easterly, William. "How Much Do Distortions Affect Growth?" *Journal of Monetary Economics* 32 (November 1993): 187–212.

Easterly, William, Michael Kremer, Lant Pritchett, and Lawrence H. Summers. "Good Policy or Good Luck?" *Journal of Monetary Economics* 32 (December 1993): 459–483.

Easterly, William, and Sérgio Rebelo. "Fiscal Policy and Economic Growth." *Journal of Monetary Economics* 32 (December 1993): 417–458.

Eden, Benjamin. "Marginal Cost Pricing When Spot Markets Are Complete." *Journal of Political Economy* 98 (December 1990): 1293–1306.

Eden, Benjamin, and Zvi Griliches. "Productivity, Market Power, and Capacity Utilization When Spot Markets Are Complete." *AEA Papers and Proceedings* 83 (May 1993): 219–223.

Eichenbaum, Martin S. "Technology Shocks and the Business Cycle." *Federal Reserve Bank of Chicago Economic Perspectives* 15 (March/April 1991): 14–32.

Eichenbaum, Martin S., Lars P. Hansen, and Kenneth J. Singleton. "A Time-Series Analysis of Representative Agent Models of Consumption and Leisure Choice under Uncertainty." *Quarterly Journal of Economics* 103 (February 1988): 51–78.

Eichenbaum, Martin S., and Kenneth J. Singleton. "Do Equilibrium Real Business Cycle Theories Explain Postwar U.S. Business Cycles?" In Stanley Fischer, ed. *NBER Macroeconomics Annual* 1 (Cambridge, MA: MIT Press, 1986): 91–134.

Eichengreen, Barry. *Golden Fetters: The Gold Standard and the Great Depression, 1919–1939* (Oxford: Oxford University Press, 1992).

Eichengreen, Barry, and Timothy Hatton. *Interwar Unemployment in International Perspective* (Dordrecht: Kluwer Academic Publishers, 1988).

Epstein, Larry G., and Stanley E. Zin. "Substitution, Risk Aversion, and the Temporal Behavior of Consumption and Asset Returns I: A Theoretical Framework." *Econometrica* 57 (July 1989): 937–969.

Epstein, Larry G., and Stanley E. Zin. "'First-Order' Risk Aversion and the Equity Premium Puzzle." *Journal of Monetary Economics* 26 (December 1990): 387–407.

Epstein, Larry G., and Stanley E. Zin. "Substitution, Risk Aversion, and the Temporal Behavior of Consumption and Asset Returns: An Empirical Analysis." *Journal of Political Economy* 99 (April 1991): 263–286.

Fair, Ray C. "Sources of Economic Fluctuations in the United States." *Quarterly Journal of Economics* 103 (May 1988): 313–332.

Fama, Eugene F., and G. William Schwert. "Human Capital and Capital Market Equilibrium." *Journal of Financial Economics* 4 (January 1977): 95–125.

Feldstein, Martin, and Philippe Bacchetta. "National Saving and International Investment." In B. Douglas Bernheim and John B. Shoven, eds. *National Saving and Economic Performance* (Chicago: University of Chicago Press, 1991): 201–220.

Feldstein, Martin, and Charles Horioka. "Domestic Saving and International Capital Flows." *Economic Journal* 90 (June 1980): 314–329.

Fischer, Stanley, and Robert C. Merton. "Macroeconomics and Finance: The Role of the Stock Market." *Carnegie-Rochester Conference Series on Public Policy* 21 (1984): 57–108.

Fisher, Irving. *The Theory of Interest* (New York: Macmillan, 1930).

Flavin, Marjorie. "The Excess Smoothness of Consumption: Identification and Interpretation." *Review of Economic Studies* 60 (July 1993): 651–666.

Fogel, Robert W. "Economic Growth, Population Theory, and Physiology: The Bearing of Long-Term Processes on the Making of Economic Policy." *American Economic Review* 84 (June 1994): 369–395.

Freeman, Scott, and Stephen Polasky. "Knowledge-Based Growth." *Journal of Monetary Economics* 30 (October 1992): 3–24.

Friedman, Milton, and Anna Schwartz *A Monetary History of the United States 1867–1960* (Princeton: Princeton University Press, 1963).

Froot, Kenneth A. "New Hope for the Expectations Hypothesis of the Term Structure of Interest Rates." *Journal of Finance* 44 (June 1989): 283–305.

Garber, Peter M., and Robert G. King. "Deep Structural Excavation? A Critique of Euler Equation Methods." NBER Technical Working Paper No. 31 (November 1983).

Gort, Michael, and Richard A. Wall. "Obsolescence, Input Augmentation, and Growth Accounting." State University of New York at Buffalo Working Paper (July 1993).

Greenig, Douglas S. "Nonseparable Preferences, Stochastic Returns, and Intertemporal Substitution in Consumption." Princeton University Undergraduate Thesis (April 1986).

Greenwood, Jeremy, Zvi Hercowitz, and Gregory W. Huffman. "Investment, Capacity Utilization, and the Real Business Cycle." *American Economic Review* 78 (June 1988): 402–417.

Greenwood, Jeremy, Zvi Hercowitz, and Per Krusell. "Macroeconomic Implications of Investment-Specific Technological Change." Federal Reserve Bank of Minneapolis Working Paper (January 1994).

Greenwood, Jeremy, and Gregory W. Huffman. "Tax Analysis in a Real Business Cycle Model." *Journal of Monetary Economics* 27 (February 1991): 167–190.

Greenwood, Jeremy, and Boyan Jovanovic. "Financial Development, Growth, and the Distribution of Income." *Journal of Political Economy* 98 (October 1990): 1076–1107.

Griliches, Zvi. "Productivity, R&D, and the Data Constraint." *American Economic Review* 84 (March 1994): 1–23.

Grossman, Gene M., and Elhanan Helpman. "Quality Ladders and Product Cycles." *Quarterly Journal of Economics* 106 (May 1991a): 557–586.

Grossman, Gene M., and Elhanan Helpman. *Innovation and Growth in the Global Economy* (Cambridge, MA: MIT Press, 1991b).

Grossman, Gene M., and Elhanan Helpman. "Endogenous Innovation in the Theory of Growth." *Journal of Economic Perspectives* 8 (Winter 1994): 23–44.

Grossman, Gene M., and Carl Shapiro. "A Theory of Factor Mobility." *Journal of Political Economy* 90 (October 1982): 1054–1069.

Hall, Robert E. "Stochastic Implications of the Life Cycle–Permanent Income Hypothesis: Theory and Evidence." *Journal of Political Economy* 86 (December 1978): 971–987.

Hall, Robert E. "Comments on: A Competitive Theory of Fluctuations and the Feasibility and Desirability of Stabilization Policy." In Stanley Fischer, ed. *Rational Expectations and Economic Policy* (Chicago: University of Chicago Press, 1980): 190–191.

Hall, Robert E. "Fluctuations in Equilibrium Unemployment." *AEA Papers and Proceedings* 78 (May 1988a): 269–275.

Hall, Robert E. "A Noncompetitive, Equilibrium Model of Fluctuations." NBER Working Paper No. 2576 (May 1988b).

Hall, Robert E. "The Relation between Price and Marginal Cost in U.S. Industry." *Journal of Political Economy* 96 (October 1988c): 921–947.

Hall, Robert E. "Consumption." In Robert J. Barro, ed. *Modern Business Cycle Theory* (Cambridge, MA: Harvard University Press, 1989): 153–177.

Hall, Robert E. "Invariance Properties of Solow's Productivity Residual." In Peter Diamond, ed. *Growth/Productivity/Unemployment* (Cambridge, MA: MIT Press, 1990): 71–112.

Hall, Robert E. *Booms and Recessions in a Noisy Economy* (New Haven: Yale University Press, 1991).

Hall, Robert E. "Macro Theory and the Recession of 1990–1991." *AEA Papers and Proceedings* 83 (May 1993): 275–279.

Ham, John C. "Testing Whether Unemployment Represents Intertemporal Labour Supply Behaviour." *Review of Economic Studies* 53 (August 1986): 559–578.

Hamilton, James D. "A Neoclassical Model of Unemployment and the Business Cycle." *Journal of Political Economy* 96 (June 1988): 593–617.

Hansen, Gary D. "Indivisible Labor and the Business Cycle." *Journal of Monetary Economics* 16 (December 1985): 309–327.

Hansen, Gary D. "The Cyclical and Secular Behaviour of the Labour Input: Comparing Efficiency Units and Hours Worked." *Journal of Applied Econometrics* 8 (January/March 1993): 71–80.

Hansen, Gary D., and Edward C. Prescott. "Did Technology Shocks Cause the 1990–1991 Recession?" *AEA Papers and Proceeding* 83 (May 1993): 280–286.

Hansen, Lars P., and Ravi Jagannathan. "Implications of Security Market Data for Models of Dynamic Economies." *Journal of Political Economy* 99 (April 1991): 225–262.

Hansen, Lars P., Thomas J. Sargent, and Thomas D. Tallarini, Jr. "Pessimism, Neurosis, and Feelings about Risk in General Equilibrium." University of Chicago Working Paper (October 1993).

Hayashi, Fumio. "Tobin's Marginal q and Average q : A Neoclassical Interpretation." *Econometrica* 50 (January 1982): 213–224.

Heaton, John. "The Interaction between Time–Nonseparable Preferences and Time Aggregation." *Econometrica* 61 (March 1993): 353–385.

Helpman, Elhanan. "Endogenous Macroeconomic Growth Theory." *European Economic Review* 36 (April 1992): 237–267.

Hercowitz, Zvi, and Michael Sampson. "Output Growth, the Real Wage, and Employment Fluctuations." *American Economic Review* 81 (December 1991): 1215–1237.

Hicks, John. *Capital and Growth* (New York: Oxford University Press, 1965).

Hillinger, Claude. "Business Cycle Stylized Facts and Explanatory Models." *Journal of Economic Dynamics and Control* 11 (June 1987): 257–263.

Hindy, Ayman, and Chi-fu Huang. "Intertemporal Preferences for Uncertain Consumption: A Continuous Time Approach." *Econometrica* 60 (July 1992): 781–801.

Hindy, Ayman, and Chi-fu Huang. "Optimal Consumption and Portfolio Rules with Durability and Local Substitution." *Econometrica* 61 (January 1993): 85–121.

Hindy, Ayman, Chi-fu Huang, and David Kreps. "On Intertemporal Preferences in Continuous Time." *Journal of Mathematical Economics* 21 (1992): 401–440.

Hodrick, Robert J., and Edward C. Prescott. "Postwar U.S. Business Cycles: An Empirical Investigation." Carnegie-Mellon University Working Paper (June 1981).

Hofstede, Geert, and Michael H. Bond. "The Confucius Connection: From Cultural Roots to Economic Growth." *Organizational Dynamics* 16 (Spring 1988): 5–21.

Hosios, Arthur J. "Unemployment and Vacancies with Sectoral Shifts." *American Economic Review* 84 (March 1994): 124–144.

Howitt, Peter. "Business Cycles with Costly Search and Recruiting." *Quarterly Journal of Economics* 103 (February 1988): 147–165.

Hulten, Charles R. "Growth Accounting When Technical Change Is Embodied in Capital." *American Economic Review* 82 (September 1992): 964–980.

Imrohoroğlu, Ayşe, and Edward C. Prescott. "Evaluating the Welfare Effects of Alternative Monetary Arrangements." *Federal Reserve Bank of Minneapolis Quarterly Review* 15 (Summer 1991): 3–10.

Jones, Irwin E. "Can a Simplified Approach to Bond Portfolio Management Increase Return and Reduce Risk?" *Journal of Portfolio Management* 18 (Winter 1992): 70–76.

Jones, Larry E., and Rodolfo Manuelli. "A Convex Model of Equilibrium Growth: Theory and Policy Implications." *Journal of Political Economy* 98 (October 1990, Part 1): 1008–1038.

Jones, Larry E., Rodolfo E. Manuelli, and Peter E. Rossi. "Optimal Taxation in Models of Endogenous Growth." *Journal of Political Economy* 101 (June 1993): 485–517.

Jorgenson, Dale W., and Barbara Fraumeni. "Investment in Education and U.S. Economic Growth." *Scandanavian Journal of Economics* 94 (Supplement 1992): 51–70.

Jovanovic, Boyan. "Micro Shocks and Aggregate Risk." *Quarterly Journal of Economics* 102 (May 1987): 395–409.

Jovanovic, Boyan, and Saul Lach. "The Diffusion of Technology and Inequality among Nations." NBER Working Paper No. 3732 (June 1991).

Jovanovic, Boyan, and Robert Moffitt. "An Estimate of a Sectoral Model of Labor Mobility." *Journal of Political Economy* 98 (August 1990): 827–852.

Jovanovic, Boyan, and Rafael Rob. "Long Waves and Short Waves: Growth through Intensive and Extensive Search." *Econometrica* 58 (November 1990): 1391–1409.

Kahn, James A. "Inventories and the Volatility of Production." *American Economic Review* 77 (September 1987): 667–679.

Kahn, James A. "Why Is Production More Volatile than Sales? Theory and Evidence on the Stockout-Avoidance Motive for Inventory-Holding." *Quarterly Journal of Economics* 107 (May 1992): 481–510.

Kaldor, Nicholas. "Capital Accumulation and Economic Growth." In Friedrich A. Lutz and Douglas C. Hague, eds. *The Theory of Capital* (New York: St. Martin's Press, 1961): 177–222.

Kandel, Shmuel, and Robert F. Stambaugh. "Asset Returns and Intertemporal Preferences." *Journal of Monetary Economics* 27 (February 1991): 39–71.

Kelly, Morgan. "On Endogenous Growth with Productivity Shocks." *Journal of Monetary Economics* 30 (October 1992): 47–56.

Kemeny, John G., Oskar Morgenstern, and Gerald L. Thompson. "A Generalization of the Von Neumann Model of an Expanding Economy." *Econometrica* 24 (April 1956): 115–135.

Kendrick, John W. *The Formation and Stocks of Total Capital* (New York: Columbia University Press, 1976).

Khan, Aubhik, and Lee E. Ohanian. "Entry and Exit in an Equilibrium Business Cycle Model." University of Virginia Working Paper (February 1993).

King, Ian. "Sectoral Shift Models of Unemployment: Measurement Ahead of Theory." *Bulletin of Economic Research* 45 (July 1993): 175–196.

King, Robert G. "Value and Capital in the Equilibrium Business Cycle Programme." In L. McKenzie and S. Zamagni, eds. *Value and Capital: Fifty Years Later* (London: Macmillan, 1990).

King, Robert G., Charles I. Plosser, and Sérgio T. Rebelo. "Production, Growth, and Business Cycles I. The Basic Neoclassical Model." *Journal of Monetary Economics* 21 (March 1988a): 195–232.

King, Robert G., Charles I. Plosser, and Sérgio T. Rebelo. "Production, Growth, and Business Cycles II. New Directions." *Journal of Monetary Economics* 21 (May 1988b): 309–341.

King, Robert G., Charles I. Plosser, James H. Stock, and Mark W. Watson. "Stochastic Trends and Economic Fluctuations." *American Economic Review* 81 (September 1991): 819–840.

King, Robert G., and Sérgio T. Rebelo. "Business Cycles with Endogenous Growth." University of Rochester Working Paper (February 1988).

King, Robert G., and Sérgio T. Rebelo. "Transitional Dynamics and Economic Growth in the Neoclassical Model." *American Economic Review* 83 (September 1993): 908–931.

Kormendi, Roger C., and Philip G. Meguire. "Macroeconomic Determinants of Growth: Cross-Country Evidence." *Journal of Monetary Economics* 16 (September 1985): 141–163.

Krane, Spencer D., and Steven N. Braun. "Production Smoothing Evidence from Physical-Product Data." *Journal of Political Economy* 99 (June 1991): 558–577.

Kremer, Michael. "The O-Ring Theory of Economic Development." *Quarterly Journal of Economics* 108 (August 1993): 551–575.

Kremer, Michael, and Jim Thomson. "Young Workers, Old Workers, and Convergence." NBER Working Paper No. 4827 (August 1994).

Krieger, Reva. "Sectoral and Aggregate Shocks to Industrial Output in Germany, Japan, and Canada." Federal Reserve Board Working Paper (June 1989).

Krueger, Anne O. "Factor Endowments and Per Capita Income Differences Among Countries." *Economic Journal* 78 (September 1968): 641–659.

Krugman, Paul. "Endogenous Innovation, International Trade, and Growth." In Paul Krugman. *Rethinking International Trade*, (Cambridge, MA: MIT Press, 1990): 165–182.

Kydland, Finn E. "Labor Force Heterogeneity and the Business Cycle." *Carnegie-Rochester Conference Series on Public Policy* 21 (1984): 173–208.

Kydland, Finn E. "Business Cycles and Aggregate Labor-Market Fluctuations." In Thomas F. Cooley, ed. *Frontiers of Business Cycle Research* (Princeton: Princeton University Press, forthcoming 1995).

Kydland, Finn E., and Edward C. Prescott. "A Competitive Theory of Fluctuations and the Feasibility and Desirability of Stabilization Policy." In Stanley Fischer, ed. *Rational Expectations and Economic Policy* (Chicago: University of Chicago Press, 1980): 169–198.

Kydland, Finn E., and Edward C. Prescott. "Time to Build and Aggregate Fluctuations." *Econometrica* 50 (November 1982): 1345–1370.

Kydland, Finn E., and Edward C. Prescott. "Business Cycles: Real Facts and a Monetary Myth." *Federal Reserve Bank of Minneapolis Quarterly Review* 14 (Spring 1990): 3–18.

Kydland, Finn E., and Edward C. Prescott. "The Econometrics of the General Equilibrium Approach to Business Cycles." *Scandinavian Journal of Economics* 93 (1991a): 161–178.

Kydland, Finn E., and Edward C. Prescott. "Hours and Employment Variation in Business Cycle Theory." *Economic Theory* 1 (1991b): 63–81.

Kydland, Finn E., and Edward C. Prescott. "Cyclical Movements of the Labor Input and Its Implicit Real Wage." *Federal Reserve Bank of Cleveland Economic Review* 29 No. 2 (1993): 12–23.

Leamer, Edward E. "Testing Trade Theory." In David Greenway and L. Alan Winters, eds. *Surveys in International Trade* (London: Basil Blackwell, 1994): 66–126.

Leonard, Jonathan S. "In the Wrong Place at the Wrong Time: The Extent of Frictional and Structural Unemployment." In Kevin Lang and Jonathan S. Leonard, eds. *Unemployment and the Structure of Labor Markets* (New York: Basil Blackwell, 1987): 141–163.

Lewis, Karen K. "What Can Explain the Apparent Lack of International Consumption Risk Sharing?" University of Pennsylvania Working Paper (July 1993).

Lilien, David M. "Sectoral Shifts and Cyclical Unemployment." *Journal of Political Economy* 90 (August 1982): 777–793.

Long, John B., and Charles I. Plosser. "Real Business Cycles." *Journal of Political Economy* 91 (February 1983): 39–69.

Long, John B., and Charles I. Plosser. "Sectoral vs. Aggregate Shocks in the Business Cycle." *AEA Papers and Proceedings* 77 (May 1987): 333–336.

Loungani, Prakash. "Structural Unemployment and Public Policy in Interwar Britain." *Journal of Monetary Economics* 28 (August 1991): 149–159.

Loungani, Prakash, and Richard Rogerson. "Cyclical Fluctuations and Sectoral Reallocation: Evidence from the PSID." *Journal of Monetary Economics* 23 (March 1989): 259–273.

Loungani, Prakash, Mark Rush, and William Tave. "Stock Market Dispersion and Unemployment." *Journal of Monetary Economics* 25 (January 1990): 367–388.

Loungani, Prakash, Mark Rush, and William Tave. "Stock Market Dispersion and Business Cycles." *Economic Perspectives* 15 (January/February 1991): 2–8.

Lucas, Robert E., Jr. "Adjustment Costs and the Theory of Supply." *Journal of Political Economy* 75 (August 1967): 321–334.

Lucas, Robert E., Jr. "Expectations and the Neutrality of Money." *Journal of Economic Theory* 4 (April 1972): 103–124.

Lucas, Robert E., Jr. "An Equilibrium Model of the Business Cycle." *Journal of Political Economy* 83 (December 1975): 1113–1144.

Lucas, Robert E., Jr. "Asset Prices in an Exchange Economy." *Econometrica* 46 (November 1978): 1429–1445.

Lucas, Robert E., Jr. *Models of Business Cycles* (Cambridge, MA: Basil Blackwell, 1987).

Lucas, Robert E., Jr. "On the Mechanics of Economic Development." *Journal of Monetary Economics* 22 (July 1988): 3–42.

Lucas, Robert E., Jr. "Why Doesn't Capital Flow from Rich to Poor Countries?" *AEA Papers and Proceedings* 80 (May 1990): 92–96.

Lucas, Robert E., Jr. "Making a Miracle." *Econometrica* 61 (March 1993): 251–272.

Lucas, Robert E., Jr., and Edward C. Prescott. "Investment under Uncertainty." *Econometrica* 39 (September 1971): 659–681.

Lucas, Robert E., Jr., and Edward C. Prescott. "Equilibrium Search and Unemployment." *Journal of Economic Theory* 7 (February 1974): 188–209.

Lucas, Robert E., Jr., and Nancy L. Stokey. "Optimal Fiscal and Monetary Policy in an Economy without Capital." *Journal of Monetary Economics* 12 (July 1983): 55–93.

Mankiw, N. Gregory. "The Term Structure of Interest Rates Revisited." *Brookings Papers on Economic Activity* No. 1 (1986a): 61–110.

Mankiw, N. Gregory. "The Equity Premium and the Concentration of Aggregate Shocks." *Journal of Financial Economics* 17 (September 1986b): 211–219.

Mankiw, N. Gregory. "Real Business Cycles: A New Keynesian Perspective." *Journal of Economic Perspectives* 3 (Summer 1989): 79–90.

Mankiw, N. Gregory. "A Quick Refresher Course in Macroeconomics." *Journal of Economic Literature* 28 (December 1990): 1645–1660.

Mankiw, N. Gregory. "Commentary: The Search for Growth." In *Policies for Long-Run Economic Growth* (Kansas City: Federal Reserve Bank of Kansas City, 1992): 87–92.

Mankiw, N. Gregory, David Romer, and David N. Weil. "A Contribution to the Empirics of Economic Growth." *Quarterly Journal of Economics* 107 (May 1992): 407–437.

Mankiw, N. Gregory, Julio J. Rotemberg, and Lawrence H. Summers. "Intertemporal Substitution in Macroeconomics." *Quarterly Journal of Economics* 100 (February 1985): 225–251.

Mankiw, N. Gregory, and Stephen P. Zeldes. "The Consumption of Stockholders and Nonstockholders." *Journal of Financial Economics* 27 (March 1991): 97–112.

Mantel, Rolf. "On the Characterization of Aggregate Excess Demand." *Journal of Economic Theory* 12 (1974): 197–201.

Manuelli, Rodolfo, and Thomas J. Sargent. "Models of Business Cycles." *Journal of Monetary Economics* 22 (November 1988): 523–542.

Mayshar, Joram, and Gary Solon. "Shift Work and the Business Cycle." *AEA Papers and Proceedings* 83 (May 1993): 224–228.

McCallum, Bennett T. "Real Business Cycle Models." In Robert J. Barro, ed. *Modern Business Cycle Theory* (Cambridge, MA: Harvard University Press, 1989): 16–50.

McCallum, Bennett T. "Unit Roots in Macroeconomic Time Series: Some Critical Issues." *Federal Reserve of Richmond Economic Quarterly* 79 (Spring 1993): 13–43.

McCloskey, Donald N. *The Rhetoric of Economics* (Madison: University of Wisconsin Press, 1985).

McCloskey, Donald N. *If You're So Smart: The Narrative of Economic Expertise* (Chicago: University of Chicago Press, 1990).

McLaughlin, Kenneth J. "A Theory of Quits and Layoffs with Efficient Turnover." *Journal of Political Economy* 99 (February 1991): 1–29.

Mehra, Rajnish, and Edward C. Prescott. "The Equity Premium: A Puzzle." *Journal of Monetary Economics* 15 (March 1985): 145–161.

Merton, Robert C. "An Intertemporal Capital Asset Pricing Model." *Econometrica* 41 (September 1973): 867–888.

Merton, Robert C. "On Estimating the Expected Return on the Market." *Journal of Financial Economics* 8 (December 1980): 323–361.

Miller, Edward M. "On the Importance of the Embodiment of Technology Effect: A Comment on Denison's Growth Accounting Methodology." *Journal of Macroeconomics* 7 (Winter 1985): 85–99.

Miller, Edward M. "The Definition of Capital for Solow's Growth Accounting Formula." *Southern Economic Journal* 56 (July 1989): 157–165.

Miller, Edward M. "Robinson's Classic Question Revisited: How to Measure Capital?" In Ingrid H. Rima, ed. *The Joan Robinson Legacy* (Armonk, NY: M.E. Sharpe, 1991): 136–151.

Mortensen, Dale, and Christopher Pissarides. "The Cyclical Behavior of Job Creation and Job Destruction." In Jan C. Van Ours, Gerard A. Pfann, and Geert Ridder, eds. *Labor Demand and Equilibrium Wage Formation* (Amsterdam: Elsevier, 1993): 201–226.

Mulligan, Casey B., and Xavier Sala-i-Martin. "Transitional Dynamics in Two-Sector Models of Endogenous Growth." *Quarterly Journal of Economics* 108 (August 1993a): 739–773.

Mulligan, Casey B., and Xavier Sala-i-Martin. "Some Evidence on the Links between Aggregate Income and Human Capital." University of Chicago Working Paper (November 1993b).

Mulligan, Casey B., and Xavier Sala-i-Martin. "Measures of the Aggregate Value of Human Capital." University of Chicago Working Paper (March 1994).

Murphy, Kevin J. "Geographic Differences in U.S. Unemployment Rates: A Variance Decomposition Approach." *Economic Inquiry* 23 (January 1985): 135–158.

Murphy, Kevin M., and Robert H. Topel. "The Evolution of Unemployment in the United States: 1968–1985." In Stanley Fischer, ed. *NBER Macroeconomics Annual* 2 (Cambridge, MA: MIT Press, 1987): 11–58.

Nelson, Charles R., and Charles I. Plosser. "Trends and Random Walks in Macroeconomic Time Series: Some Evidence and Implications." *Quarterly Journal of Economics* 102 (November 1987): 857–880.

Neumann, George R., and Robert H. Topel. "Employment Risk, Diversification, and Unemployment." *Quarterly Journal of Economics* 106 (November 1991): 1341–1365.

Pack, Howard, and John Page. "Accumulation, Exports, and Growth in the High Performing Asian Economies." *Carnegie-Rochester Conference Series on Public Policy* 40 (June 1994): 199–235.

Parente, Stephen L., and Edward C. Prescott. "Changes in the Wealth of Nations." *Federal Reserve Bank of Minneapolis Quarterly Review* 17 (Spring 1993): 3–16.

Parente, Stephen L., and Edward C. Prescott. "Barriers to Technology Adoption and Development." *Journal of Political Economy* 102 (April 1994): 298–321.

Phelps, Edmund S. *Seven Schools of Macroeconomic Thought: The Arne Ryde Memorial Lectures* (Oxford: Clarendon Press, 1990).

Pindyck, Robert S. "A Note on Competitive Investment under Uncertainty." *American Economic Review* 83 (March 1993): 273–277.

Pissarides, Christopher A. "Loss of Skill During Unemployment and the Persistence of Employment Shocks." *Quarterly Journal of Economics* 107 (November 1992): 1371–1391.

Plosser, Charles I. "Understanding Real Business Cycles." *Journal of Economic Perspectives* 3 (Summer 1989): 51–77.

Plosser, Charles I. "The Search for Growth." *Policies for Long-Run Economic Growth* (Kansas City: Federal Reserve Bank of Kansas City, 1992): 57–86..

Poterba, James M., and Lawrence H. Summers. "Reporting Errors and Labor Market Dynamics." *Econometrica* 54 (November 1986): 1319–1338.

Prescott, Edward C. "Efficiency of the Natural Rate." *Journal of Political Economy* 83 (December 1975): 1229–1236.

Prescott, Edward C. "Theory Ahead of Business Cycle Measurement." *Federal Reserve Bank of Minneapolis Quarterly Review* 10 (Fall 1986): 9–22.

Prescott, Edward C. "Real Business Cycle Theory: What Have We Learned?" *Revista de Analisis Economico* 6 (1991): 3–19.

Prescott, Edward C., and Rajnish Mehra. "Recursive Competitive Equilibrium: The Case of Homogeneous Households." *Econometrica* 48 (September 1980): 1365–1379.

Przeworski, Adam, and Fernando Limongi. "Political Regimes and Economic Growth." *Journal of Economic Perspectives* 7 (Summer 1993): 51–69.

Quah, Danny. "The Relative Importance of Permanent and Transitory Components: Identification and Some Theoretical Bounds." *Econometrica* 60 (January 1992): 107–118.

Ramey, Garey, and Valerie A. Ramey. "On the Cost of Economic Fluctuations." University of California at San Diego Working Paper (April 1994).

Ramey, Valerie A. "Nonconvex Costs and the Behavior of Inventories." *Journal of Political Economy* 99 (April 1991): 306–334.

Rebelo, Sérgio. "Long-Run Policy Analysis and Long-Run Growth." *Journal of Political Economy* 99 (April 1991): 500–521.

Rebelo, Sérgio. "Growth in Open Economies." *Carnegie-Rochester Conference Series on Public Policy* 36 (1992): 5–46.

Rios-Rull, José-Víctor. "On the Quantitative Importance of Market Completeness." *Journal of Monetary Economics* 34 (December 1994).

Rissman, Ellen R. "Wage Growth and Sectoral Shifts." *Journal of Monetary Economics* 31 (June 1993): 395–416.

Rogerson, Richard. "An Equilibrium Model of Sectoral Reallocation." *Journal of Political Economy* 95 (August 1987): 824–834.

Rogerson, Richard. "Indivisible Labor, Lotteries, and Equilibrium." *Journal of Monetary Economics* 21 (January 1988): 3–16.

Rogerson, Richard. "Sectoral Shocks, Human Capital, and Displaced Workers." Stanford University Working Paper (October 1990).

Rogerson, Richard. "Sectoral Shifts and Cyclical Fluctuations." *Revista de Analisis Economico* 6 (1991): 37–46.

Rogerson, Richard, and Peter Rupert. "New Estimates of Intertemporal Substitution." *Journal of Monetary Economics* 27 (February 1991): 255–269.

Romer, Christina D. "Is the Stabilization of the Postwar Economy a Figment of the Data?" *American Economic Review* 76 (June 1986): 314–334.

Romer, Christina D. "The Prewar Business Cycle Reconsidered: New Estimates of Gross National Product, 1869–1908." *Journal of Political Economy* 97 (February 1989): 1–37.

Romer, Christina D. "The Great Crash and the Onset of the Great Depression." *Quarterly Journal of Economics* 105 (August 1990): 597–624.

Romer, Christina D. "The Cyclical Behavior of Individual Production Series, 1889–1984." *Quarterly Journal of Economics* 106 (February 1991): 1–31.

Romer, Christina D., and David H. Romer. "Credit Channel or Credit Actions? An Interpretation of the Postwar Transmission Mechanism." In Barbara Sagraves, ed. *Changing Capital Markets: Implications for Monetary Policy* (Kansas City: Federal Reserve Bank of Kansas City, 1994): 71–116.

Romer, Paul M. "Increasing Returns and Long-Run Growth." *Journal of Political Economy* 94 (October 1986): 905–926.

Romer, Paul M. "Growth Based on Increasing Returns Due to Specialization." *American Economic Review* 77 (May 1987a): 56–62.

Romer, Paul M. "Crazy Explanations for the Productivity Slowdown." In Stanley Fischer, ed. *NBER Macroeconomics Annual* 2 (Cambridge, MA: MIT Press, 1987b): 163–202.

Romer, Paul M. "Capital Accumulation and Long-Run Growth." In Robert J. Barro, ed. *Modern Business Cycle Theory* (Cambridge, MA: Harvard University Press, 1989): 51–127.

Romer, Paul M. "Are Nonconvexities Important for Understanding Growth?" *American Economic Review* 80 (May 1990a): 97–103.

Romer, Paul M. "Endogenous Technical Change." *Journal of Political Economy* 98 (October 1990b): S71–S102.

Romer, Paul M. "Two Strategies for Economic Development: Using Ideas and Producing Ideas." In *Supplement to the Proceedings of the World Bank Conference on Development Economics 1992* (March 1993): 63–91.

Rotemberg, Julio J., and Lawrence H. Summers. "Inflexible Prices and Procyclical Productivity." *Quarterly Journal of Economics* 105 (November 1990): 851–874.

Rotemberg, Julio J., and Michael Woodford. "Is the Business Cycle a Necessary Consequence of Stochastic Growth?" Massachusetts Institute of Technology Working Paper (February 1994).

Rouwenhorst, K. Geert. "Time to Build and Aggregate Fluctuations." *Journal of Monetary Economics* 27 (February 1991): 241–254.

Ryder, Harl E., Jr., and Geoffrey M. Heal. "Optimum Growth with Intertemporally Dependent Preferences." *Review of Economic Studies* 40 (January 1973): 1–33.

Saint-Paul, Gilles. "Productivity Growth and the Structure of the Business Cycle." *European Economic Review* 37 (May 1993): 861–890.

Sala-i-Martin, Xavier. "Lecture Notes on Economic Growth (II): Five Prototype Models of Endogenous Growth." NBER Working Paper No. 3564 (December 1990).

Samson, Lucie. "Fluctuations in Employment Growth." *Japan and the World Economy* 3 (1991): 271–283.

Sargent, Thomas J. "A Classical Macroeconometric Model for the United States." *Journal of Political Economy* 84 (April 1976): 207–237.

Sargent, Thomas J. "Tobin's q and the Rate of Investment in General Equilibrium." *Carnegie-Rochester Conference Series on Public Policy* 12 (1980): 107–154.

Schmitz, James A., Jr. "Early Progress on the 'Problem of Economic Development'." *Federal Reserve Bank of Minneapolis Quarterly Review* 17 (Spring 1993): 17–35.

Schultz, Theodore W. "Investment in Human Capital." *American Economic Review* 51 (March 1961): 1–17.

Shapiro, Matthew D. "Cyclical Productivity and the Workweek of Capital." *AEA Papers and Proceedings* 83 (May 1993): 229–233.

Shiller, Robert J. "Ultimate Sources of Aggregate Variability." *AEA Papers and Proceedings* 77 (May 1987): 87–92.

Shiller, Robert J. *Market Volatility* (Cambridge, MA: MIT Press, 1989).

Shoven, John B., and John Whalley. *Applying General Equilibrium* (Cambridge, UK: Cambridge University Press, 1992).

Singleton, Kenneth J. "Econometric Issues in the Analysis of Equilibrium Business Cycle Models." *Journal of Monetary Economics* 21 (March/May 1988): 361–386.

Solow, Robert M. "A Contribution to the Theory of Economic Growth." *Quarterly Journal of Economics* 70 (February 1956): 65–94.

Solow, Robert M. "Technical Change and the Aggregate Production Function." *Review of Economic Studies* 39 (August 1957): 312–320.

Solow, Robert M. "Growth Theory and After." *American Economic Review* 78 (June 1988): 307–317.

Solow, Robert M. *The Rate of Return and the Rate of Interest* (Stockholm: Industrial Institute for Economic and Social Research, 1991).

Solow, Robert M. "Perspectives on Growth Theory." *Journal of Economic Perspectives* 8 (Winter 1994): 45–54.

Sonnenschein, Hugo. "Do Walras' Identity and Continuity Characterize the Class of Community Excess Demand Functions?" *Journal of Economic Theory* 6 (1973): 345–354.

Stadler, George W. "Business Cycle Models with Endogenous Technology." *American Economic Review* 80 (September 1990): 763–778.

Starr-McCluer, Martha. "Cyclical Fluctuations and Sectoral Reallocation." *Journal of Monetary Economics* 31 (June 1993): 417–425.

Startz, Richard. "Growth States and Sectoral Shocks." University of Washington Working Paper (March 1994).

Stock, James H., and Mark W. Watson. "Variable Trends in Economic Time Series." *Journal of Economic Perspectives* 2 (Summer 1988): 147–174.

Stockman, Alan C. "Sectoral and National Aggregate Disturbances to Industrial Output in Seven European Countries." *Journal of Monetary Economics* 21 (March/May 1988): 387–409.

Stockman, Alan C., and Linda L. Tesar. "Tastes and Technology in a Two-Country Model of the Business Cycle: Explaining International Comovements." *American Economic Review* 85 (forthcoming 1995).

Stokey, Nancy L. "Human Capital, Product Quality, and Growth." *Quarterly Journal of Economics* 106 (May 1991): 587–616.

Summers, Lawrence H. "Some Skeptical Observations on Real Business Cycle Theory." *Federal Reserve Bank of Minneapolis Quarterly Review* 10 (Fall 1986): 23–27.

Summers, Lawrence H. "The Scientific Illusion in Empirical Macroeconomics." *Scandinavian Journal of Economics* 93 (1991): 129–148.

Summers, Robert, and Alan Heston. "The Penn World Table (Mark 5): An Expanded Set of International Comparisons, 1950–1988." *Quarterly Journal of Economics* 106 (May 1991): 327–368.

Sundaresan, Suresh M. "Intertemporally Dependent Preferences and the Volatility of Consumption and Wealth." *Review of Financial Studies* 2 (1989): 73–89.

Tamura, Robert. "Income Convergence in an Endogenous Growth Model." *Journal of Political Economy* 99 (June 1991): 522–540.

Uzawa, Hirofumi. "Optimum Technical Change in an Aggregate Model of Economic Growth." *International Economic Review* 6 (January 1965): 18–31.

Uzawa, Hirofumi. "Time Preference, the Consumption Function, and Optimum Asset Holdings." In James N. Wolfe, ed. *Value Capital and Growth: Papers in Honour of Sir John Hicks* (Chicago: Aldine, 1968): 485–504.

Von Furstenberg, George M. "Corporate Investment: Does Market Valuation Matter in the Aggregate?" *Brookings Papers on Economic Activity* No. 2 (1977): 347–397.

Von Neumann, John. "A Model of General Economic Equilibrium." *Review of Economic Studies* 13 (1945, Part 1): 1–9.

Von Neumann, John, and Oskar Morgenstern. *Theory of Games and Economic Behavior* (Princeton: Princeton University Press, 1946).

Walras, Léon. *Elements of Pure Economics.* (Lausanne: L. Borbax, 1874). Definitive edition published in Paris by R. Pichon and R. Durand-Auzias, 1926. Translated by William Jaffé (London: George Allen and Unwin, 1954. Reprinted in New York by Augustus M. Kelley, 1969).

Weil, Philippe. "The Equity Premium Puzzle and the Risk-Free Rate Puzzle." *Journal of Monetary Economics* 24 (November 1989): 401–421.

Weiss, Laurence. "Asymmetric Adjustment Costs and Sectoral Shifts." In Jerry Green, ed. *Essays in Honor of Kenneth Arrow* (Chicago: University of Chicago Press, 1984): 251–264.

West, Kenneth D. "The Sources of Fluctuations in Aggregate Inventories and GNP." *Quarterly Journal of Economics* 105 (November 1990): 939–971.

Williamson, Stephen D. "Sectoral Shifts, Labor Market Sorting, and Aggregate Fluctuations." *International Economic Review* 31 (November 1990): 935–952.

Yang, Xiaokai, and Yew-Kwang Ng. *Specialization and Economic Organization: A New Classical Microeconomic Framework* (Amsterdam: North-Holland, 1993).

Young, Alwyn. "A Tale of Two Cities: Factor Accumulation and Technical Change in Hong Kong and Singapore." In Olivier J. Blanchard and Stanley Fischer, eds. *NBER Macroeconomics Annual* 7 (Cambridge, MA: MIT Press, 1992): 13–63.

Young, Alwyn. "Substitution and Complementarity in Endogenous Innovation." *Quarterly Journal of Economics* 108 (August 1993): 775–807.

Zarnowitz, Victor. "Recent Work on Business Cycles in Historical Perspective: A Review of Theories and Evidence." *Journal of Economic Literature* 23 (June 1985): 523–580.

Zarnowitz, Victor. *Business Cycles* (Chicago and London: University of Chicago Press, 1992).

Index

Abel, Andrew B.
  on equity premium puzzle (1990),
    22, 132–133
  on investment under uncertainty
    (1994), 133
Abraham, Katharine
  on aggregate and allocative shocks
    (1986), 134
  on aggregate demand (1986), 214
  Davis on (1987b), 174
  on help-wanted ads and
    unemployment (1987), 133
  on labor mobility (1986), 102
Abramovitz, Moses, on economic
    growth (1989), 134
Added risk, 46
Adjustment costs, 14, 20, 26, 33, 87.
  See also Irreversible investments;
    Tobin's q
  and capital reallocation, in Kydland
    and Prescott (1991b), 210
  and imperfect competition, 104
  irreversibility as, 150
  in Kydland and Prescott (1982), 209
  in Lucas (1967), 214–215
  modeling of, 50
  Pindyck on (1993), 133
  and reallocation of capital, 93, 128
  and roundabout production, 122
  and Tobin's q, 115
Aggregate demand, 15, 53, 61, 87–88
  in Abraham and Katz (1986), 214
  in Blanchard and Wyplosz (1981),
    154–155
  in Bosworth (1975), 157
  in Christiano and Eichenbaum
    (1992), 167

  in Eichenbaum (1991), 180
  in Loungani, Rush, and Tave (1990),
    214
Aggregate shocks, 101, 153–154.
  See also Shocks, aggregate and
    allocative
  Abraham and Katz on (1986), 134
  in Loungani, Rush, and Tave (1991),
    214
  as shocks to government purchases,
    in Barro (1981), 141
  in Stadler (1990), 248–249
Aggregate supply, in Blanchard and
    Wyplosz (1981), 155
Aggregation, 88
  in Miller (1989), 223; (1991), 223–224
Aghion, Philippe, xii
  on growth and fluctuations (1993),
    135
  on negative externalities in market
    stealing (1992), 41, 134–135, 184,
    196, 241, 248
Aiyagari, S. Rao, on role of technology
    shocks in business cycles (1994),
    135–136
Alchian, Armen, xii
  on adjustment costs (1959), 209
  and business fixed investment (1959),
    215
  and constant returns (1959), 197
  on costs and outputs (1959), 136, 234
  on marginal cost (1959), 115
  production smoothing and (1959),
    155
  on replacement cost (1959), 121
  and returns to scale (1959), 191
Alchian's Q, 136

Printed in the United States
by Baker & Taylor Publisher Services